Life and Afterlife in Ancient Egypt during the Middle Kingdom and Second Intermediate Period

Edited by

Silke Grallert – Wolfram Grajetzki

Golden House Publication
Egyptology 7

London 2007

This title is published by
Golden House Publications
GoldenHouse100@aol.com

Life and Afterlife in Ancient Egypt during the Middle Kingdom and Second Intermediate Period,
edited by Silke Grallert and Wolfram Grajetzki

Printed in the United Kingdom
by
CPI, Antony Rowe Limited

London 2007

ISBN-10: 1-906137-01-3
ISBN-13: 978-1-906137-01-4

Front Cover Picture:
Model of a Tomb Chapel of *Kmz*, © copyright Ägyptisches Museum der Universität Bonn
(Photograph by D. Klein)
Back Cover Picture:
Fragment of a false door belonging to a Middle Kingdom queen, © copyright Eva Lange

Contents

Preface

The Middle Kingdom is certainly one of the most diversified periods in the long history of ancient Egyptian civilization. Learned from the downfall of the Old Kingdom central government and a universal crisis of the formerly centralized state in the First Intermediate Period, the rulers of the country reunified in the later Eleventh Dynasty had to respond to the changes in the world and in the society. Given the current situation, kings initiated a program of monumental construction oriented to building and rebuilding of gods' temples over the whole country in order to secure divine blessings for a successful rule and a support of the central government. At the same time, residential cemeteries centred on by the royal pyramids remained, as in the Old Kingdom, the main architectural focus of Egypt. Newly discovered pieces from a queen's burial place may have come from such sites (E. Lange).

Long hieroglyphic inscriptions on temple walls as well as didactic literature on papyrus scrolls were used to explain royal politics and to draw a picture of a harmonious society based on the "Maat" where every person loyal to the king had a fixed place in the world to live and to die peacefully. Along with this intensive use of the written language at the elite level, less wealthy strata of the society could commission or acquire inscribed monuments to be placed in temples, tombs or holy places like Abydos. Such monuments, mainly stelae and statues, for the first time show a high degree of personal influence of the owners of the monuments on their aesthetic treatment and the concepts of their written and pictorial decoration. Thus, we face numerous Middle Kingdom monuments revealing the creativity of craftsmen and their employers that may be considered almost unique (B. Backes, P. Whelan). Such a bent for individualism seems to contradict to the tendency to burying several bodies in the same tomb chamber, especially from the later Middle Kingdom onwards, but is in keeping with the so called "family stelae" depicting not only the members of the tomb owner's family but also his colleagues (W. Grajetzki).

Another product of the Middle Kingdom funerary industry famous for the great variety of items are rectangular wooden coffins, often covered with well preserved polychromous painting. They are not only of great value for the study of ancient Egyptian painting and colour conventions, but also contain religious texts almost unknown in the Old Kingdom. Besides the well known Coffin Texts written in cursive hieroglyphs or hieratic mostly in text blocks on the inner and outer walls of the coffins, several rectangular coffins bear a hitherto neglected group of texts hidden in the mitre joints that partly became very common on the coffins and sarcophagi of the New Kingdom and later periods (S. Grallert). Three coffins of two officials, Khenu and Amenemhat, can boast the presence of three main liturgical sequences – uniquely separated by CT 62 – that later became a part of chapter 178 of the Book of the Dead preserved on the walls of Theban Tomb 82 and on three Twenty-first Dynasty funerary papyri, which raises a question of the structure of religious texts and how certain sequences were used over long time in the creative field of compiling religious texts anew over centuries (S. Quirke). Both papers demonstrate clearly how the rituals centred around the embalming situation gained more and more importance in the Middle Kingdom.

Besides the traditional rectangular coffins, the funerary industry of the Middle Kingdom developed a new anthropoid shape of wooden coffins resembling the outlines of a wrapped mummy. According to G. Miniaci the well-known *rishi* coffins of the Second Intermediate Period loaned, of course, their shape from the earlier examples of the Twelfth and Thirteenth Dynasties as well as some parts of their decoration that seems not to be an entire new design of the Theban Seventeenth Dynasty, but showing also strong connections with the decoration of the traditional rectangular coffins.

Another source of materials demonstrating the wide spread of literacy among some parts of the population are the extensive archives of the Middle Kingdom that survived at several sites (el-Lahun archives, Reisner papyri, Semna Despatches). A sarcastic letter from el-Lahun seems to question the postulated existence of a temple of the goddess Heqet in the swampy Fayum region (Z. Horváth), whereas especially the Semna Despatches offer deeper information on the activities of Middle Kingdom soldiers (D. Stefanović).

The broad scope of articles collected in this volume considering various aspects of the culture of the Middle Kingdom and its great influence on the following Second Intermediate Period may contribute in different ways to a deeper and more detailed insight into the period that lasted for approximately 330 years so important in the history of Ancient Egypt.

Silke Grallert & Wolfram Grajetzki
Bonn and London August 2007

Principles of Decoration on Middle Kingdom Stelae*

Burkhard Backes

"Middle Kingdom stelae are a mass of signs and symbols. They are a manifestation of unconscious and conscious cultural codes and the deliberate intentions and agreements of the customer(s) and artist(s)".[1]

1. Introduction

The various mortuary stelae, and stelae found in the cultic landscape of Abydos are an important source for the ancient Egyptian religion of the Middle Kingdom. However, this essay is not a contribution to the history of ancient Egyptian religion, but deals with the outer appearance of these monuments. It is well known that there are several artistic innovations on stelae. From a limited repertoire of motifs were created through changing of details und through different arrangements, new compositions.[2] They can affect the overall arrangement of the stela but also single depictions in the form of a development of already existing motifs. Our knowledge is not sufficient for writing a complete stylistical and iconographical history of Middle Kingdom stelae. The precise datings are often missing. Instead I want to look at some motifs of the Middle Kingdom or at least show their importance in the arrangement of the stelae relating to the development of a new motive and as individual solutions.[3]

The following remarks relate to the knowledge that the form and the contents appear together and influence each other. The aim of this contribution is to demonstrate the influence of the form, with selected examples. A science that aims to interpret, to look for the non-material sense in the written and pictorial remains of a culture, is in danger of neglecting the outer appearance. Most motifs for the development of a new depiction can be summarised in two points. They can be categorised under the keywords "contents" and "aesthetic".

1. "contents": Certain depictions should appear on a stela or are arranged in a certain way because the religious value is desired for the monument.
2. "aesthetic": A depiction appears in a certain way on a stela – alone or in combination with others – because it "looks better". The available space and its best use are important in this context. The content is not affected, this means that several arrangements with the same information are possible.

* I am grateful to Ingrid Blom-Böer and Gabriele Pieke for reading a first draft of this article and to Silke Grallert for practical help.

1 D. FRANKE, The Middle Kingdom Stelae Publication Project, exemplified by stela BM EA 226, *British Museum Studies in Ancient Egypt and Sudan* 1 (2002), 7-19, reference p. 7-8.

2 An overview on the variations is visible in the lists in R. HÖLZL, *Die Giebelfelddekoration von Stelen des Mittleren Reichs* (*Veröffentlichungen der Institute für Afrikanistik und Ägyptologie der Universität Wien* 55 = *Beiträge zur Ägyptologie* 10), Vienna 1990.

3 There is a consistent and strong tendency to provide stelae with an individual appearance, *pace* HÖLZL, *Giebelfelddekoration*, 162.

Researchers, such as Jacques Vandier, already pointed to aesthetic reasons for use of certain depictions. A harmonious arrangement of lines was desirable (e.g. the wedjat eyes fitting perfectly into the pediment of the stela).[4] A clarification of this fundamental knowledge is still missing. In the following text will be presented stelae, where aesthetical conceptions played obviously an important role, regardless of the quality of craftsmanship.

2. Stelae with Niches or Perforation and "ʿnḫ-Stelae"

2.1 Stelae with Groups of Figures

Some stelae have a rectangular niche with the figure of the stela owner standing in it. Not so often several people are standing in the niche, very rarely there are several niches, indeed, I only know one example.[5] The figure can be produced of one piece, together with the stela. In these cases it is a very high relief, almost already a three dimensional sculpture. In other cases the figure is made separately from the stela. The niche breaks fully through the stela, the figure is a freestanding statuette. In these cases the figure is most often missing.[6]

The popularity of depictions showing the stela owner does not need to be explained in detail. It has its origin on false doors of the Old Kingdom, from which the decoration of the Middle Kingdom stelae developed.[7] Because of the "potency" of ancient Egyptian pictures as well as writing, a depiction immortalises the presence of the stela owner very clearly. However, why does a three dimensional image appear in these rare cases? Relief was obviously more popular. The stelae with the niche are only a small group. A relief suits better the general form of a plain stela. This is an aesthetic argument. Perhaps it was the higher technical expenditure, which caused stelae with niches and perforation. At any rate, the popularity of reliefs in general and on stelae shows that it was a common instrument for an "effective" depiction. For us the interesting feature is the opposition of both forms of depictions of the stela owner. They both immortalised his presence, whether three or two-dimensional. It seems that the Egyptians thought about the function and the difference between three-dimensional depictions and relief, but without any discrepancy in result, as the different solutions show. One reason for the three-dimensional depictions might come from interpretation of the false door as shrine for a statue, as developed in the Old Kingdom und made clear by torus moulding and a cornice.[8] Torus moulding and cornice were found on some Middle Kingdom stelae with aperture but not on all of them.[9] Once appearing on a stela, the statue could be combined with different elements widening the meaning of the stelae to pure framing of the statue.

It is not possible to make a valuation between thinkable "contents" or more "aesthetic" reasons for the invention of the stelae with niche or perforation. On one side, they demonstrate very well our

---

4 J. VANDIER, *Manuel d'archéologie égyptienne* II. *Les grandes époques. L'architecture funéraire*, Paris 1954, 489-490.

5 Stela Vienna, Kunsthistorisches Museum ÄS 109. For this special case see infra page 4.

6 Their original existence is proven: A. BADAWY, La stèle funéraire égyptienne à ouverture axiale, *Bulletin de l'Institut d'Égypte* 35 (1954), 117-139, especially 117 with example Cairo CG 20748.

7 S. WIEBACH, *Die ägyptische Scheintür. Morphologische Studien zur Entwicklung und Bedeutung der Hauptkultstelle in den Privat-Gräbern des Alten Reiches* (*Hamburger Ägyptologische Studien* 1), Hamburg 1981; see also H.W. MÜLLER, Die Totendenksteine des Mittleren Reiches, ihre Genesis, ihre Darstellungen und ihre Komposition, *Mitteilungen des Deutschen Instituts für Ägyptische Altertumskunde in Kairo* 4 (1933), 165-206.

8 Cf. in detail WIEBACH, *Scheintür*, chapter IV.

9 For a summary see BADAWY, *Bulletin de l'Institut d'Égypte* 35 (1954), 120-21, fig. 1.

initial question about the two viewpoints. On the other side they served as starting point for the invention of a rare stela type, the so-called "*ʿnḫ*-stelae"[10].

2.2 Stelae with *ʿnḫ*-Hieroglyph Sign

There are reasons in contents for placing a single *ʿnḫ*-Hieroglyph sign on an Abydos stela. The meaning of the hieroglyphic sign for life/living on a stela at the main cult centre of the most important funerary god do not need to be explained. We might ask rather ourselves why the *ʿnḫ*-sign does not appear more often. For this contribution, it is important where and how the *ʿnḫ*-sign outside the text was placed on a stela. One reason for the rarity of that sign might be that originally there was no space for that sign because it stood in competition with a number of other obvious pictures. One possibility was to place the *ʿnḫ*-sign between the pair of wedjat eyes, instead of the *šn*-rings or other signs or objects, often placed between these two eyes.[11] In one instance it is even placed between two jackals (Fig. 1: Stela Tübingen 461[12]). Another much more striking possibility is the *ʿnḫ*-sign placed as the dominant decoration pattern of the whole stela. Like the stelae with statuettes and groups of statuettes the "*ʿnḫ*-stelae" appear in a frame (Fig. 2: Cairo CG 20353), but also within a perforation. Instead of the figure of the stela owner, there is a large *ʿnḫ*-sign (Vienna ÄS 109, see also infra). The *ʿnḫ* can also appear on the stela without any framing. In this case, the space within the "loop" is hollowed out (Abydos-tomb 78[13], but also Cairo CG 20353) or even perforated (University of Liverpool E.30[14]). In a certain way it takes over the pictorial function of the niche or perforation. This means, that an already existing decoration scheme – figure in niche/perforation – is varied. One of its elements is exchanged for another. For example the *ʿnḫ*-sign between the Wedjat-eyes is one of several solutions.

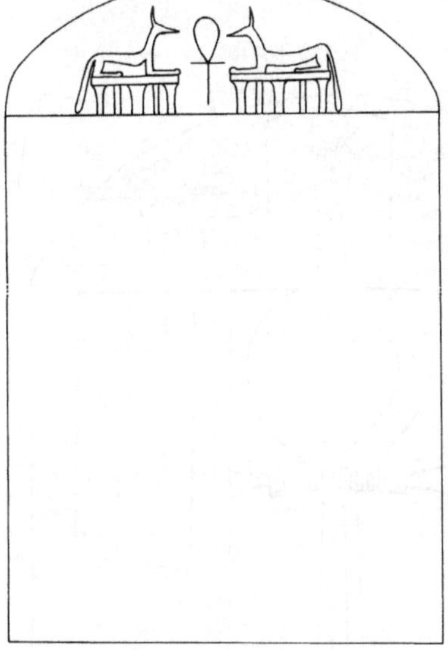

Fig. 1: Stela Tübingen 461

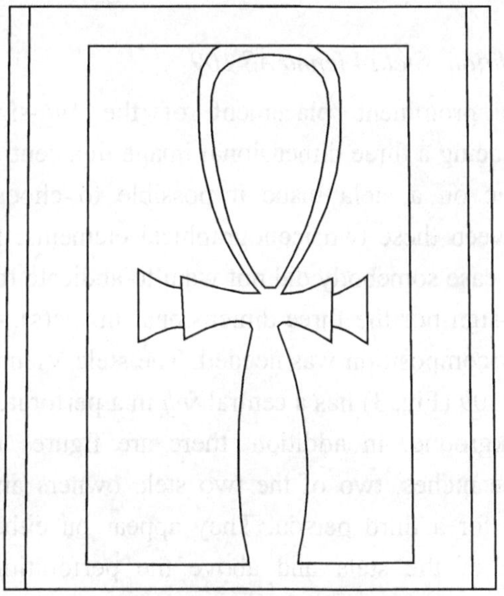

Fig. 2: Stela Cairo CG 20353

---

[10] The term is called "Anch-Stele" in I. Hein/H. Satzinger, *Stelen des Mittleren Reiches einschließlich der I. und II. Zwischenzeit* II (*Corpus Antiquitatum Aegyptiacarum. Kunsthistorisches Museum Wien Ägyptisch-Orientalische Sammlung* 7), Mainz 1993, 39.

[11] Examples presents Hölz, *Giebelfelddekoration*, 17, 27.

[12] E. Brunner-Traut/H. Brunner, *Die Ägyptische Sammlung der Universität Tübingen*, Mainz 1981, 91-92 and pl. 59.

[13] D. Randall-MacIver/A.C. Mace, *El Amrah and Abydos 1899-1901* (*Egypt Exploration Fund* 23), London 1902, 87 and pl. 43.

[14] J. Bourriau, *Pharaohs and Mortals. Egyptian Art in the Middle Kingdom* (exhibition catalogue), Cambridge 1988, 60-62, Nr. 48.

There are several questions concerning these observations. Two of them are at this juncture of special interest. Why did, following my opinion, the *ʿnḫ*-sign replace the statuettes and not vice versa? Why did the *ʿnḫ*-sign appear especially at the place of the statuettes? The niches are built up like a shrine. They often have a torus moulding and a cornice and therefore play the role of shrine for a statue.[15] For *ʿnḫ*-signs or objects in a similar shape, there are no comparable prototypes known. They are also very new on stelae, while the depiction of a stela owner is not new, at least in other form, such as relief. Another important point for replacing a statuette by an *ʿnḫ*-sign, coming to the second question, is the shape of the *ʿnḫ*-sign. The proportions of the *ʿnḫ*-sign closely resemble those of a human figure. This all seems more plausible than assuming, that the *ʿnḫ*-sign was conceived "out of the blue" and replaced thereafter a statuette of the stela owner, who could appear in any form anyway on the stela. Regardless of these questions we have here one example for different solutions of an aesthetic problem (the harmonious incorporation of the large *ʿnḫ*-sign), which is solved by a symbolic demand (an *ʿnḫ*-sign should be placed in a striking way on a stela). Two fundamental solutions were found, both via replacing another element with the *ʿnḫ*-sign. It can replace the *šn*-rings in the middle of the upper register or it can emerge as a big hieroglyphic sign in the middle of the monument, where sometimes a statuette appears.

Regardless of the motivation – contents or aesthetics –, this shows the broad scope of the stonecutter and their client regarding the creative development of new depictions. This observation is well visible especially in the group of the *ʿnḫ*-stelae. They remain rare and disappeared from the programme of the stonecutters before different types of depictions were established. Therefore, they reveal an enjoyment in experimenting in searching for new solutions.

Addition: Stela Vienna ÄS 109

The prominent placement of the *ʿnḫ*-sign replacing a three dimensional image in a central niche on a stela made it possible to choose between these two iconographical elements. In one case somebody did not want to abdicate the *ʿnḫ*-sign nor the three dimensional image(s). A new composition was needed. The stela Vienna ÄS 109 (Fig. 3) has a central *ʿnḫ* in a perforated background. In addition, there are figures in three niches, two of the two stela owners and one for a third person. They appear on either side of the stela and above the perforation. However, in general existing schemata were reproduced, perhaps combined. Therefore, we can recognise them as schemata. Perhaps it is no accident, that the complex composition, which certainly needed careful planning, is combined with a high degree of artisanship in execution. Possibly, it is really a unique piece.

Fig. 3: Stela Vienna ÄS 109

15 Cf. BADAWY, *Bulletin de l'Institut d'Égypte* 35 (1954), 117.

3. Wedjat-eyes and Jackals

Far more complex than the stelae with niche and perforation is the situation with two of the most popular elements on Abydos stelae. These are the two wedjat eyes and the jackals, most often also shown in pairs and representing the jackals animal form of Anubis and Upuaut. Vandier[16] already has several useful remarks, but a detailed study to the form and style of these two elements would certainly add to our knowledge. For the question of the aesthetic motivation of a certain arrangement, I will concentrate on the cases where both motifs appear together. For these monuments it can be assumed that the question of contents for the pair of eyes and jackals was undecided. They were both needed. This wish is understandable in regard of the different but fundamental function of both elements.[17] They were both preferably placed near the upper end of a stela. Thanks to their form they could easily and harmonically fill the semicircle of the stela's upper register. Certainly, there is an aesthetic reason for the choice of placement, but this is not the only one. The association with the human body advises the placement of the eyes at the top.[18] The solution of placing both motifs on a stela was a new task for a craftsman. A new harmonic arrangement was needed. This trivial fact is not self-evident. There are enough other elements which could be combined without problems or obstruction. One example is the niche. Its placement on a stela was no problem for the eyes or the jackals in the upper register, as it was placed on a stela far under the others. The jackals, as protector, most often represent Upuaut, and appear quite often together with the niche. They could be placed above the niche or next to it.[19] The stonecutter or draughtsman had to face a new, more aesthetically challenging task depicting the eyes and jackals together on a stela, a solution which was guided by symbolic reasons dominated by the meaning of these pictures. The task was solved in different ways. Several solutions were in use at the same time. It was decided in each case anew.

Vandier concluded that the combination of pairs of eyes and jackals was unpopular, because it is relatively rare.[20] Unpopular, perhaps because the combination looks some how overcrowded. Rarity is no proof for unpopularity. Besides the wedjat eyes all elements of decorations could be called unpopular. Furthermore, most often nothing is known about the original context of stelae. It is possible that several stelae erected together, formed one text and picture programme, in which one stela shows the pairs of eyes, the other the two jackals. In such cases it was obviously not necessary to place both motifs on a single stela. In his assessment Vandier rightly considers the ambition of the stonecutters for a balanced composition. Nevertheless, the conception of "overcrowded" depends too much on personal and cultural taste. It is not useful for judging 4000 year old compositions. Aesthetic motives certainly played an important part, but these were those of the craftsmen (and possible clients of them) about 4000 years ago, and not ours. For us overcrowded, the solution was used and was therefore an acceptable possibility. The following arrangements of wedjat-eyes and jackals on a stela are attested:

---

16 VANDIER, *Manuel d'archéologie* II, 487-492.

17 Especially "regeneration" through eyes, "protection" through the (gods of the) jackals, cf. HÖLZL, *Giebelfelddekoration*, 13-15 (for wedjat eyes) und 96 (for jackals).

18 This does not mean that the stela was regarded on purpose in analogy to a person. It is just important to note the human self-perception in terms of aesthetical questions.

19 HÖLZL, *Giebelfelddekoration*, 94-96.

20 VANDIER, *Manuel d'archéologie* II, 490: "Il est rare qu'ils [les yeux] soient encadrés par des chiens, car cette accumulation de motifs donnait l'impression d'une décoration trop chargée".

1. *Jackals on the Outside, Pair of Eyes in between*

- Jackals lying on standard or shrine, at the outer side of the pediment (in the middle most often a *šn*-ring): CG 20104 (jackals smaller), CG 20718 (the same), Chicago University Museum E312[21], Leiden 14 (AP. 2)[22] (the same), London BM 240[23] (the same), MMA 63.154[24] (the same), Stuttgart 3[25], Stuttgart 12[26] (block of inscriptions between the eyes and jackals), Tübingen 459[27] (Fig. 4).
- The eyes are framed by a box: Stockholm Nationalmuseum NME 19[28], London UC 14551[29] (Fig. 5; only left side preserved).
- Jackals at the outer side on standards, something below: CG 20255, Paris Louvre C.29, C.30, C.189 (jackals a little bigger than the eyes), CG 20761 (under the eyes on either side a figure of Osiris, on the same height as the standard of the jackals), Zagreb 592[30] (Fig. 6; eyes of a falcon above line of inscription, standard on base line of inscription).
- Jackals on the outside, lying without standards or shrines: CG 20030, CG 20154 (jackals are lying just above the baseline), CG 20160 (jackals much smaller than the eyes and very high placed, as if they are resting on a standard, instead there is a kneeling figure under them), CG 20334[31], CG 20600[32] (jackals are today no longer visible, perhaps they were once painted), CG 20706 (jackals smaller and placed higher, there would have been space for a standard under them), CG 20102 (similar), Berkeley Bt. 9[33], Leiden 34 (V. L. D. J. 2)[34] (front and back side very similar, in the pediment almost identical. The back parts of the wedjat eyes end in circles. Above there are the head and the front legs of the much smaller jackals. Standards were possibly once painted, compare the human figures on the stela, which are without inner details), Vienna ÄS 142[35] (Fig. 7; jackals slightly over basis line, their long tails cut through the basis line and occupy almost the whole length of the uppermost text line. Their bodies are so big that they occupy harmoniously the space between the pair of eyes and edge of the stela), Leiden 13 (AP. 38)[36] (Fig. 8; jackals much bigger than the eyes).

---

21 Cf. HÖLZL, *Giebelfelddekoration*, 118.

22 P.A.A. BOESER, *Beschreibung der Aegyptischen Sammlung des Niederländischen Reichsmuseums der Altertümer in Leiden* II. *Die Denkmäler der Zeit zwischen dem Alten und Mittleren Reich und des Mittleren Reiches. Erste Abteilung: Stelen*, Den Haag 1909, 6 (no. 14), pl. 15.

23 *Hieroglyphic Texts from Egyptian Stelae, &c., in the British Museum* II, London 1912, Pl. 32.

24 HÖLZL, *Giebelfelddekoration*, 99.

25 After HÖLZL, *Giebelfelddekoration*, 117; cf. W. SPIEGELBERG/B. PÖRTNER, *Aegyptische Grabsteine und Denksteine aus süddeutschen Sammlungen* I, Strasbourg 1902, 2 (without picture).

26 Cf. HÖLZL, *Giebelfelddekoration*, 106.

27 BRUNNER-TRAUT/BRUNNER, *Ägyptische Sammlung Tübingen*, 85 and pl. 55.

28 B.J. PETERSON, Ägyptische Privatstelen aus dem Mittleren Reich. Neun Denkmäler in schwedischem Besitz, *Orientalia Suecana* 17 (1967), 11-27, esp. 15-16 with fig. 2.

29 H.M. STEWARD, *Egyptian Stelae, Reliefs and Paintings from the Petrie Collection* II: *Archaic Period to Second Intermediate Period*, Warminster 1979, 29 (no. 121), pl. 31.4; cf. HÖLZL, *Giebelfelddekoration*, 119.

30 J. MONNET SALEH, *Les antiquités égyptiennes de Zagreb. Catalogue raisonné des antiquités égyptiennes conservées au Musée Archéologique de Zagreb en Yougoslavie*, Paris/Den Haag 1970, 22-23 (no. 8).

31 No photo in H.O. LANGE/H. SCHÄFER, *Catalogue général des antiquités du musée du Caire N°s 20001-20780, Grab- und Denksteine des Mittleren Reichs im Museum von Kairo* IV, Berlin 1902; cf. LANGE/SCHÄFER, *Grab- und Denksteine* I, 1902, 346-347 und HÖLZL, *Giebelfelddekoration*, 115.

32 No photo in LANGE/SCHÄFER, *Grab- und Denksteine* IV; cf. LANGE/SCHÄFER, *Grab- und Denksteine* II, Berlin 1908, 240 and HÖLZL, *Giebelfelddekoration*, 115.

33 After HÖLZL, *Giebelfelddekoration*, 115.

34 BOESER, *Beschreibung der Aegyptischen Sammlung* II, 9 (no. 34), pl. 24.

35 I. HEIN/H. SATZINGER, *Stelen des Mittleren Reiches einschließlich der I. und II. Zwischenzeit* I (*Corpus Antiquitatum Aegyptiacarum. Kunsthistorisches Museum Wien Ägyptisch-Orientalische Sammlung* 4), Mainz 1989, 62-67.

36 BOESER, *Beschreibung der Aegyptischen Sammlung* II, 6, no. 13, pl. 14.

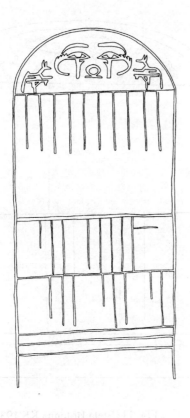

Fig. 4: Stela Tübingen 459

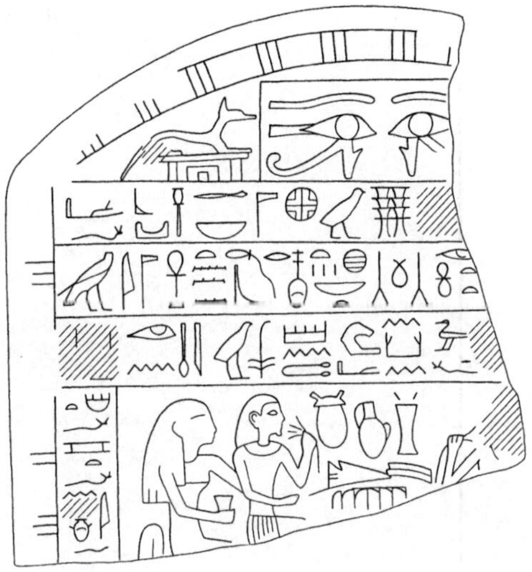

Fig. 5: Stela London UC 14551

Fig. 6: Stela Zagreb 592

Fig. 7: Stela Vienna ÄS 142

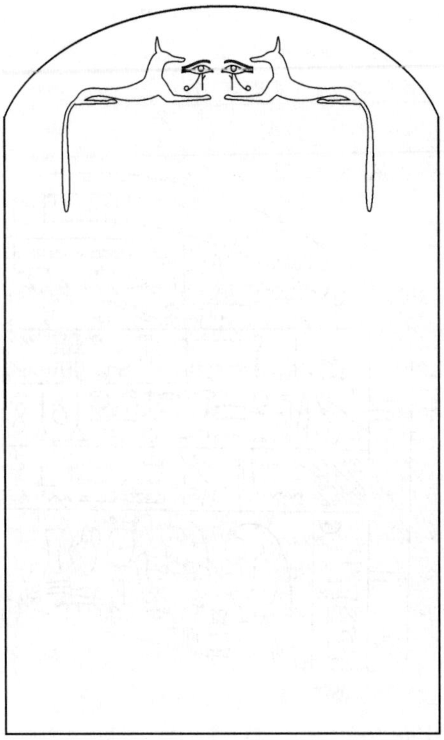

Fig. 8: Stela Leiden 13

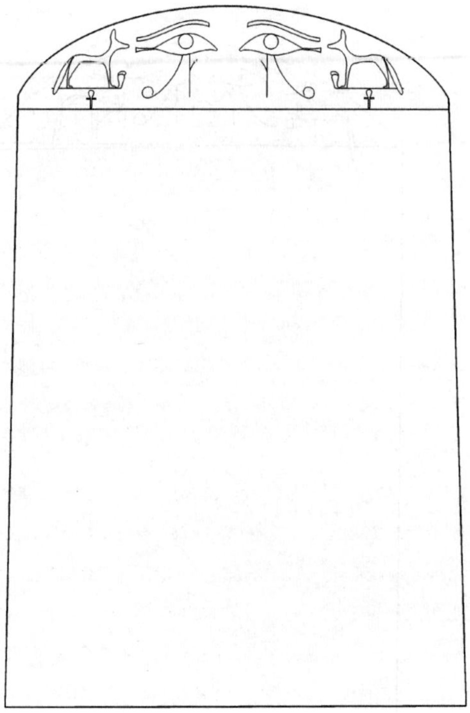

Fig. 9: Stela Cairo CG 20155

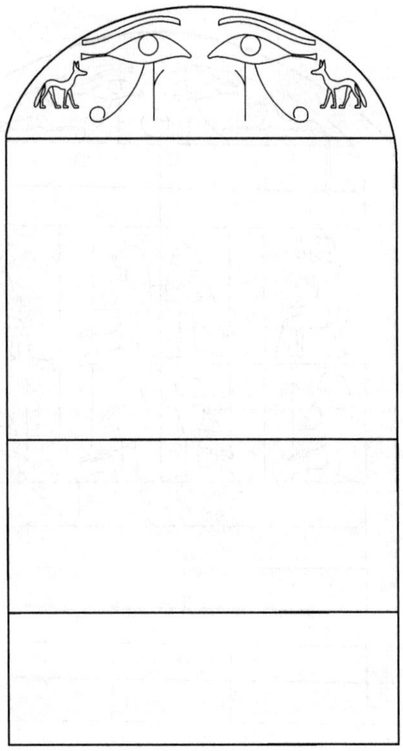

Fig. 10: Stela Cairo CG 20656

Fig. 11: Stela Bologna KS 1930

- CG 20155: ˁnḫ-signs as standards (Fig. 9).
- Only one jackal: CG 20640.[37]
- Jackals, standing: CG 20656[38] (Fig. 10; jackals much smaller than the eyes, which already fill the pediment), CG 20716[39], Marseille without no.[40] (the left jackal is higher positioned than the right one, certainly providing space for three columns of hieroglyphs; both are place on the standard "table").
- One jackal, staying, the other one lying on a standard: Bologna KS 1930[41] (Fig. 11; left jackal, standing, behind it *šmˁ*; right one on standard, behind it *mḥw*).
- On rectangular stela with torus moulding and cornice: Vienna ÄS 156[42] (Fig. 12; text line under the pair of eyes, vertical line between left and right, at the outer side there is a shrine in big proportions on the basis line of the text line, the heads of the jackals are high as the eye brows, jackals and eyes about the same size).

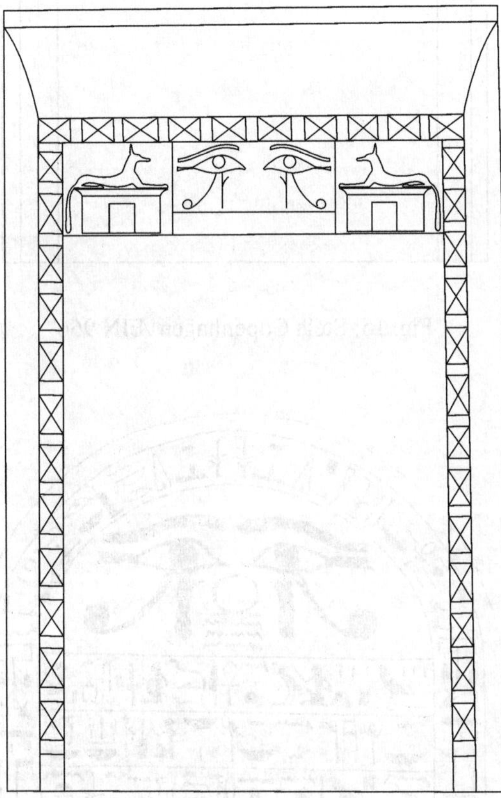

Fig. 12: Stela Vienna ÄS 156

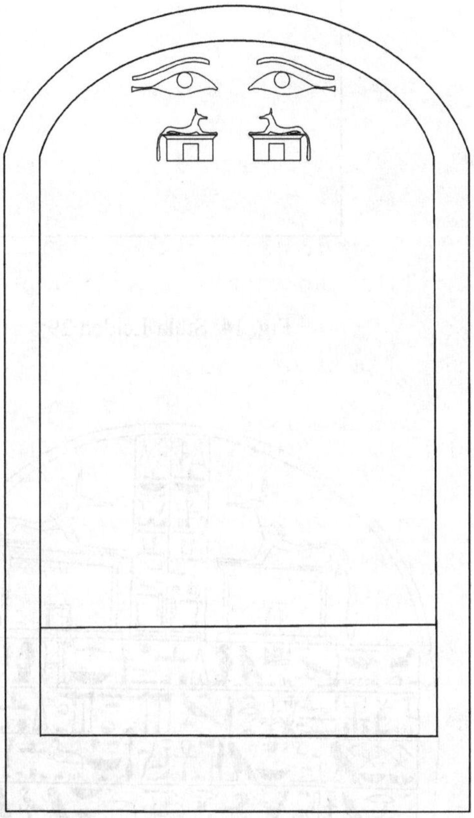

Fig. 13: Stela Cairo CG 20100

[37] No photographic picture in LANGE/SCHÄFER, *Grab- und Denksteine* IV; and LANGE/SCHÄFER, *Grab- und Denksteine* II, 277 and HÖLZL, *Giebelfelddekoration*, 116.

[38] Hard to recognise on the photo in LANGE/SCHÄFER, *Grab- und Denksteine* IV, pl. L; cf. LANGE/SCHÄFER, *Grab- und Denksteine* II, 289 and HÖLZL, *Giebelfelddekoration*, 115.

[39] No photo in LANGE/SCHÄFER, *Grab- und Denksteine* IV; see also LANGE/SCHÄFER, *Grab- und Denksteine* II, 342-343 and HÖLZL, *Giebelfelddekoration*, 114.

[40] M. GAUTHIER-LAURENT, Une stèle du Moyen-Empire, *Revue d'Égyptologie* 1 (1933), 75-80, pl. VII.

[41] E. BRESCIANI, *Le stele egiziane del Museo Civico Archeologico di Bologna* (*Cataloghi delle Collezioni del Museo Civico Archeologico di Bologna*), Bologna 1985, 30 (no. 6), pl. 9.

[42] HEIN/SATZINGER, *Stelen des Mittleren Reiches* I, 84-92.

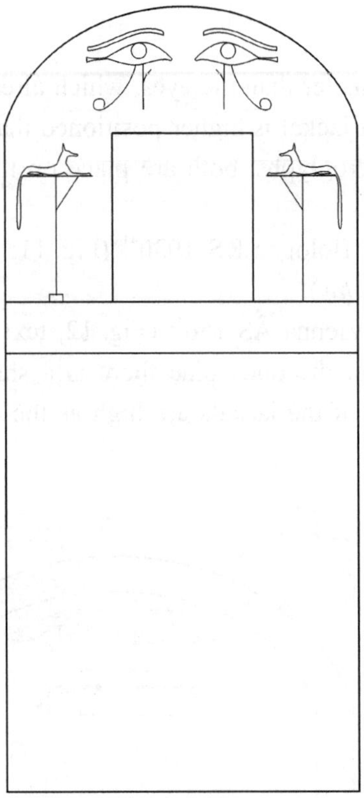

Fig. 14: Stela Leiden 29

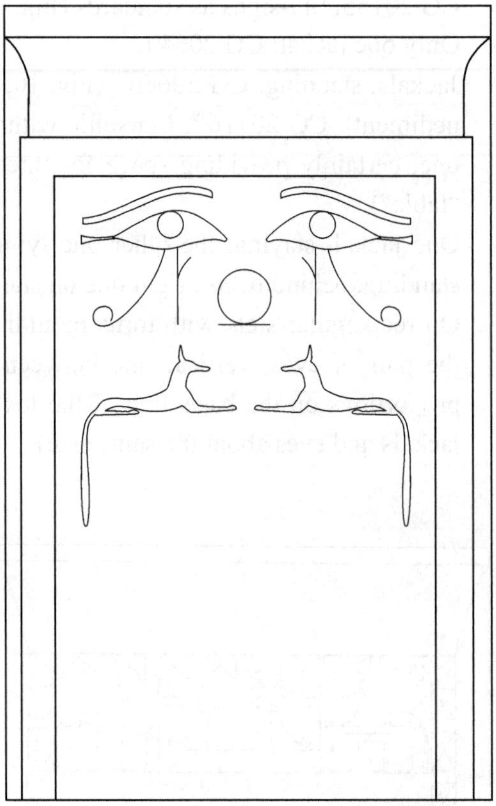

Fig. 15: Stela Copenhagen ÆIN 966

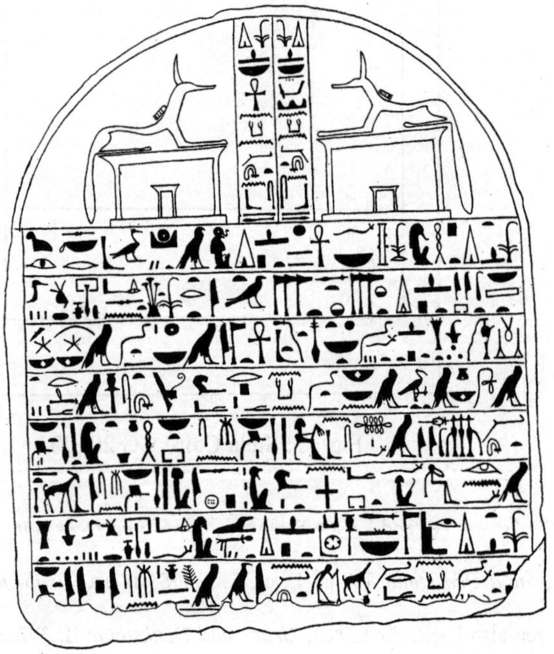

Fig. 16a: Stela Copenhagen ÆIN 1539

Fig. 16b: Stela Copenhagen ÆIN 1539

2. *One on Top on the Other: top Pair of Eyes, under it Two Lying Jackals*

– Eyes and jackals on shrine in the pediment: CG 20087, CG 20100 (Fig. 13; human eyes, jackals quite small: both because of lack of space[43]), CG 20101 (falcon eyes).
– Jackals under the pediment: CG 20299.[44]
– Combination with niche and jackals on either side: CG 20397 (in the pediment above the eyes there is *Bḥd.ti*), Leiden 29 (L. XI. 1; Fig. 14).[45]
– Rectangular stela with torus moulding and cornice: CG 20459, Copenhagen ÆIN 966[46] (Fig. 15).

3. *Front and Back*

– Copenhagen ÆIN 1539[47] (Fig. 16 a-b).

4. *One Jackal between a Pair of Eyes*

– Cairo CG 20746 (Fig. 17; standing between two wedjat-eyes, stylised jackal on baseline, in front the uraeus of its standard is visible).

Fig. 17: Stela Cairo CG 20746

Before discussing no. 1 and 2 it should be mentioned that two possible arrangements are not attested. These are the jackals above the eyes or between them. This can readily be explained from the close relation of a pair of eyes. Eyes appear closely placed in a human face. For the high placement of the eyes on stelae see above page 5.[48]

43 So M. MARÉE, A Remarkable Group of Egyptian Stelae from the Second Intermediate Period, *Oudheidkundige Mededelingen uit het Rijksmuseum van Oudheden te Leiden* 73 (1993), 7-22, especially 8 note 3. The human eyes appear also elsewhere, but much less often.

44 No picture in LANGE /SCHÄFER, *Grab- und Denksteine* IV; cf. LANGE/SCHÄFER, *Grab- und Denksteine* I, 312-313 and HÖLZL, *Giebelfelddekoration*, 119.

45 BOESER, *Beschreibung der Aegyptischen Sammlung* II, 8-9 (no. 29), pl. XII.

46 M. JØRGENSEN, *Catalogue Egypt* (*3000 – 1550 B.C.*) *Ny Carlsberg Glyptotek* I, Copenhagen 1996, 200-201, no. 84.

47 JØRGENSEN, *Catalogue Egypt* I, 196-197, no. 82 (wrongly designated as ÆIN 967, cf. 199); R. ENGELBACH/B. GUNN, *Harageh* (*British School of Archaeology in Egypt* 28), London 1923, pl. LXXII.

48 However, it is possible to imagine a pair of jackals above a cornice, which is the upper end of a false door. In the upper field of this false door eyes might appear which are under the jackals. However, this combination is not attested, only the single elements (eyes on false door, jackals in the cornice).

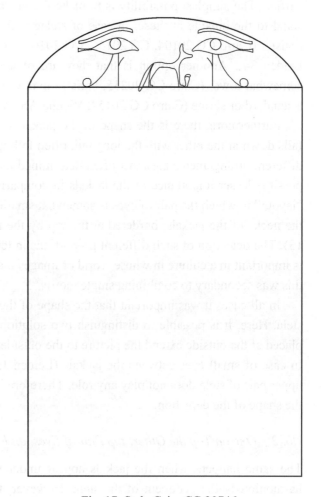

Commentary

No. 1: Jackals on the Outside, Pair of Eyes in between

The relation in size between the eyes and the jackals varies greatly. Evidently, the main intention was to fill the space in the pediment harmonically, although one of these two elements would already suffice. The simplest possibility is to make the jackals somewhat smaller than the eyes, because they stand to the outside of these. In case of stelae with a rounded top they have less space at the upper register (Cairo CG 20104, CG 20155, CG 20160, CG 20706, CG 20718, Leiden 14, London BM 240, Leiden 34). Another option is that they are of about the same size as the eyes and were placed somewhat lower (Cairo CG 20255, Paris Louvre C 189). In this case it is helpful not to place them on a standard or shrine (Cairo CG 20154, Vienna ÄS 142).

Furthermore, there is the shape of the jackal. It starts high at one side, with the raised head and falls down at the other with the long tail, often falling down to the next register (Vienna ÄS 142). The different arrangements are most often determined by the available space and say very little about the possible lesser importance of the jackals in comparison to the eyes. This is demonstrated by another "layout" in which the pair of eyes is somewhat smaller. It is so small, that it fits into the space between the necks of the jackals, bordered at the top by the mouth and at the bottom by the forelegs (Leiden 13). The detection of such different proportions in terms of size between two iconographical elements is important in a culture in whose world of images many relations are expressed by the scale.[49] Clearly, this was secondary to combining single motifs[50].

In all cases it was important that the shape of the figures fitted harmoniously in the roundel of the stela. Here, it is possible to distinguish two solutions. Several combinations of eyes with the jackals placed at the outside extend the picture to the outsides. Their shapes add up to a new, combined shape. In case of small eyes between the jackals (Leiden 13), the combination of these two elements in the upper part of stela does not play any role. Therefore, a conflict was avoided. The jackals alone provide the shape of the depiction.

No. 2 : One on Top the Other: top Pair of Eyes, under it Two Lying Jackals

The same happens when the jackals appear under the pair of eyes. In this case the eyes alone fill harmoniously the pediment of the stela. However, there are also in this combination differences in detail. The animals can be placed on a cornice instead of a standard or shrine, if the stela has a perforation under them (Cairo CG 20748, similar Cairo CG 20177).[51] In these cases, the whole decoration of the stela gave the opportunity for a compact combination of two elements, cornice and jackals. With the placement of the pairs of eyes directly above the cornice, the jackals had to be placed somewhere else and are arranged on either side of the niche (Leiden 29, Cairo CG 20397). Finally, other possibilities to present two jackals should be mentioned. They can be depicted lying, with or without shrine or standard, or, another variable on a standard or not. Furthermore different captions

[49] See e.g. H. SCHÄFER, *Principles of Egyptian Art. Edited, with an epilogue, by Emma Brunner-Traut. Translated and edited, with an introduction, by John Baines. Foreword by E.H. Gombrich*, Oxford 1986, 230-234 (chapter 4.4.7)

[50] Cf. V. VASILJEVIĆ, Über die relative Größe der Darstellungen des Grabherrn im Alten Reich, *Studien zur Altägyptischen Kultur* 25 (1998), 341-351.

[51] Examples for jackals, placed on a cornice at stelae with a niche or false door instead of a perforation are not known to me. In regards to the structure, these options should also have been open for a craftsman in charge. The relevant motif is an Anubis on a cornice.

can appear.[52] In a certain sense there was almost a catalogue of combinations available for designing a whole stela.

At the end, it should be mentioned that there are many combined depictions of eyes and jackals following the Middle Kingdom down to the coffins of the Late and Ptolemaic Periods. They do not only attest the transmission or reuse of the motifs "pair of eyes" and "jackals", but also the processing as fixed combination.[53]

No. 3: Front and Back, and No. 4: One Jackal between a Pair of Eyes

The decoration schemes nos. 3 and 4 must be indeed regarded as special cases, although there were once possibly more examples with these combinations. In the case of no. 3 the rarity is simply a reflection of the circumstance that there are not many stelae decorated on both sides. The extraordinary solution no. 4 is to my knowledge without parallel. However, the asymmetry is for example attested by stelae with the depiction of only one jackal without pair of eyes (Cairo CG 20192[54], Vienna ÄS 104[55], Cairo CG 20596[56]) or the confrontation of two different gods (Cairo CG 20085[57], Vienna ÄS 136[58], London BM 222[59], BM 233[60], Louvre C.6[61], Louvre C.7[62], Leiden 8 [AP. 21][63], Cairo CG 20089[64]). As regards the dating of the examples presented, there is the impression that the reign of Amenemhat III was a time of innovations and experiments concerning asymmetrical arrangements. However, three out of eight examples are certainly not yet enough to confirm this observation. It is worth mentioning, in particular as research on sculpture of Amenemhat III came to the same result.[65]

---

52 For the variable identification of the jackals as Anubis and Upuaut, regardless of the possible appearance of the pair of eyes on the stela, cf. J. SPIEGEL, *Die Götter von Abydos. Studien zum ägyptischen Synkretismus* (*Göttinger Orientforschungen IV.Reihe Ägypten* 1), Göttingen 1973, 49-53.

53 One good example is provided by the head and foot ends of the Late Period to Ptolemaic coffin Cairo CG 29307, where eyes and jackals are placed one on each other; in this case the space between them is filled by a *šn*-ring, three waterlines and a *wsḫ*-pot at the bottom. Through this frame form, all depicted motifs form one picture.

54 One canid on a shrine, facing to the right, placed in the middle, before him a column in the direction of reading: *tp.i-ḏw=f.*

55 Similar, but caption on the right in two columns: *Wpj-wꜣ.wt nb tꜣ-ḏsr*. HEIN/SATZINGER, *Stelen des Mittleren Reiches* I, 13-17.

56 Identical, but inscription on the other side, therefore from left to right in three columns: *Wpj-wꜣ.wt nb ꜣbḏ.w*.

57 *Hieroglyphic Texts in the BM* II, pl. 31: left Upuaut-standard, right Osiris.

58 Similar, but the small field with the standard of Upuaut and Osiris is placed slightly to the left, removed from the middle, HEIN/SATZINGER, *Stelen des Mittleren Reiches* I, 48-54.

59 Similar, also slightly placed to the left. The standard is standing on the *nb*-sign of *nb tꜣ-ḏsr*.

60 Osiris to the left, canid on standard on the right, in the middle cartouche of Amenemhat III, on the outer sides captions. Very shallow upper roundel of stela (*Hieroglyphic Texts from Egyptian Stelae, &c., in the British Museum* IV, London 1913, pl. 14).

61 E. GAYET, *Musée du Louvre. Stèles de la XII*e *dynastie* (*Bibliothèque de l'Ècole des Hautes Études, Sciences philologiques et historiques* 68), Paris 1886, pl. X: similar to the former one, also with name of Amenemhat III.

62 E. GAYET, *Stèles de la XII*e *dynastie*, pl. VI. Rectangular stela, in the middle there is a small box with wedjat eyes und a *šn*-ring, at the outside there is on each side a shrine, the one on the left with Osiris, the one on the right with the standing Upuaut (human shape with jackal head); captions appear between central field and the shrine. Also dated under Amenemhat III.

63 BOESER, *Beschreibung der Aegyptischen Sammlung* II, 4 (no. 8), pl. 7: In the pediment there is a winged sun, under that is on the right an Osiris figure with the name behind and opposite of a Horus falcon on a palace facade (Horus name), as the beginning of the names of Amenemhat III. This is a variation of the Osiris-Upuat opposition in which the king as Horus occupies his position and function.

64 Min on the left, jackal on a shrine on the right.

65 Cf. R.E. FREED, Another Look at the Sculpture of Amenemhat III, *Revue d'Égyptologie* 53 (2002), 103-124; I. BLOM-BÖER, *Die Tempelanlage Amenemhets III. in Hawara. Das Labyrinth. Bestandsaufnahme und Auswertung der Architektur- und Inventarfragmente* (*Egyptologische Uitgaven* 20), Leiden 2006, 74-77 (chapter 2.8.2).

4. Conclusion

It is true that the size and arrangement of individual elements of a picture in a composition provide important hints for the meaning of Egyptian pictures. The discussed examples demonstrate that the contents is not everything. There is also the desire for an aesthetic arrangement. The longing for "beauty", whatever it means, is a basic need of people. It is visible in all degrees. The placement of the *ꜥnḫ*-sign in a harmonious image format, as well as the different combinations of the pairs of eyes and jackals is less important than the size, which often implies rank. It is unlikely that each new combination of eyes and jackals implies a new meaning. Our idea of the importance of size and sequence of reading are correct observations as before, but do not explain everything.

On the other hand asymmetrical arrangements of individual elements seem to prove that a harmonic image format was not everything. With Vandier we might call these cases "moins heureux".[66] However, some Egyptian regarded these solutions as fully appropriate, whether they liked the effect of asymmetry[67], or whether they accepted for symbolic advantages the aesthetic disadvantage. Especially this openness of the system made it possible that on stelae of the Middle Kingdom always new depictions appear. Each client could hope for a satisfying result in terms of contents as well as aesthetic whenever he could find able craftsmen. Also time and place related aspects, in other words "fashions", must have played an important part. How far the imagination of single individuals were influential show unique designs as on stela Vienna ÄS 109.

The selected examples show the unit of contents and optical harmonious depictions. Not only for the stelae of the Middle Kingdom, they remind us to be cautious about one-sided interpretations.

List of Illustrations

Fig. 1: Adapted from E. BRUNNER-TRAUT/H. BRUNNER, *Die Ägyptische Sammlung der Universität Tübingen*, Mainz 1981, pl. 59.

Fig. 2: Adapted from H.O. LANGE/H. SCHÄFER, *Catalogue général des antiquités du Musée du Caire N°s 20001-20780, Grab- und Denksteine des Mittleren Reiches im Museum von Kairo* IV, Berlin 1902, pl. XXVI.

Fig. 3: Adapted from I. HEIN/H. SATZINGER, *Stelen des Mittleren Reiches einschließlich der I. und II. Zwischenzeit* II (*Corpus Antiquitatum Aegyptiacarum Kunsthistorisches Museum Wien Ägyptisch-Orientalische Sammlung* 7), Mainz 1993, 7,42.

Fig. 4: Adapted from E. BRUNNER-TRAUT/H. BRUNNER, *Die Ägyptische Sammlung der Universität Tübingen*, Mainz 1981, pl. 55.

---

66 VANDIER, *Manuel d'archéologie* II, 489. Vandier asked himself why there was sometimes only one instead of two jackals depicted.

67 It is received Egyptological opinion that in Egyptian art, one hundred percent symmetry was avoided and not wanted, see e.g. E. HORNUNG, *Geist der Pharaonenzeit*, Zurich-Munich 2nd ed. 1990, 85-87 with fig. 13.

Fig. 5: H.M. STEWARD, *Egyptian Stelae, Reliefs and Paintings from the Petrie Collection* II: *Archaic Period to Second Intermediate Period*, Warminster 1979, pl. 31.4.

Fig. 6: Adapted from J. MONNET SALEH, *Les antiquités égyptiennes de Zagreb. Catalogue raisonné des antiquités égyptiennes conservées au Musée Archéologique de Zagreb en Yougoslavie*, Paris/Den Haag 1970, 23.

Fig. 7: Adapted from I. HEIN/H. SATZINGER, *Stelen des Mittleren Reiches einschließlich der I. und II. Zwischenzeit* I (*Corpus Antiquitatum Aegyptiacarum Kunsthistorisches Museum Wien Ägyptisch-Orientalische Sammlung* 4), Mainz 1989, 4,63 and 4,67.

Fig. 8: P.A.A. BOESER, *Beschreibung der Aegyptischen Sammlung des Niederländischen Reichsmuseums der Altertümer in Leiden* II. *Die Denkmäler der Zeit zwischen dem Alten und Mittleren Reich und des Mittleren Reiches. Erste Abteilung: Stelen*, Den Haag 1909, pl. 14 (no. 13).

Fig. 9: Adapted from H.O. LANGE/H. SCHÄFER, *Catalogue général des antiquités du Musée du Caire N°s 20001-20780, Grab- und Denksteine des Mittleren Reiches im Museum von Kairo* IV, Berlin 1902, pl. XIV.

Fig. 10: Adapted from H.O. LANGE/H. SCHÄFER, *Catalogue général des antiquités du Musée du Caire N°s 20001-20780, Grab- und Denksteine des Mittleren Reiches im Museum von Kairo* IV, Berlin 1902, pl. L.

Fig. 11: E. BRESCIANI, *Le stele egiziane del Museo Civico Archeologico di Bologna* (*Cataloghi delle Collezioni del Museo Civico Archeologico di Bologna*), Bologna 1985, 31, pl. 9.

Fig. 12: Adapted from I. HEIN/H. SATZINGER, *Stelen des Mittleren Reiches einschließlich der I. und II. Zwischenzeit* I (*Corpus Antiquitatum Aegyptiacarum Kunsthistorisches Museum Wien Ägyptisch-Orientalische Sammlung* 4), Mainz 1989, 4,85 and 4,91.

Fig. 13: Adapted from H.O. LANGE/H. SCHÄFER, *Catalogue général des antiquités du Musée du Caire N°s 20001-20780, Grab- und Denksteine des Mittleren Reiches im Museum von Kairo* IV, Berlin 1902, pl. X.

Fig. 14: P.A.A. BOESER, *Beschreibung der Aegyptischen Sammlung des Niederländischen Reichsmuseums der Altertümer in Leiden* II. *Die Denkmäler der Zeit zwischen dem Alten und Mittleren Reich und des Mittleren Reiches. Erste Abteilung: Stelen*, Den Haag 1909, l. XII (no. 29).

Fig. 15: Adapted from M. JØRGENSEN, *Catalogue Egypt* (*3000 – 1550 B.C.*) *Ny Carlsberg Glyptotek* I, Copenhagen 1996, 200-201, no. 84.

Fig. 16a-b: R. ENGELBACH/B. GUNN, *Harageh* (*British School of Archaeology in Egypt* 28), London 1923, pl. LXXII.

Fig. 17: Adapted from H.O. LANGE/H. SCHÄFER, *Catalogue général des antiquités du Musée du Caire N°s 20001-20780, Grab- und Denksteine des Mittleren Reiches im Museum von Kairo* IV, Berlin 1902, pl. LVII.

Multiple Burials in Ancient Egypt to the End of the Middle Kingdom

Wolfram Grajetzki

1. Introduction

A prominent phenomenon in Egyptian funerary culture is the practice of multiple burial, very well attested in the Pre-Dynastic Period, not very common in the Early Dynastic Period and Old Kingdom, but then from the late Old Kingdom on again widespread. They became especially regular in the late Twelfth Dynasty and in all further periods down to the Christian era. To date there have been few attempts to explain the practice and its historical development, in Egyptian archaeology. In many cases it is simply assumed that they represent family-burials.[1] Sometimes this is indeed demonstrated by the inscribed material, in other cases the context indicates it, for example, when a man and a woman are placed side by side in a single tomb chamber. However, very often it is impossible to say anything about the relations between the people placed in one tomb, especially when more than two bodies were found.

Before going into further discussion, a definition is required. Multiple burials are here defined as the burials/graves/tombs where in one tomb chamber or pit more than one body was placed. There are already in the First Dynasty the subsidiary tombs, built side by side as an integrated architectural context around the cult enclosure and burials of the kings at Abydos and around other monumental tombs of that period at Saqqara and Gizeh. However, on the definition adopted here these are not multiple burials: each individual is placed in a separate unit. In the late Old Kingdom shafts with several chambers at the bottom appear. If only one body was placed in each chamber, this is also not a multiple burial. However, especially the older excavation reports are not always very detailed. The number of bodies for such shafts is normally stated, but it is often not mentioned in which of the chambers they were found. Obviously, such evidence should be treated with caution. There are also graves, which are often called "mass burials". Here a very high number of people was placed in one tomb or one tomb chamber. The most famous example is perhaps the "second cache" at Thebes, where the elite of the 21st Dynasty was laid to rest. This tomb contained about 150 mummies with coffins. For this study the difference between multiple and mass burials is not relevant. To my knowledge, I do not know any discussion on definition and distinction between mass and multiple burials.

Another problem are intrusive burials; e.g. dead bodies added to an already existing burial, which was not built for the intrusive/later deceased (while multiple burials always seems to have been arranged from the beginning for several dead). At many cemeteries, tombs were reused in later times, leaving the old burial in the tomb and placing a new one over it. It is arguable in many concrete cases, whether a burial could be called intrusive. However, looking at several cemeteries as a whole, the picture becomes quite clear, that multiple burials appear in certain periods, while at other periods the tombs for a single person are more common.

1 P.F. Dorman, Family Burial and Commemoration in the Theban Necropolis, in: N. Strudwick/J.H. Taylor (eds.), *The Theban Necropolis. Past, Present and Future*, London 2003, 30-41.

2. Pre-Dynastic, Old Kingdom to about the Fifth Dynasty

The usual burial in the Badarian Period is the single inhumation: one body in one tomb (shaft) is the rule.[2] In the Naqada period multiple burials are quite common, though not the norm. In the small Naqada cemetery excavated at Elkab about 20 % of the tombs contained more than one body. In many cases these are burials of an adult with a child. Stan Hendrickx comments: "children were buried in the graves of adults whenever the occasion existed".[3] The important point, following Hendrickxs, seems to be that the tomb was only opened once to introduce both bodies. Even these single-moment, multiple burials disappear at the end of the Naqada period. In the early Dynastic period the single interment is the rule. This is also true for the following early Old Kingdom, when multiple burials are still rare. A short survey of some better documented cemeteries can demonstrate this.

From about 150 burials in the Old Kingdom cemetery of Gurob only four graves contained each one adult (two women, two men) and one child. Only one burial contained one man and one woman buried together.[4] Interestingly the tomb register states: "bodies side by side, very old".[5] At Matmar[6], Mostagedda,[7] Badari and Qau[8] and other places multiple burials are also very rare and generally restricted to burials of a woman with a child.

At the same time, there are also important developments in the Old Kingdom concerning the mastabas and the number of burial shafts, reflecting the same tendency. Mastabas of the Early Dynastic Period are always reserved for one person. This seems to be true for all social levels and in all parts of the country. The royal tombs of Abydos may be compared with the palace facade tombs at Saqqara or Tarkhan or with the more modest sized burials at Helwan, Tarkhan or Naga ed-Deir.[9] Although the architecture of these mastabas is often very different from place to place in detail, the burial chamber seems to be taken always only by one person. Husband and wife are clearly buried at different places, architecturally separated. At the end of the Second Dynasty mastabas appear with two cult chapels and two different burial chambers. George Andrew Reisner called them "twin Mastabas", because they are almost double the length of the more or less contemporary "single mastabas" and therefore they seem for us a little out of proportion.[10] Mastabas of the Third Dynasty with two shafts are already more "in proportion" (in general about 1 to 2 - width to length).

---

2 M.A. MURRAY, Burial Customs and Beliefs in the Hereafter in Predynastic Egypt, *Journal of Egyptian Archaeology* 42 (1956), 87.

3 S. HENDRICKX, *Elkab* V. *The Naqada III Cemetery*, Brussels 1994, 154.

4 G. BRUNTON/R. ENGELBACH, *Gurob* (*British School of Archaeology in Egypt* 41), London 1927, pl. IV-V, IX (tomb register).

5 BRUNTON/ENGELBACH, *Gurob*, pl. X.

6 G. BRUNTON, *Matmar* (*British Museum Expedition to Middle Egypt 1929-1931*), London 1948, pl. X (three tombs with each two bodies – no. 3111, 3112, 5119).

7 G. BRUNTON, *Mostagedda and the Tasian Culture* (*British Museum Expedition to Middle Egypt First and Second Years 1928, 1929*), London 1937, pl. XLV, tomb 2677 (fc - about Fourth Dynasty), tomb 683 (cc - Fifth Dynasty). Abbreviation used here and hereafter: f - human remains of a female person, m - human remains of a male, c - human remains of a child.

8 No multiple burials for the Fourth and Fifth Dynasty, only three examples for the end of the Old Kingdom: G. BRUNTON, *Qau, Badari* II (*British School of Archaeology in Egypt* 45), London 1928, pl. LVI-LVII, tomb 3113 (ff), 3169 (mmf), 4852 (mmfc).

9 See in general G.A. REISNER, *The Development of the Egyptian Tomb down to the Accession of Cheops*, Oxford/London 1936.

10 REISNER, *Development of the Egyptian Tomb*, 285-86.

However, in the Third and Fourth Dynasties there are still many mastabas with only one shaft, and many of them are datable to the time of Snefru (Dahshur)[11] and Khufu. A husband and his wife are clearly buried at different places with a separate cult chapel.[12] In the Fourth and Fifth Dynasties the number of shafts per mastaba increased.[13] The available inscribed material indicates that these tombs represent family burial places.[14] Therefore the Old Kingdom provides a clear development from mastabas reserved just for one person to mastabas for several people, most likely family members. In connection with this development the decoration of the false door and tomb chapel in general should be mentioned. Tomb stones of the First and Second Dynasties always mention only one person. The same holds true for the false door in the early phase of its development, in the Third Dynasty. However, at the beginning of the Fourth Dynasty the whole family is sometimes shown in the tomb decoration, false doors depict in the main field the tomb owner and his wife together at the funerary meal.[15] These false door panels seem to be especially popular in the Fourth Dynasty,[16] but are also attested in the later Old Kingdom.[17] However, they are not very common, and it appears still quite often that a tomb decoration is just made for one man, without even mentioning a wife.[18]

3. Late Old Kingdom, First Intermediate Period and Early Middle Kingdom

In terms of multiple burials the period from the end of the Old Kingdom to the early Middle Kingdom (until about Senusret II) constitutes one single period, although the development of burial customs underwent important changes in detail. Multiple burials are still not common, but they appear in higher number than before. It is particularly important to note that now not only an adult and a child were placed into tombs but more often also an adult man and an adult woman, who are most likely a couple. There are also cases of burials with more than two individuals, whose relationship is not always clear.

Examples of Innovations in Burial Customs

The following list offers an overview of tombs at several sites in Egypt. These are just some examples which are better recorded or which provide further insight into the custom of placing more than one body into a tomb chamber. The list does not aim to be complete.

---

11 N. ALEXANIAN, *Dahschur* II. *Das Grab des Prinzen Netjer-aperef. Die Mastaba II/1 in Dahschur* (*Archäologische Veröffentlichungen* 56), Mainz 1999, fig. 4.

12 H. JUNKER, *Bericht über die von der Akademie der Wissenschaften in Wien auf gemeinsame Kosten mit Dr. Wilhelm Pelizaeus unternommenen Grabungen auf dem Friedhof des Alten Reiches bei den Pyramiden von Gîza* I (*Denkschriften der Akademie der Wissenschaften in Wien* 69), Wien-Leipzig 1929, 38.

13 See for example the mastaba of Rawer with its high number of shafts datable to the Fifth Dynasty. S. HASSAN, *Excavations at Giza 1929-1930*, Oxford 1932, frontispiece. It is not certain whether all shafts are contemporary or whether some of them are later.

14 Y. HARPUR, *Decoration in Egyptian Tombs of the Old Kingdom* (*Studies in Egyptology*), London 1987, 16-20.

15 HARPUR, *Decoration in Egyptian Tombs*, 79.

16 For example L. BORCHARDT, *Catalogue général des antiquités égyptiennes du Musée du Caire. N°s 1295-1808, Denkmäler des Alten Reiches* (*außer den Statuen*) *im Museum von Kairo* I-II, Berlin 1937-1964, no. 1392; D. ARNOLD (ed.), *Egyptian Art in the Age of the Pyramids* (exhibition catalogue), New York 1999, 296-97, no. 85 (Fourth Dynasty); H. JUNKER, *Gîza* V, Wien-Leipzig 1941, 185, fig. 57; 61, fig. 48; 145, fig. 40; for the dating compare N. CHERPION, *Mastabas et hypogées d'Ancien Empire* (*Connaissance de l'Égypte Ancienne* 2), Brussels 1989, 83-103, 116, 128; compare the discussion: A.M. ROTH, Social Change in the Fourth Dynasty. The Spatial Organization of Pyramids, Tombs, and Cemeteries, *Journal of the American Research Centre in Egypt* 30 (1993), 42.

17 M. JØRGENSEN, *Catalogue Egypt* (*3000 - 1550 B.C.*) *Ny Carlsberg Glyptotek* I, Copenhagen 1996, 84-87, nos. 29-30 (Sixth Dynasty); C.M. FIRTH/B. GUNN, *Teti Pyramid Cemeteries* II (*Excavations at Saqqara*), Le Caire 1926, pl. 62.

18 Discussed A.M. ROTH, *A Cemetery of Palace Attendants* (*Giza Mastabas* 6), Boston 1995, 43-45.

Late Old Kingdom and First Intermediate Period

Beni Hasan: A tomb chamber, dating to the late Old Kingdom contained three bodies; one of them belongs to a woman (the *king's ornament* Senet), and two belong to other women (called "daughters" in the publication).[19]

Gebelein: One well documented Old Kingdom tomb was found in 1911 by Ernesto Schiaparelli. The burial consists of four rock cut chambers, one of which was found intact and contained two coffins and one sarcophagus (coffin in stone).[20] No inscriptions were found and it is therefore not possible to determine the relations between the people buried here. The use of a sarcophagus and the quality of some objects found in the tomb suggest that members of the local elite were buried here. In the tomb were found a wooden model of a boat and wooden (model) sandals.

Gurob: The First Intermediate Period cemetery with about 70 burials contained only one double burial, again a man and a woman.[21]

Harageh: A shaft tomb (no. 651)[22], probably to be dated to the First Intermediate Period, contained the body of four people, two men, one woman and one person for whom it was not possible to determine the sex. Another tomb in the same cemetery (no. 99) contained the bodies of six children placed in coffins.[23] Tomb no. 87 contained two coffins, and according to the publication, the human remains of a man and of a woman. They were each placed in inscribed coffins, which were both produced, following the names and titles on them, for men. If the publication is correct concerning the sexing of the bodies, at least one coffin was therefore reused for a woman. There are also other tombs at Harageh with two burials, sometimes a man and a woman (tombs no. 44, 198), which makes it very likely that these are cases of couples (or son and mother?). However, there are again other instances where two men (tomb no. 84), and two men, one woman and a fourth person were found (tomb no. 651). Here it is not so easy to give such a simple explanation for the combination of these people, unless we assume that the sexing of the excavators was wrong and that these burials are all couples. However, altogether these pair and multiple burials are not very common and single burials are still the rule.

Hagarsa: Two multiple burials were found, one containing six coffins, the other two. The tomb with the six coffins had functioned – following the assumption of the publication – as a family tomb, which was opened and used over two or three generations.[24] However, the style of the coffins and mummy-masks found seems so homogeneous (although the offering formula differs) that one may wonder whether all six burials were more or less contemporarily placed into the tomb. Nevertheless, it is possible to argue against this that the burial goods might have been made by a local workshop that produced objects in the same style over a longer period.

19 J. GARSTANG, *The Burial Customs of Ancient Egypt as Illustrated by Tombs of the Middle Kingdom Being a Report of Excavation Made in the Necropolis of Beni Hasan during 1902-3-4*, London 1907, 36-41, pl. VIII.

20 E. D'AMICONE, Gli edifici religiosi e la necropoli di Gebelein nel III millennio a.C., in: A.M. DONADONI ROVERI (ed.), *Museo Egizio di Torino, Civiltà degli Egizi. Le Credenze Religiose*, Milano 1988, 68-81. The publication (p. 77) dates the tomb to about 2400 BC which is about the Fifth Dynasty; A.M. DONADONI ROVERI, *I sarcofagi Egizi dalle origini alla fine dell' Antico Regno* (*Università di Roma – Istituto di studi del vicino oriente serie archeologica* 16), Rome 1969, 171-173 (no. C 39-43).

21 BRUNTON/ENGELBACH, *Gurob*, 6 and see the tomb register.

22 R. ENGELBACH, *Harageh* (*British School of Archaeology in Egypt* 28), London 1923, 14.

23 ENGELBACH, *Harageh*, 14.

24 N. KANAWATI, *The Tombs of El-Hagarsa* II (*The Australian Centre for Egyptology Reports* 6), Sydney 1993, passim, especially 11-15, compare the short discussion on p. 24.

Naga ed-Deir: The Old Kingdom cemetery of Naga ed-Deir, possibly belonging to a small rural community, is well published. About 250 tombs, belonging to the Fifth and Sixth Dynasty are recorded.[25] 23 tombs contained more than one body. In three cases two different burials were found in two separated chambers (tomb no. N 717, N 723, N 832). However, most often two or three skeletons were found placed together in one chamber. The relation between the individuals in each burial is never clear; inscribed material is very rare at this cemetery and no analysis of the human remains has been undertaken to investigate this question. In three cases it can be assumed that a mother and her child were buried together (N 508, N 754, N 961). In some tombs were found three (N 705) or even more bodies (N 745, N 777, N 783, N 879).

Saqqara/Abusir/Gizeh: The picture is not so clear for the residential cemeteries in the late Old Kingdom and First Intermediate Period. The tomb chamber of the vizier Ptahshepses at Abusir contained two sarcophagi, obviously for Ptahshepses himself and his wife.[26] The burial is of special importance because it is well dated (end of Fifth Dynasty) and the people buried here belong to the highest social level. The wife of Ptahshepses is a *king's daughter*. However, most of the burials at Saqqara and Gizeh seem still to be placed as single bodies into the burial chambers. There are remarkably few recorded exceptions in the residential region, where a multiple burial is datable to the First Intermediate Period, notably some tombs around the Teti pyramid.[27]

In the late Old Kingdom, many mastabas but also many rock cut tombs in Upper Egypt are more packed with shafts than before. At some parts of the residential cemeteries, there is a very high density of shaft tombs. Regardless of this observation, there are not many multiple burials.

In the development of tomb architecture, there are some new tomb types in the late Old Kingdom and First Intermediate. There are tombs with several burial chambers built in a close architectural context, which seem not to belong to people connected by family ties, although the missing or scant written record might be misleading. Many of them were excavated in Saqqara South around the pyramid of Pepy II.[28] Some large mastabas with several burial chambers had several cult places (false door and offering table) in the superstructure. Some of the burial chambers were decorated with relief showing friezes of objects. Stephan Seidlmayer, who discussed these burial places, distinguished between (1) tombs with a hierarchical structure, e.g. tombs with one or more main burials and several subsidiary burials and (2) tombs with an egalitarian structure, where each burial is more or less equal in size. The latter he interprets as family tombs, the hierarchical as tombs of a master and his servants.[29] The burial of a servant in close context to his master is not new. The subsidiary tombs of the First Dynasty are particularly well known, but there are also many Old Kingdom examples where a servant (often depicted in serving role in the reliefs of the master's tomb) is buried in his small mastaba next to that of his master.[30] The innovation of the late Old Kingdom is that the servant tombs are architecturally part of the mastaba of the master. However, most of the inhumations inside these new

---

25 G.A. REISNER, *A Provincial Cemetery of the Pyramid Age. Naga-ed-Dêr* Part III (*University of California Publications Egyptian Archaeology* 6), Oxford 1932.

26 M. VERNER, *Forgotten Pharaohs. Lost Pyramids*, Prague 1994, 190 (figure at the top).

27 C.M. FIRTH/B. GUNN, *Teti Pyramid Cemeteries* I (*Excavations at Saqqara*), Le Caire 1926, 39-40, 50-51 (dated in the report to the Heracleopolitian Period, but an early Middle Kingdom date seems also be possible).

28 G. JÉQUIER, *Tombeaux de particuliers contemporains de Pepi II* (*Excavations at Saqqara*), Le Caire 1929.

29 S. SEIDLMAYER, *Gräberfelder aus dem Übergang vom Alten zum Mittleren Reich* (*Studien zur Archäologie und Geschichte Altägyptens* 1), Heidelberg 1990, 403-408.

30 S. HASSAN, *Excavations at Giza* VI *Part III, 1934-1935*, Cairo 1950, 67-71 (mastaba of a *steward* buried next to the mastaba of the *king's daughter* Hemetre, in whose tomb he is depicted). A similar case: H. JUNKER, *Gîza* III, Wien-Leipzig 1938, 124, 142.

types are single burials. The tomb chambers seem to have been opened only once for burial of its owner. They are therefore not essentially different from mastabas with several shafts.

Early Middle Kingdom

In terms of multiple burials the picture changed little in the Middle Kingdom. Sadly there are not many well recorded and well excavated cemeteries which could give an idea of the development and which would make it possible to determine a date for the beginning of new developments. For places such as Rifeh[31] or el-Tarif[32] the objects found are in the publication almost the only point of discussion, without further information on human remains. El-Lisht is a key site, yet to be published.

Abusir: Ludwig Borchardt excavated a Middle Kingdom cemetery at Abusir next to the pyramids of the Fifth Dynasty. Most of the tombs contained burials for a single person, but there is one grave with four inscribed coffins, two for men, two for women. The style of the coffins suggests a date around the mid Twelfth Dynasty.[33]

Asyut: This is one of the main cemeteries of the Middle Kingdom. There were not many proper excavations and therefore the evidence from the place remains very patchy. However, tombs excavated by Émile Chassinat and Charles Palanque are important because many inscribed coffins were found, providing a clue of the social status and the sex of the people buried here. Most of the tombs published contained more than one coffin. More than once it is possible to observe that a man and a woman were placed together.[34] In other tombs several coffins only belonging to men were found.[35] The bodies found in the coffins were not sexed by the excavators. The identification of the sex relies therefore very much on the inscription on the coffins. It is possible to argue that some women were placed in a "male" coffin. However, the impression remains that in some tombs men were placed together. Their relation remains unknown.

Beni Hasan: Through inadequate publication, it is hard to gain a clear picture about the number of people buried in single tombs, but the evidence points to a similar picture as observed in Assyut. The tomb register in the publication lists only the objects found, without mentioning the quantity of coffins or burials.[36] There is also a list of tombs for people published whose names and titles are known, but this offers only a rough guide, because it excludes uninscribed coffins or people whose name and title are lost.[37] There are many tombs with several coffins, but without inscriptions. These tombs do not appear in any list, but are in a few instances described.

From about 800 tombs there are 16 with more than one buried person listed in the name and title list. Quite often it seems clear that these are a man and his wife (tomb no. 81, 90, 94, 134, 177, 181,

---

31 W.M. Flinders Petrie, *Gizeh and Rifeh* (*British School of Archaeology in Egypt* 13), London 1907, 11-26.

32 W.M. Flinders Petrie, *Qurneh* (*British School of Archaeology in Egypt* 16), London 1909, 2-4; the note books indicate that only a small number of tombs contained human remains.

33 H. Schäfer, *Priestergräber und andere Grabfunde vom Ende des Alten Reiches bis zur griechischen Zeit vom Totentempel des Ne-User-Rê* (*Wissenschaftliche Veröffentlichungen der Deutschen Orient-Gesellschaft* 8), Leipzig 1908, 18-39 (mR.1); H. Willems, *Chests of Life. A Study of the Typology and Conceptual Development of Middle Kingdom Standard Class Coffins* (*Mededelingen en Verhandelingen van het Vooraziatisch-egyptisch Genootschap "Ex oriente lux"* 25), Leiden 1988, 107 (date of the coffins).

34 É. Chassinat/C. Palanque, *Une campagne des fouilles dans la nécropole d'Assiout* (*Mémoires publiés par les membres de l'Institut français d'archéologie orientale du Caire* 24), Le Caire 1911, 168-172 (tomb no. 16), 114-125 (tomb no. 7.2), 135-154 (tomb no. 7.4).

35 Chassinat/Palanque, *Campagne Assiout*, 4-28 (tomb no. 6 – seven coffins); 155-159 (tomb 8, two coffins); 172-178 (tomb no. 17 – three coffins mmf).

36 Garstang, *Burial Customs*, 211-244.

37 Garstang, *Burial Customs*, pl. VII-VIII.

516, 861), although this is never explicit. Another tomb contained four burials, explicable as two couples (tomb no. 23 - two women with the title *lady of the house*, two men without title). In other cases such an explanation does not fit so well. One example is tomb no. 294 in which four burials were found, three of them belonging to women with the title *lady of the house*, the fourth to a man with the title *overseer of the house of the god*. However, it is possible to argue that this is the burial of a husband with his three contemporary or succeeding wives.[38] Tomb no. 140, which is briefly described in the publication, contained six coffins. Only one preserved the name of its owner (Hetep). A seventh coffin of a certain *steward* Khnumhotep was placed in a "recess" behind these coffins. The tomb was found undisturbed but the objects were already badly decayed.[39]

Riqqeh: This is one of the few relatively well-recorded cemeteries with tombs dating to the Middle and New Kingdom. About 200 tombs belong to the Middle Kingdom[40], for about 66 of which there is information on the individuals. They are all sexed. This provides the impression that in the publication only bodies are mentioned for which it was possible to determine the sex. However, there remain problems in interpreting the material of the cemetery. Most tombs in the cemetery are shaft tombs with one or two tomb chambers, but there is also a number of simple shafts without any chamber. In general, it seems that each chamber was reserved for one body. Of the 66 tombs recorded with human remains, 36 burials are single burials, 20 tombs still contained two bodies and the rest are burials with three (4), four (3) and once six bodies. For the burials with two bodies, there are some cases where only one chamber was found.[41] Altogether, the remains of 113 people were found. Multiple burials seem to be used by more people, although they are still not the most common burial type.

tomb number	number of burials	number of chambers	sex of buried persons
4	2	1	mf
15	2	1	ff
18	2	1	mc
23	2	1	ff
28	2	1	mf
76	2	1	mm
20	3	2	mmf
177	3	2	mmf
3	3	2	mmf
9	3	2	mff
13	4	1	mmfc
21	4	2	mmmf
183	4	2	mmff
2	6	2	mmmmff

38 GARSTANG, *Burial Customs*, pl. VII-VIII.

39 GARSTANG, *Burial Customs*, 173.

40 WILLEMS, *Chests of Life*, 102 (about Amenemhat II - Amenemhat III).

41 Abbreviations used here and in the following: m - male body; f - female body; c - body of a child. Mm means two male bodies found; fm - one female and one male body - and so on.

Rifeh: In this cemetery was found the so-called tomb of the two brothers. Two men were buried in the same shaft tomb. They are sons of a person called Khnum-aa.[42] Another elite tomb with gilded and silver decorated coffins contained four burials for two men and two women.[43]

Thebes: One tomb of the Twelfth Dynasty was found which was made or at least used for a high number of people. It still contained the bodies of about 60 soldiers, known in Egyptological literature as the "tomb of the slain soldiers". Only two of them were buried in an undecorated coffin. All others were wrapped in linen and then placed directly into the tomb. Some of the linen bandages bore the name of the soldier. The tomb might date under king Senusret I or slightly later. It is highly exceptional and must have something to do with special circumstances under which these soldiers died, perhaps in a Nubian campaign of Senusret I. The examination of their bodies showed that at least some were killed or wounded in battles. This gives the impression that soldiers were buried here who fought for their king and then were buried by him in honour.[44] The tomb is obviously not a family tomb. The circumstances make it very likely that all the soldiers were killed about the same time (although there is no final proof for it) and that they were all buried together at about the same time. The tomb was therefore most likely only opened once, and then closed (in theory) forever. This is an important point. For most cases where a man and a woman were found together it must be assumed that the tomb was once opened and closed and later opened and closed again.

Final Remarks for the Early Middle Kingdom

The burials of couples and the burial places with more than two people are not easy to explain. The evidence from the tomb of the "slain soldiers" suggests that the tomb was only opened once to place all the dead individuals in it. Is it possible that the same holds true for all multiple burials of the period? This would easily explain why we find not only couples, but a wide range of combinations of sexes buried in tombs. It is possible that at least some couples, but also other combinations of men and women (mother and son, father and daughter etc.) died at about the same time and could therefore have been buried together. It also seems possible to assume that families or parts of families died at about the same time (disease and plagues must have killed many people) and were therefore buried together. In such cases, a tomb would also have been opened only once. Finally it is possible to argue that, when the partner of a couple or a member of a family died, the body in its coffin was kept in store until other family members, especially partners were buried, so that both could be placed together in one tomb. However, all these suggestions are speculative and it seems safer to state simply that at a certain point from the late Old Kingdom some tombs were reserved for more than one burial. With very few exceptions the number of people buried in each tomb remains low.

42 M.A. MURRAY, *Museum Handbooks. The Tomb of Two Brothers* (*Manchester Museum Publication* 68), Manchester 1910, pl. 17-20.

43 FLINDERS PETRIE, *Gizeh and Rifeh*, 12-13.

44 H.E. WINLOCK. *The Slain Soldiers of Neb-Hetep-Re Mentuhotpe* (*Publications of the Metropolitan Museum of Art Egyptian Expedition* 16), New York 1945; for the dating: D. FRANKE, review of W.K. Simpson, Personnel Accounts of the Early Twelfth Dynasty: Papyrus Reisner IV, Transcription and Commentary, Boston 1986, *Bibliotheca Orientalis* 45 (1988), 102; R. MÜLLER-WOLLERMANN, review of L. Gestermann, Kontinuität und Wandel in Politik und Verwaltung des frühen Mittleren Reiches in Ägypten, *Discussions in Egyptology* 13 (1989), 110; C. VOGEL, Fallen Heroes? Winlock's "slain soldiers" reconsidered, *Journal of Egyptian Archaeology* 89 (2003), 239-245.

4. Late Middle Kingdom

Multiple burials on a larger scale seem to have been introduced at all social levels around the same time, under Senusret III. The best examples are the burials of queens and other royal women around the royal pyramid. The royal women of the Eleventh and early Twelfth Dynasty are always placed in single tomb chambers, which were most often shaft tombs situated very close to the royal funerary monument. The best known examples are the six queens/royal women buried at Deir el-Bahari inside the mortuary temple of Mentuhotep II.[45] The royal women of Senusret I were placed under small pyramids around the pyramid of the king.[46] The princesses who had their tombs next to the pyramid of Amenemhat II were buried in gallery tombs next to the pyramid.[47] The latter tombs consist of a corridor from which there was access to two separated burial chambers. Although it is possible to argue, that these galleries are already multiple burials, it should be pointed out that each burial chamber was closed separately and was always an unit on its own. The burials of the royal women of Senusret II were again placed next to the pyramid of the king.[48] Each woman had her own shaft and her own burial. The situation under Senusret III in Dahshur is different. At the north side of the pyramid a corridor system was found to include many burials of queens and daughters of the king. Although some of these burials were blocked, and therefore formed single isolated burials in this gallery, there are at least eight sarcophagi just placed into niches without further closing or special blocking. There is evidence that the galleries were still in use under Amenemhat III.[49] The place was therefore designed and built from the beginning for use over a certain period.

The development of the burials of the royal family for the rest of the Twelfth and for the Thirteenth Dynasty is hard to follow. Inside the pyramid of Amenemhat III in Dahshur there were buried several women, but each in a separate chamber.[50] It is therefore not reasonable to call his Dahshur pyramid a multiple burial place. The pyramid complex of the king at Hawara is heavily destroyed, and inadequately excavated, so that further evidence is missing; however, next to the sarcophagus of the king was prepared a burial for his daughter Neferuptah, which is until now a unique feature.[51] Neferuptah was never buried next to the king. Her burial was found elsewhere in the vicinity of Hawara. Evidence for the Thirteenth Dynasty is patchy. The pyramid of king Khendjer has been assumed to be one of the few finished royal burial places of the period, because fragments of the decorated pyramidion were found.[52] Next to the pyramid of the king a smaller pyramid was excavated, which contained two sarcophagi and two canopic chests.[53] A shaft tomb found inside the pyramid complex contained three sarcophagi and three canopic chests. It is not known who was buried here and in the small pyramid, but the fragment of a canopic jar with the name of the *king's wife* Seneb... was

45 D. ARNOLD, *Der Tempel des Königs Mentuhotep von Deir el-Bahari* I: *Architektur und Deutung* (*Archäologische Veröffentlichungen* 8), Mainz 1974, 64.

46 D. ARNOLD, *The Pyramid Complex of Senwosret I: The South Cemeteries of Lisht* III (*Publications of the Metropolitan Museum of Art Egyptian Expedition* 25), New York 1992.

47 J. DE MORGAN, *Fouilles à Dahchour 1894-1895*, Vienne 1903.

48 A recent summary P. JÁNOSI, *Die Pyramidenanlagen der Königinnen. Untersuchungen zu einem Grabtyp des Alten und Mittleren Reiches* (*Untersuchungen der Zweigstelle Kairo des Österreichischen Archäologischen Instituts* 13 = *Österreichische Akademie der Wissenschaften Denkschriften der Gesamtakademie* 13), Wien 1996, 60-62.

49 J. DE MORGAN, *Fouilles a Dahchour Mars-Juin 1894*, Vienne 1895, 58, fig. 128 (plan); 64, 66, pl. XX (objects with the name of Amenemhat III).

50 D. ARNOLD, *Der Pyramidenbezirk des Königs Amenemhet III. in Dahschur* I: *Die Pyramide* (*Archäologische Veröffentlichungen* 53), Mainz 1987, 37-53, compare JÁNOSI, *Pyramidenanlagen der Königinnen*, 65-67.

51 W.M. FLINDERS PETRIE, *Kahun, Gurob and Hawara*, London 1890, 8, 16-17, pl. IV, V.

52 G. JÉQUIER, *Deux pyramides au moyen empire* (*Fouilles à Saqqara*), Le Caire 1933, pl. II.

53 JÉQUIER, *Deux pyramides*, 36 fig. 26.

found. She was perhaps the wife of Khendjer buried in the small pyramid, which raises the question, who was the other person for which a sarcophagus was prepared. Although the evidence is not abundant, in general it seems that from the reign of Senusret III onwards multiple burials are common in royal circles.

Dahshur/Hawara: Going down the social hierarchy the tombs of the high officials around the pyramid of Senusret III should be mentioned first. As far as it is possible to judge, most of them are individual burials, indicating that this type was still very common. At Hawara the private cemeteries around the burial complex of the king have yet to be extensively examined, but a few undisturbed tombs have been recorded. Tomb 64 contained three coffins: the largest one belonged to the *lady of the house* Bebut. On top of it was placed the small coffin of a child, while another coffin of a child was placed directly next to the Bebut coffin.[54]

Lisht: This is one of the main cemeteries of the royal residence. Several expeditions excavated there, but so far only little is published. It is therefore very hard to gain a full picture. Of some interest are tombs with one shaft and several burial chambers. One of these is a shaft tomb with six small chambers at the bottom. In each chamber there was placed one burial. Jewellery and the fact that one coffin was inscribed for a certain Satsobek, indicate that the people buried here were of not very low status.[55] Other information seems to indicate that multiple burials are quite common.[56]

Abydos: Similar tombs have been excavated at Abydos, where extensive Middle Kingdom and Second Intermediate Period cemeteries existed. Multiple burials – quite often two bodies in one chamber – are common, although the publication of the cemetery is very limited. Some tombs are of special interest and are similar to tombs already discussed for Lisht. They contained several underground chambers with one shaft. Tomb V 21 consisted of one shaft with three chambers in three levels. One chamber still contained two bodies side by side, adorned with golden jewellery.[57] Tomb μ50 contained six chambers in three levels, but was found already looted.[58] Tomb D 152 and D 241 each had two chambers; one of them still contained two bodies.[59]

Thebes: Here, there was found the burial place of at least five persons; the titles on some objects provide a clue to the social status of the tomb owners, who are middle ranking court officials. The grave consisted of a shaft and two chambers. In the southern chamber was found a box with the name of Kemni, an *official responsible for a chamber* depicted serving king Amenemhat IV; this chamber contained three mummies, one being that of a child. The other chamber contained several coffin fragments, of which one belonged to a woman called Henut, born of Senet. The inscribed coffin of the *great one of the tens of Upper Egypt* Ren-seneb, was found in the shaft but must have stood originally

54 W.M. FLINDERS PETRIE/G.A. WAINWRIGHT/E. MACKAY, *The Labyrinth, Gerzeh and Mazghuneh* (*British School of Archaeology in Egypt* 21), London 1912, 35.

55 A.C. MACE, Egyptian Expedition 1921-22. Excavations at Lisht, *Part II of the Bulletin of the Metropolitan Museum of Art* (December 1922), 6-7.

56 J. BOURRIAU, The Dolphin Vase from Lisht, in: P. DER MANUELIAN (ed.), *Studies in Honor of William Kelly Simpson* I, 110 (at least two burials in one tomb); EAD., Patterns of Change in Burial Customs during the Middle Kingdom, in: S. QUIRKE (ed.), *Middle Kingdom Studies*, New Malden 1991, 17; J.P. ALLEN, Coffin Texts from Lisht, in: H. WILLEMS (ed.), *The World of the Coffin Texts. Proceedings of the Symposium Held on the Occasions of the 100th Birthday of Adrian de Buck, Leiden December 17-19, 1992* (*Egyptologische Uitgaven* 9), Leiden 1996, 4; compare: A.C. MACE, Egyptian Expedition 1920-1921: I. Excavations at Lisht, *Part II of the Bulletin of the Metropolitan Museum of Art* (November 1921), 16.

57 E.R. AYRTON/C.T. CURRELLY/A.E.P. WEIGALL, *Abydos Part III 1904* (*Egypt Exploration Fund* 25), London 1904, 8.

58 AYRTON/CURRELLY/WEIGALL, *Abydos Part III*, 47, pl. XX.

59 T.E. PEET/W.L.S. LOAT, *The Cemeteries of Abydos Part III 1912-1913* (*Egypt Exploration Fund Excavation Memoir* 35), London 1913, 24-26.

in one of the chambers.[60] It is not known how these people relate to each other. In theory it is possible that these are at least two couples, related in some way such as parents and child with husband/wife. Another tomb, obviously cut in the early Middle Kingdom and then reused in the Second Intermediate Period, was found full of coffins and was used as burial place until the early New Kingdom.[61]

Another well preserved multiple burial was excavated at Thebes. Five undecorated coffins were found in a small and rather shallow shaft tomb. A sixth coffin was found destroyed, lying under the other coffins, indicating that already in ancient times the first burial was quite old when the others were placed in the chamber. Finally there was the burial of a child without a coffin. There are no inscriptions to give us a title or any other clue.[62]

Harageh: The cemeteries of Harageh are relatively well published, about 280 tombs dating to the late Middle Kingdom. Human remains were excavated in 138 tombs. In 63 examples remains of more than one body were found. Most tombs found are shafts with more than one chamber at the bottom, two chambers being common. There are 45 tombs for which it seems probable that in at least one burial chamber more than one body was placed. This is about one third of the tombs with human remains. There are some cases where a woman and a child were found together (tombs 264, 347, 373- with two chambers), and in other cases the remains of a woman and a man were discovered, suggesting that these were couples (tombs 117, 348, 395). Other tombs are not so easy to explain on the "core family" assumption. Tomb 56 contained the remains of six women and of four men. In Tomb 59 two men and two women were buried, which could be interpreted as two couples. Tomb 71 contained three women, tomb 82 two men and three women.

Qau/Badari: There are many burials dating to the Second Intermediate Period. A high number of the tombs are heavily robbed, so that the tomb register does not mention any bodies. However, most of the burials seem to have contained single bodies placed in shallow pits. There are only a few exceptions. In tomb 3712 were found three women. In tomb 7131 were found a man and a woman. In tomb 7323 one woman and three children and finally in tomb 7578 were found six bodies. The whole Second Intermediate Period cemetery at Qau/Badari gives an impression of poverty. The region seems to have been provincial; burial customs might have been therefore rather conservative.[63] Elite burials were perhaps placed somewhere else and the excavated areas are just the poorest parts of the cemetery.

Naga ed-Deir/Sheik Farag: The main cemeteries are datable from the Pre-Dynastic to the First Intermediate Period. Few burials belong to the Middle Kingdom or Second Intermediate Period. Many of the tombs excavated and belonging to these periods are multiple burials. Most have been heavily looted in antiquity, so that it is not possible to gain a clear picture. However, the site is of some importance because Reisner and his team made plans of the tombs (now in Boston[64]) and detailed descriptions, helpful for reconstructing the original appearance.

---

60 FIFTH EARL OF CARNARVON/H. CARTER, *Five Years Exploration at Thebes*. London-New York-Toronto-Melbourne 1912, 54-60.

61 CARNARVON/CARTER, *Five Years Exploration*, 64-88 (tomb no. 37); B. PORTER/R.L.B. MOSS, *Topographical Bibliography of Ancient Egyptian Hieroglyphic Texts, Reliefs and Paintings* I. *The Theban Necropolis* Part 2. *Royal Tombs and Smaller Cemeteries*, Oxford 1964, 615-616.

62 R. ANTHES, Die deutschen Grabungen auf der Westseite von Theben in den Jahren 1911 und 1913, *Mitteilungen des Deutschen Instituts für ägyptische Altertumskunde in Kairo* 12 (1943), 6-15.

63 This conservative attitude is also visible in the position of the body, compare J. BOURRIAU, Change of Body Position in Egyptian Burials from the Mid XIIth Dynasty until the Early XVIIIth Dynasty, in: H. WILLEMS (ed.), *Social Aspects of Funerary Culture in Egyptian Old and Middle Kingdom* (*Orientalia Lovaniensia Analecta* 103), Leuven-Paris-Sterling Virginia 2001, 17.

64 At this point I want to thank Rita Freed for providing me with the possibility to view Reisner's records.

Naga ed-Deir 284: The tomb consists of two chambers, one substantially larger than the other (Fig. 1). The main chamber contained two coffins; one of the coffins was inscribed with vertical texts on the outside (about mid Twelfth Dynasty).

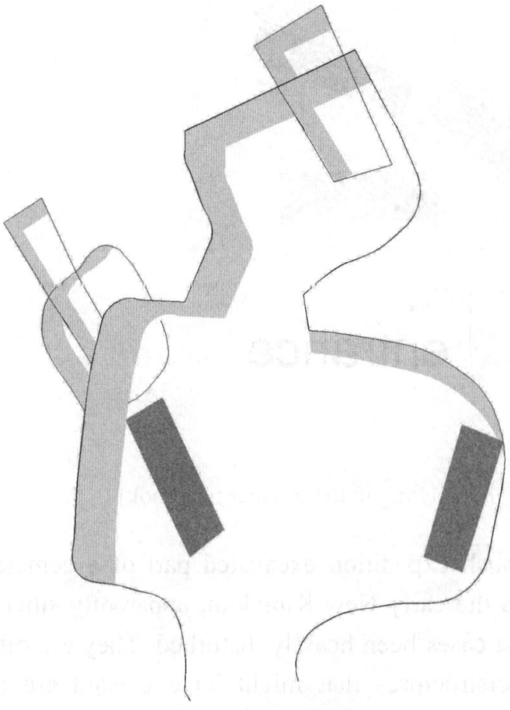

Fig. 1: Plan of Naga ed-Deir Tomb 284 (Sketch after the drawing in the Reisner notebook)

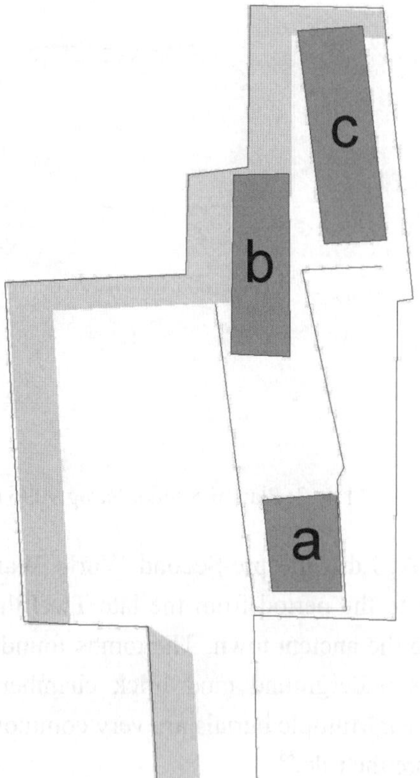

Fig. 2: Plan of Naga ed-Deir Tomb 408 (Sketch after the drawing in the Reisner notebook)

Naga ed-Deir 408: The tomb consists of one chamber with one "sub" chamber (Fig. 2). Three coffins were found, one of them belonging to a child placed in a contracted position (a - on the figure). The tomb is of special interest because the famous *Reisner papyri* were found lying on the innermost coffin (c), in which a mummy adorned with a mask was found. A date *post quem* is given for the tomb by the papyri, which belong to the reign of Senusret I. However, only the publication of the pottery might confirm the date or demonstrate that it is later; papyri in tombs are better attested for the late Middle Kingdom and not earlier.

Sheikh Farag 9096: The tomb consists of a shaft and two chambers, one main chamber and a smaller one. The chambers are roughly cut into the rock without any further attempt to shape them. The tomb seems to have been disturbed. Different kinds of objects were found. In the main chamber lay three box shaped coffins; six skulls were found. One of the coffins (a) was inscribed with Coffin Texts (?) and belonged to a person called Ameny. Several scarabs were found, maybe of late Middle Kingdom date; there were also three flat wooden dolls, two pieces of head-rests, a piece of a broken wooden stick, "a quantity of cloth", "a painted stucco mask, with (gilt?) foil" and some pottery. A date in the Twelfth Dynasty seems likely.

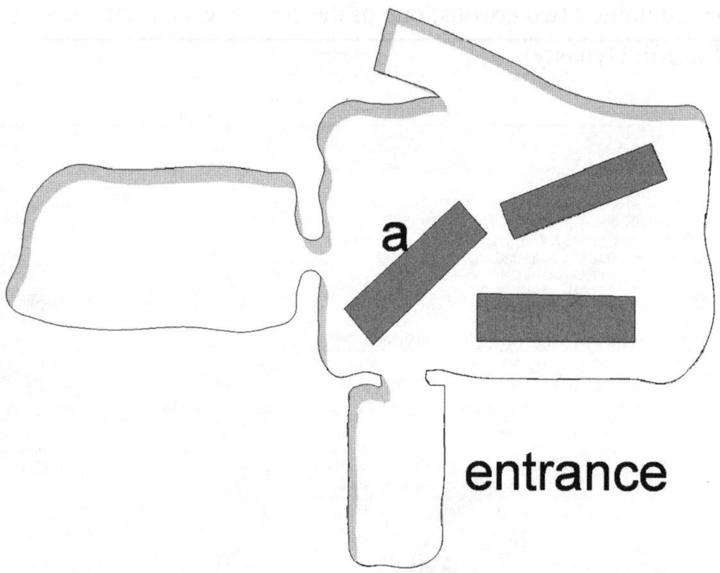

Fig. 3: Plan of Sheikh Farag 9096 (Sketch after the drawing in the Reisner notebook)

Edfu: At Edfu the pre-Second World War Franco-Polish expedition excavated part of a cemetery datable to the period from the late Twelfth Dynasty to the early New Kingdom, apparently situated close to the ancient town. The tombs found had in most cases been heavily disturbed. They are often built as underground mud brick chambers; any superstructures that might have existed are not preserved. Multiple burials are very common. Inhumations with more than two bodies, often four, five or six are the rule.[65]

Nubia: The best documented and published examples of multiple burials were found not in Egypt, but in Nubia at Mirgissa and Buhen where Egyptian soldiers lived at the end of the Middle Kingdom. In Mirgissa (the site of a Middle Kingdom fortress) about 260 burials belonging to the late Middle Kingdom and Second Intermediate Period were found, including a high number of multiple burials.[66]

The cemeteries around the fortress are concentrated in groups. M.X is the main focus for burials. Altogether 628 people were buried in 44 multiple burial tombs; 14.2 burials for each tomb can be calculated as the average. Beside the tombs with several bodies, 69 burials were found reserved for individuals. Finally there are about 44 tombs for which the number of burials is not certain[67], though single burials seem to be most likely. The burials in the case of multiple burials are often quite rich. Mummy masks, as well as inscribed and decorated coffins are common. Tomb 117, for example, is by far the largest, with the remains of at least 68 people, some of them in a coffin or adorned with a mummy mask.[68] In most cases the burials seem to display attention to relations between individuals; coffins and bodies are often placed in a certain order side by side. In tomb no. 5 the bodies were found arranged in two layers and in tomb no. 104 the bodies were in three layers. In tomb no. 114 were

65 K. MICHAŁOWSKI/CH. DESROCHES/J. DE LINAGE/J. MANTEUFFEL/M. ZEJMO-ZEJMIS, *Tell Edfou 1939* (*Fouilles Franco-Polonaises Rapports* III), Le Caire 1950, 61-100; a summary: SEIDLMAYER, *Gräberfelder*, 66.

66 J. VERCOUTTER, *Mirgissa* II. *Les nécropoles*, Paris 1975.

67 Unknown: 9, 14, 21, 27, 48, 49, 50, 54, 56, 61, 63, 64, 66, 67, 68, 74, 81, 88, 89, 92, 93, 94, 95, 96, 97, 98, 107, 109a, 110, 111, 120, 122a, 126, 132a-g, 137b-c, 139c, d, 143, 144.

68 VERCOUTTER, *Mirgissa* II, 154-164.

found the remains of at least 31 individuals also arranged in several levels (see Fig. 4 below). On the lowest level people were placed in coffins side by side (with the head to North-West - maybe intending the West), giving the burial place a well organised impression. People at the second and third level seem to have been arranged mainly at the entrance of the tomb and not in such neat order.[69] This impression is perhaps misleading given the looting of the tomb, which must have affected especially the higher levels. Nevertheless there is the impression that some tombs were used for quite a long period, although the coffins might have been just cached here in a short period.

Final Remarks on Late Middle Kingdom Burials

Local Distribution

One main observation for multiple burials in the late Middle Kingdom is that they are very well attested at the political and religious centres such at Thebes and Abydos, but are not so common at other places, such as Qau/Badari or even Harageh. Therefore, the evidence of the Nubian sites (Mirigissa, Buhen) might come as a surprise, and one wonders whether the custom was directly influenced by the centres of cultural development in Egypt and not by local traditions. For the pottery it has been possible to show that many vessels in Nubia were brought from the residence,[70] which supplied the fortresses at the periphery of the state. Egyptians living here, at least the first generations might also have come directly from the residence region, although this is not proven. Is it possible that these people brought their burial customs to their new home? The evidence from the "provincial" cemeteries Qau/Badari is harder to explain, but also in terms of orientation of the bodies this area seems to be quite conservative. Therefore, it seems possible that the region was something of a backwater in terms of the general development.

Social Distribution

Multiple burials seem to be common at almost all social levels. They are attested at the royal court and at the level of the administrative elite, throughout the country. However, there are also still many single burials especially at Qau/Badari and the question arises why these people chose the older form. The previous paragraph proposed that this might have something to do with a more conservative attitude of the population living here. Another reason might be the poverty of these people. Cutting a multiple burial is more complicated than just digging a shaft or shallow hole in the ground for one person. Therefore, it is possible that a multiple burial is already the sign of a slightly higher social status, of people who had the resources to create an artificial cave, big enough for several burials.

Family Tombs?

One important question about multiple burials is: How were the people buried together connected? Are they all members of the same family? Evidence that multiple burials were at least sometimes family tombs comes from the New Kingdom. From written sources it is known, that Ramose and Hatnefer,[71] Tuya and Yuya[72] and the people in the tomb of Sennedjem[73] were related by family ties, to

69 VERCOUTTER, *Mirgissa* II, figs. 51, 53.

70 J. BOURRIAU, *Patterns of Change*, 7.

71 A. LANSING/W.C. HAYES, Egyptian Expedition: the Museum's Excavations at Thebes, *Part II of the Bulletin of the Metropolitan Museum of Art* (January 1937), 5-39; PORTER/MOSS, *Topographical Bibliography* I, Part 2, 669.

72 PORTER/MOSS, *Topographical Bibliography* I, Part 2, 562.

73 G. DARESSY/E. TODA, La découverte et l'inventaire du tombeau de Sen-nezem, *Annales du service des antiquités de l'Égypte* 20 (1920), 147-160.

give just three secure examples of the period. For the Middle Kingdom such well documented examples are missing, but it should be remembered that there are instances where two men ("tomb of two brothers" in Rifeh) or other combinations were found. It is not so easy to explain them. The attribution to a family tomb for the higher number of burials per tomb at Mirgissa and the "tomb of the slain soldiers" seems very unlikely. However, in the latter tomb men were buried who were at least in close social contact; the same might be true for the burials at Mirgissa, although the evidence is missing.[74]

Another question arises from that: Were the tombs just left open for a short period and did all people buried in a multiple burial die within a short period or were these tombs opened several times to introduce the later burials? A burial with three coffins, found at Saqqara, seems in this respect less ambiguous. Parts of the burial equipment, in this case wooden models, were found under a coffin, which was placed there without giving attention to the older burial. The original burial dates to the early Middle Kingdom, while the later one belongs already to the late Middle Kingdom. The later coffin therefore must be intrusive.[75] A similar situation was observed at Thebes where a new coffin was placed on an older coffin, which was crushed by the weight of the new arrival.[76]

From the evidence collected at different cemeteries in Egypt and Nubia it is clear that multiple burials became commoner in the late Middle Kingdom. The reason for this change is not clear.

1. Economical Reasons. It was certainly cheaper to cut one big tomb for several people, than to cut many small tombs for them. This idea would fit our picture of a less wealthy state at the end of the Middle Kingdom. However, already queens and princesses were buried in a multiple burial ground already in the reign of Senusret III, one of the most powerful kings of the Twelfth Dynasty.

2. Lack of Space. Multiple burials seem to be common at centres such as Thebes and Abydos, where there was probably limited space and it is possible to argue that this burial type was forced by the circumstances of a packed burial ground. However, there are some cemeteries of the late Old Kingdom (Saqqara, Gizeh), which are packed with shaft tombs, but they seem to be in most cases single burials. The cemetery of Mirgissa is on the other side not in a densely populated region. Furthermore, a distinction must be drawn between tombs which were reused and which give the impression of a multiple burial, although the original intention was to provide a single burial place for a single individual.

3. Changes in Object Culture. The new burial customs are related to other changes in Middle Kingdom. It was noted above that burial customs changed radically towards the end of the Twelfth Dynasty. The wooden models and longer religious texts and depictions fall out of regular use in elite burials. In their place other object types, which are in many cases also found in domestic contexts, were deposited in tombs.[77]

Not only burial customs, but also the way people are depicted on stelae is different in the late Middle Kingdom, revealing a new approach to the way groups of people represent themselves. The

---

74 It is tempting to assume that in Mirgissa (a fortress town) also mainly soldiers were buried, but the few written sources found there do not support this idea.

75 FIRTH/GUNN, *Teti Pyramid Cemeteries* I, 50.

76 ANTHES, *Mitteilungen des Deutschen Instituts für ägyptische Altertumskunde in Kairo* 12 (1943), 15.

77 BOURRIAU, *Patterns of Change*, 3-20.

stelae of the early Middle Kingdom focussed very much on the owner of the stela and his family. Most common on stelae is a picture of its owner together with his wife sitting at an offering table. Other people include the family and the household, but these figures tend to be secondary. Most late Middle Kingdom stelae are different. Many present a high number of people side by side in almost the same position and they have therefore a more "egalitarian" appearance. Perhaps the clearest example is the stela of the *king's mother* Iuhet-ibu found at Abydos; members of her family (excluding her son, the king) are shown side by side in several registers and almost equal in position, only distinguished by the titles and the costume.[78] There are many examples of similar stelae, though there are at least the same number of stelae, which are clearly hierarchical (compare another example - stela found at Abydos, fig. 5).

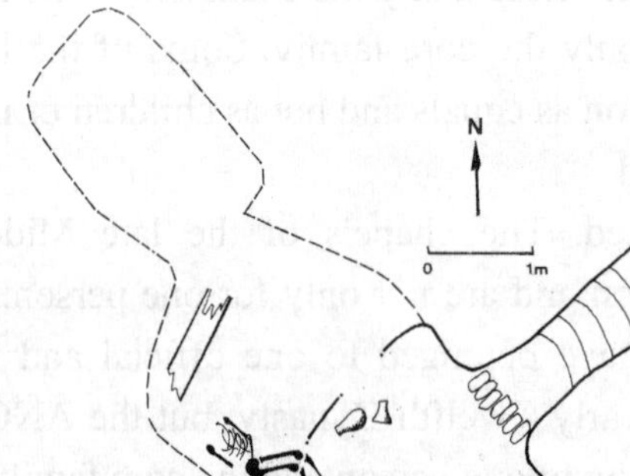

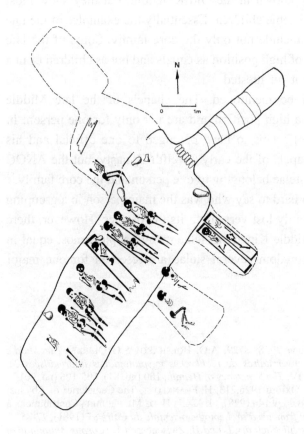

Fig. 4: Multiple Burial, Mirgissa, Tomb 114 (after VERCOUTTER, *Mirgissa* II, 141, fig. 53)

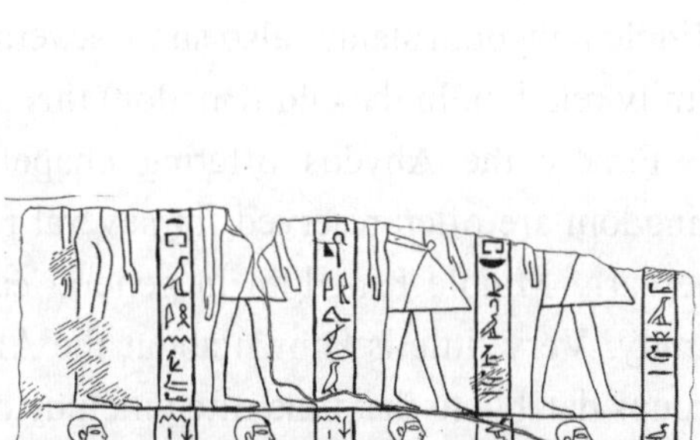

Fig. 5: Stela fragment of (late?) Thirteenth Dynasty Date (after PETRIE/GRIFFITH, *Abydos* II, pl. XXX.5)

78 AYRTON/CURRELLY/WEIGALL, *Abydos Part* III, 48, pl. XIII; K. RYHOLT, The *Political Situation in Egypt during the Second Intermediate Period* (*Carsten Niebuhr Institute Publications* 20), Copenhagen 1997, 246-248 (with further literature).

There are also other ways of referring to a group of people, not known before. A number of stelae just give a list of people with titles and name, without giving a picture of them.[79] There are formulae on several stelae, referring to groups of people. The phrase *n kꜣ n nti nb rn.f ḥr wḏ pn* (*for the ka of all who appear on this stela*) is common at the end of the Twelfth Dynasty (under Amenemhat III).[80] On stela Vienna ÄS 5900 appears the phrase *n kꜣ n nn n ꜣḫw nti ḥr wḏ* (*for the ka of these spirits who are on the stela*).[81]

With these stelae it is possible to compare other object groups such as offering tables and statues. Offering tables of the early Middle Kingdom are normally dedicated to one person, while in the middle of the Twelfth Dynasty it appears more often that several people are mentioned on them.[82] Statues showing not only one or two persons, but bigger groups appear sometimes (but not very often) in the late Middle Kingdom. The group statue Louvre E 11573 shows no fewer than four persons around the *chamberlain of the beer chamber* Senpu.[83] Louvre A 47 depicts three high priests of Ptah, standing side by side.[84] Group statues are already known in the Old Kingdom, but they show most often only the core family: a husband, his wife and some children. Essentially the examples of the late Middle Kingdom are not very different, but they include not only the core family. Some of the late Middle Kingdom statues also show several people of high position as equals and not as children or in a family relation. In the Old Kingdom this is so far not yet attested.

Finally the Abydos offering chapels should be mentioned. The chapels of the late Middle Kingdom are often reserved for several people in a high position and are not only for one person. In the early Middle Kingdom in general each chapel seems to have belonged to one official and his family. Very little is known about the Abydos chapels of the early Twelfth Dynasty, but the ANOC groups datable to that time often include different stelae belonging to one person and the core family.[85] In contrast, for the late Middle Kingdom it is often hard to say who was the main person in a grouping of several stelae belonging together.[86] The core family lost very often its importance. However, there are again numerous exceptions, where on early Middle Kingdom stelae many people almost equal in position appear and where in the late Middle Kingdom several stelae are reserved for one major official.[87]

---

79 Just a few examples of many: St. Petersburg, Hermitage 2958, 8729, A.O. BOLSHAKOV/S.G. QUIRKE, *The Middle Kingdom Stelae in the Hermitage* (*Publications interuniversitaires de recherches égyptologiques informatisées* 3), Utrecht-Paris 1999, 50-52, 68-70; HABACHI, *Elephantine* IV. *The Sanctuary of Heqaib*, 100 (no. 81), 105-106 (no. 90).

80 For example: Leiden 30 (datable under Amenemhat III); Oxford 1926.213, H. FRANKFORT, The Cemeteries of Abydos: Work of the Season 1925-26, *Journal of Egyptian Archaeology* 14 (1928), pl. XX.1; H. DE MEULENARE, Contributions à la prosopographie du Moyen Empire, *Bulletin de l'Institut français d'archéologie orientale du Caire* 81 (1981), 77-85.

81 I. HEIN/H. SATZINGER, *Stelen des Mittleren Reiches einschließlich der I. und II. Zwischenzeit* II (*Corpus Antiquitatum Aegyptiacarum Kunsthistorisches Museum Wien* 7), Mainz 1993, 160- 161. The writing of *nn* with the "negative arms" is exceptional. The line may end "*wḏ pn*" (*this stela*).

82 P. LACAU, *Catalogue général des antiquités égyptiennes du Musée du Caire Nos 28001-28126, Sarcophages antérieurs au Nouvel Empire*, Le Caire 1904-1906, No. 23027, 23035, 23045, 23047.

83 E. DELANGE, *Catalogue des statues égyptiennes du Moyen Empire 2060 – 1560 avant J.-C.*, Paris 1987, 144-147.

84 DELANGE, *Statues du Moyen Empire*, 81-83; see also Philadelphia 59-23-1, D.P. SILVERMAN (ed.), *Searching for Ancient Egypt. Art, Architecture, and Artefacts from the University of Pennsylvania Museum of Archaeology and Anthropology*, Dallas 1997, no. 35.

85 ANOC (Abydos North Offering Chapel) 2-4, 13, 23, 29, 30, 40, see W. K. SIMPSON, *The Terrace of the Great God at Abydos. The Offering Chapels of Dynasties 12 and 13* (*Publications of the Pennsylvania-Yale Expedition to Egypt* 5), New Haven 1974.

86 One example discussed: W. GRAJETZKI, *Two Treasurers of the Late Middle Kingdom* (*British Archaeological Reports International Series* 1007), Oxford 2001, 72.

87 ANOC 10, 34.

To sum up it can be observed that there is a general tendency in the late Middle Kingdom in mortuary practices to put together several individuals. In tombs the multiple burials appear, while on objects relating to the cult of the dead groupings of a high number of people introduce a new way of representing people not known before. However, there are still many single burials, at all social levels attested and there are still many stelae, statues etc. showing one main owner. This is a way of representation not very different from before.

5. Concluding Remarks

Multiple burials are complex archaeological contexts and a serious challenge to the excavators recording tombs. The single burials of Prehistory and the Old Kingdom are often well documented. The publications very often record the arrangement and orientation of the body. For Naga ed-Deir Reisner published for each Old Kingdom tomb a detailed plan, as did Junker for Giza, while Brunton provided often similar information in his tomb registers for Qau, Badari, Gurob and other sites. For later tombs, mainly Middle Kingdom and onwards, no such detail can be found in many publications. The excavation reports of Harageh by Engelbach offer very limited information on the arrangement of the bodies, and even on the tomb cards (field records) not much more information is given. The same is true for other cemeteries in Egypt excavated before the 1950's such as Riqqeh. More recent publications are more detailed, such as the report on the cemeteries of Mirgissa cited above. Evidently the "disorder" found in many burials deterred excavators from a more careful examination of the finds and bodies.[88]

The introduction of multiple burials on a greater scale in the late Middle Kingdom also has a direct effect on our way of looking at Old and Middle Kingdom cemeteries. The cemetery of Mirgissa discussed above contained over 100 tombs. This sounds like a rather small cemetery. The total number of burials found is around 600, which is much higher. In the Old Kingdom this would be a cemetery bigger than the Old Kingdom tomb field excavated for the Fifth and Sixth Dynasty at Naga ed-Deir. In a heavily looted cemetery a single tomb used as multiple burial place appears in the statistics of a tomb register just as one grave. False impressions may arise concerning demography, from just counting numbers of tombs, which might have originally contained many burials. Tomb 117 at Mirgissa contained 67 burials. Two tombs of this size would already supply the number of burials placed in a single small cemetery such as Zaraby with its 126 burials.[89]

With all reservation, it can be assumed that most of the multiple tombs before the late Middle Kingdom were only opened once. People related to each other and dying at about the same time seem to have been buried together. In the late Middle Kingdom multiple burials became increasingly common. Notably the number of people placed in one tomb can be sometimes very high. It is no longer possible to assume that all people buried in a multiple burial were placed there at about the same time, but it seems that the tombs must have been reopened to introduce new burials over a longer period. This high number of multiple burials seems to be related to new ways of representing people on monuments. While in former times the family and close servants were always the focus on stelae, there are now many stelae and other inscriptions mentioning many people, often not related by family ties but related by their work. Interestingly multiple burials appear at a time for which, especially

88 Further problems are disturbed chambers against disturbed surface burials. Even robbed, a surface burial still provides information on the arrangement of the objects. In a chamber, this is not often the case.

89 FLINDERS PETRIE, *Gizeh and Rifeh,* 10.

recently the rise of individuality has been postulated, but just from the viewpoint of sculpture and literature, which are two products almost exclusively reserved for a social elite.[90] In terms of burial customs the opposite picture could be drawn. The development from the Old to the Middle Kingdom seems to be a line from single individuals to groups of people (in art and in the burials). Individuality seems here not apparent at all. This observation raises questions on the meaning of individuality in Ancient Egypt and is a clear example of how different sources can produce starkly different results.

90 G. BURKARD, Aufbruch des Individuums. Literatur im Mittleren Reich, in: D. WILDUNG (ed.), *Ägypten 2000 v. Chr. Die Geburt des Individuums*, München 2000, 13 (on individuality in literature).

The Mitre Inscriptions on Coffins of the Middle Kingdom: A New Set of Texts for Rectangular Coffins?

Silke Grallert

Coffins and sarcophagi[1] are a phenomenon inherent in many cultures, both ancient and modern, always creating a certain habitat for the dead person placed in them. From the earliest times a coffin is an important element of rich Egyptian burials endowing social status and knowledge to the deceased through the décor. As the innermost surrounding of the corpse it offers shelter against destruction, perhaps the first and most important reason to introduce this funerary object into the burial customs, since the integrity of the body is of predominant significance in Egyptian funerary beliefs. Regularly inscribed with the name and titles of the deceased from the beginning of the Sixth Dynasty, it quickly develops into a highly decorated and sophisticated container to help the dead to a new existence after his physical death. Originally covered only with simple offering formulas, it comes to be decorated by images of gods and goddesses from the Middle Kingdom onwards. Coffins entirely decorated with hundreds of scenes and inscriptions are produced in the Third Intermediate Period as a first peak of richness in decoration. These brief notes serve just to recall the concern of the ancient Egyptians for the welfare of their deceased in the beyond by using the surfaces of coffins to express and ensure their hopes for eternity. The magic potential of the Egyptian writing made this an easy task on the one hand, but it might cause danger to the dead corpse by harmful animals depicted on the other hand. With this in mind we may join Willems in calling a coffin or sarcophagus a "ritual machine".[2]

A history of the development of the coffin decoration is still far from realisation in Egyptology. Although the coffins and their decoration gained in importance in Egyptological publications and were studied in several of their manifold aspects over the last decades[3], the researchers specialising in the decoration of the Middle Kingdom coffins are nonetheless few. Thousands of Egyptian coffins stored in museums are not published at all, sometimes they are even not documented, which makes a thorough study of these artefacts extremely difficult and time consuming. This situation increases even more with the hidden inscriptions on coffins recorded from the Old Kingdom onwards and most often written on their mitres. Since they can be only detected and documented when a box-shaped coffin is dismantled to its six main boards[4], the possibility to incorporate a greater part of them into a study is

[1] The term "coffin" will refer in this paper to a wooden repository if not otherwise stated (cf. clay coffin), a sarcophagus is a repository made of stone. Both can be of rectangular or anthropoid shape.

[2] H.O. Willems, *Chests of Life. A Study of the Typology and Conceptual Development of Middle Kingdom Standard Class Coffins* (*Mededelingen en Verhandelingen van het Vooraziatisch-Egiptisch Genootschap "Ex Oriente Lux" XXV*), Leiden 1988, 239.

[3] Willems, *Chests of Life*; G. Lapp, *Typologie der Särge und Sargkammern von der 6. bis 13. Dynastie* (*Studien zur Archäologie und Geschichte Ägyptens* 7), Heidelberg 1993; E. Meyer-Dietrich, *Nechet und Nil. Ein ägyptischer Frauensarg des Mittleren Reiches aus religionsökonomischer Sicht* (*Acta Universitatis Upsaliensis Historia Religionum* 18), Uppsala 2001; Ead., *Senebi und Selbst. Personenkonstituenten zur rituellen Wiedergeburt in einem Frauensarg des Mittleren Reiches* (*Orbis Biblicus et Orientalis* 216), Fribourg-Göttingen 2006; R. Hannig, *Zur Paläographie der Särge aus Assiut* (*Hildesheimer Ägyptologische Beiträge* 47), Hildesheim 2006; H. Willems (ed.), *The World of the Coffin Texts. Proceedings of the Symposium Held on the Occasion of the 100th Birthday of Adriaan de Buck Leiden, December 17-19,1992* (*Egyptologische Uitgaven* 9), Leiden 1996; H. Willems (ed.), *Social Aspects of Funerary Culture in the Egyptian Old and Middle Kingdoms. Proceedings of the International Symposium Held at Leiden University 6-7 June, 1996* (*Orientalia Lovaniensia Analecta* 103), Leuven-Paris-Sterling 2001.

[4] The following abbreviations will be used as references to the different parts of a rectangular coffin: H(ead board), F(oot board), Fr(ont board), B(ack board), Bo(ttom board), L(id board). The corpse is supposed to lie in the box on the left

not very good. For example, at the moment, out of 67 known Middle Kingdom coffins with hidden inscriptions only a half of the material is available for study through publications or hand copies by the author. Of the published inscriptions, only some could be collated by the author personally in museum collections. Thus, a purpose of this paper is to bring these hidden inscriptions into the focus of a greater scientific community, and to gain knowledge of more texts in the future. Therefore, I shall first give a broad overview of these texts on Middle Kingdom coffins, followed by an attempt of interpretation. At the end a brief summary of their transmission from the New Kingdom until the Late Period will demonstrate their importance for coffin decoration. Some still unidentified and very fragmentary spells on coffins will not be discussed here and need further research.

1. General Remarks on the Development of Coffin Decoration

Wooden box coffins are a distinctive class of monuments that can be regarded as typical of Middle Kingdom burials, although they existed already in the Old Kingdom and even earlier. During that earlier period the decoration of both wooden coffins and stone sarcophagi consisted mainly of horizontal bands of inscriptions running along the upper edge of the outer walls. More seldom such bands of inscriptions were placed by the vertical edges of the rectangular repositories for human bodies. The band inscriptions contain usually the offering formulas addressed to Osiris (B = West side) and Anubis (Fr = East side) or just the title(s) and the name(s) of the owner. Besides texts, Old Kingdom coffins and sarcophagi were often decorated with architectural patterns like false-doors or palace-façades. Only at a later stage of the development of their decoration (late Fifth Dynasty) the motif of the two eyes of Horus was introduced on the outer East side (Fr) near the head end of the container. Starting from that moment it is clear that the dead person was considered to communicate with the outer world (seeing sunrises and daily offerings placed in front of the false door in the offering chapel). The idea of the dead receiving his offerings is manifest in a monolithic limestone sarcophagus discovered at Abusir South. Hewn out of the same stone block as the sarcophagus, a false door occupies the head end of the East side where usually the eye panel is placed.[5] Contemporary royal sarcophagi are decorated also very sparely at that time. Only the royal sarcophagus of Teti is inscribed with short religious texts on its inner walls and on the outer surface of the lid (PT spell 1-6), whereas later sarcophagi mention only royal titles and the names of their owners.[6] These Pyramid spells are never used on private sarcophagi or coffins in the Old Kingdom.

In the First Intermediate Period stone built private tombs almost disappeared and painted and relief decoration diminished greatly, so wooden coffins became the main focus of a burial for several levels of society. Accordingly, the importance and richness of their decoration increased much and they became more widespread than in the Old Kingdom. As a result of the political situation in Egypt at that time, we can ascertain the development of certain local traditions in the patterns of decoration that continue well into the Middle Kingdom. For example, the Book of Two Ways is a product of the funerary industry of el-Bersheh and is mainly written on the bottom; the colour palette of coffins from Asyut is reduced to yellow and blue on the outer walls, thus giving them a distinctive appearance

---

side, facing the front board (= East); thus, the head is in the North, the feet in the South, the back in the West. This ideal orientation predetermines the structure of any coffin decoration.

5 M. Verner, *Abusir. Realm of Osiris*, Cairo-New York 2002, 219.

6 Cf. A.M. Donadoni Roveri, *I sarcofagi egizi dalle origini alla fine dell'Antico Regno* (*Università di Roma – Istituto di studi del vicino oriente serie archeologica* 16), Rom 1969, Appendice A 103-108; J.P. Allen, *The Ancient Egyptian Pyramid Texts* (*Society of Biblical Literature: Writings from the Ancient World* 23), Atlanta 2005, 67, 396-397.

incomparable with other cemeteries. In the hieroglyphic text bands scribes/painters show some preference to important gods of their localities, for example, to Geb in el-Bersheh or to Nut and Ra in Asyut.

The basic elements of the Old Kingdom coffin decoration were taken over and new texts and images loaned from the former decoration of tomb chapels were added. The new corpus of the Coffin Texts appears regularly on the inner walls of Middle Kingdom coffins, the frieze of objects providing the dead with necessary equipment for his eternal life occupies more and more space. The great offering list is located besides the false door on the inner head end of the East wall. Horizontal and vertical bands with hieroglyphic inscriptions are placed on each side of the coffin according to specific patterns developed in certain cemeteries. New types of hieroglyphic texts are the *im3ḫ ḫr GN PN*[7] formula ("the revered one by god N, PN") in the vertical lines on the outer sides and some speeches of deities. In general, for the first time in Egyptian history a double strategy – a sophisticated combination of texts and images on a single funerary object – is used to ensure the well-being of the dead.[8]

The main attention of Egyptologists is still directed to the aforementioned corpus of the Coffin Texts as it was the case from the very beginning of the study of coffins. These spells are assembled uniquely on each single coffin and are clearly separated from other texts on the coffins by the type of the script used (cursive hieroglyphs set in columns), their colour (black and red ink on a light background), and the program of their arrangement (mainly on the inner surfaces of the walls, preferably on their lower parts, and on the bottom and the lid). As a whole they form quite a new part of the coffin decoration that had not been known in the Old Kingdom but was introduced in the First Intermediate Period.[9] Less attention was paid by scholars to hieroglyphic inscriptions on the Middle Kingdom coffins because of their allegedly less thrilling tenor and variety. Nevertheless, since these texts are clearly visible on the coffins, they can be scrutinized in museums and collections more or less easily. The state of affairs is quite opposite as concerns the third group of texts to be found on Middle Kingdom coffins: the hidden inscriptions on the mitres.

2. Hidden Inscriptions and Images on Middle Kingdom Coffins

Besides the visible decoration on the inner and outer coffin walls, there is a third group of texts and sometimes even images, invisible when the coffin is assembled. They sporadically appear first in the Old Kingdom and First Intermediate Period, but are more common on Middle Kingdom rectangular coffins. Before the Middle Kingdom they consist, in accordance with the common funerary beliefs of that time, only of a title and/or the name of the coffin or sarcophagus owner.[10] The pharaoh of the Old

---

7 The following abbreviations are used to replace proper names in Egyptian texts: GN for a god's name, PN for a private name of a non-royal person, and KN for a King's name.

8 A.O. Bolshakov, Representation and Text: Two Languages of Egyptian *Totenglauben*, *Altorientalische Forschungen* 30 (2003), 128-140.

9 In the late Old Kingdom burial of *Mdw-nfr* the inscriptions of the inner coffin walls survived as negative imprints on the mummy bandages, whereas the wooden coffin walls disappeared due to humidity. The few text fragments suggest that they belong to the corpus of the Coffin Texts and would be one of the earliest attestations of them. Cf. M. Vallogia, *Balat* I. *Le Mastaba de Medou-Nefer* (*Fouilles de l'Institut français d'archéologie orientale du Caire* 31), Le Caire 1986, 74-78, pl. 62-63.

10 Sarcophagus of *K3(=j)-m-nfr.t* Hildesheim RPM 3177 published in W. Seipel, *Ägypten. Götter, Gräber und die Kunst, 4000 Jahre Jenseitsglauben* I, Linz 1989, 56; coffin of *Wsr* (Sq32 of Lapp, *Typologie der Särge*): *im3ḫ zš ꜥ nsw.t ḫft-ḥr Wsr*, published by A. el-Khouli, An Old Kingdom Tomb in the Teti Pyramid Cemetery, Saqqara, *Journal of the Society for the Study of Egyptian Antiquities* 11 (1981), 90-92, dated by Lapp to his Sixth Dynasty type that may perhaps also be placed into Seventh/Eighth Dynasty.

Kingdom, who provided his officials with necessary goods during their lifetime, was also responsible for their posthumous welfare and guaranteed their funerary income. On the contrary, the short texts or spells on the Middle Kingdom coffins are of religious contents and are intended to prepare the deceased for his new life in the beyond in the role of a king or of Osiris. Like the Old Kingdom inscriptions they are hidden from view and placed on the vertical and horizontal mitre joints of the walls (see below Fig. 1) or even of the single planks of a coffin (see below Fig. 3). As compared with other texts on coffins, this group of inscriptions is not well documented, since only single walls of dismantled coffins or their fragments are easily accessible in museums. Occasionally the joint of two vertical mitres of an assembled coffin edge can be so widened that a look inside the join could at least verify the existence of inscriptions. The fading of the ink through time is another problem that would make application of infrared photography a useful method of research.

There is still no general accepted Egyptological terminology for these inscriptions. Lesko calls them "edge inscriptions"[11], Lüscher entitles them as "Dübelinschriften"[12]. Both terms seem to be insufficient to highlight the specific position of these texts on the coffins: "edge inscriptions" may also designate the bands of ornamental hieroglyphic texts nearby the edges of the coffin, while dowels ("Dübel") that can bear the same inscriptions, are not a common medium for them. In contrast, the German term "Fugeninschriften" used by the present author[13] and corresponding to the English term "mitre (joint) inscriptions" proposed by Willems[14] clearly describes the location of these texts on a coffin.

Besides the spells referred to as mitre inscriptions in this study, there is another kind of inscriptions on the Middle Kingdom coffins known already in the Old Kingdom and First Intermediate Period. They have a distinct function in building up a coffin during all periods and, therefore, they may be described best as simple labels or construction signs placed mainly on the foot or head board.[15] These labels mark the position of the wall in the process of assembling a coffin box or give a hint at the arrangement of the body inside the coffin. Therefore, they are placed either on the inner or on the outer surface of the sidewalls. On the H of coffins of the Old Kingdom and the First Intermediate Period we sometimes recognize the hieroglyphic sign of a head (Gardiner-Sign D 1) or human legs on the F (Gardiner-Sign D 54 or 56).[16] S65L bears a similar construction sign on the mitre of H/Bo,

---

11 L.H. LESKO, *Index of the Spells on Egyptian Middle Kingdom Coffins and Related Documents*, Berkeley 1979, 4.

12 B. LÜSCHER, *Untersuchungen zu Totenbuchkapitel 151* (*Studien zum Altägyptischen Totenbuch* 2), Wiesbaden 1998, 68-70.

13 S. GRALLERT, Die Fugeninschriften auf Särgen des Mittleren Reiches, *Studien zur altägyptischen Kultur* 23 (1996), 147-165 and EAD., *Die Fugeninschriften auf Särgen des Mittleren Reiches. Ein Beitrag zur Entwicklungsgeschichte der Sargdekoration seit dem Mittleren Reich* (unpublished MA thesis Freie Universität Berlin), Berlin 1994. It is also used by MEYER-DIETRICH, *Nechet und Nil* and *Senebi und Selbst*.

14 H.O. WILLEMS, *The Coffin of Heqata* (*Cairo JdE 36418*). *A Case Study of Egyptian Funerary Culture of the Early Middle Kingdom* (*Orientalia Lovaniensia Analecta* 70), Leuven 1996, 138-139.

15 Cf. a thorough study of such labels on the golden shrines of Tutankhamun by M. BELL, Notes on the Exterior Construction Signs from Tutankhamun's Shrines, *Journal of Egyptian Archaeology* 76 (1990), 107-124.

16 Cf. LAPP, *Typologie der Särge*, § 95: Sq68, Gi4a-b, M1, M7, M14; DONADONI ROVERI, *Sarcofagi dell'Antico Regno*, 91, 172 and fig. 19; H. JUNKER, *Bericht über die von der Akademie der Wissenschaften in Wien auf gemeinsame Kosten mit Dr. Wilhelm Pelizaeus unternommenen Grabungen auf dem Friedhof des Alten Reiches bei den Pyramiden von Giza* VIII (*Denkschriften der Akademie der Wissenschaften Wien* 73), Wien 1947, 147 fig. 71; S. HASSAN, *Excavations at Saqqara 1937-1938* III: *Mastabas of Princess Hemet-R^{c} and Others Re-Edited by Z. Iskander* (*Excavations at Saqqara*), Cairo 1975, 8, pl. IV F; P. MUNRO, Der Unas-Friedhof Nord-West. 6. Vorbericht über die Arbeiten der Gruppe Berlin/Hannover in Saqqara (Teil 1), *Göttinger Miszellen* 74 (1984), 76 (all four sidewalls).

whereas S1C uses a *nfr* sign in the same way to mark the junction of a sidewall with the lid (H and L).[17] Since they serve an obvious technical or practical purpose, they are excluded from this study.

2.1 Provenance and Date of Coffins with Mitre Inscriptions

Coffins with mitre inscriptions are well attested in many cemeteries of the Middle Kingdom. Nineteen coffins from el-Bersheh and twenty coffins from Meir bear them, followed by twelve examples from Asyut, six from Saqqara, three from Western Thebes and one piece from both Aswan and Asyut.[18] The complete absence of documented coffins with these inscriptions in the residential cemeteries at Dahshur and el-Lisht[19] is surprising and may be due more to incompleteness of Egyptological publications than to their actual absence. The same may be true as concerns the coffins from Beni Hasan. In general the total of 67 coffins is a very small number as compared with hundreds of known Middle Kingdom coffins.[20] It may be altogether a result of their well hidden location that makes them inaccessible for research.

The elite tombs in the necropolis of Beni Hasan date from the late Eleventh Dynasty down to about Senusret III. The only coffin with mitre inscriptions belongs to the very end of this period. The rock tombs at Meir are attested from the second half of the reign of Amenemhet I until the reign of Senusret III. Here far more coffins are dated to the early Twelfth Dynasty than to the middle of the Dynasty. The rock-cut tombs of el-Bersheh range from the late Eleventh Dynasty to Senusret III, and the coffins cover the whole period continuously. Almost the same time span is covered by the elite tombs at Asyut that started to be hewn somewhat later in the early Twelfth Dynasty. Here the peak of using mitre inscriptions was obviously reached in the late Eleventh and early Twelfth Dynasty. Tombs of nobles in Western Thebes were built mainly during the Eleventh and early Twelfth Dynasty, afterwards the importance of the necropolis ceased much; accordingly, two coffins are from that early period and one is from the middle or later Twelfth Dynasty.

The extensive group of well recognizable coffins from the necropolis of Asyut is not well published yet, although very recently the study of Rainer Hannig on their palaeography appeared. Since he introduced the newest and most extensive numbering system for these coffins it is used in this paper. Where necessary, additional numbers for coffins from Asyut in the British Museum are added to Hannig´s sigla by the present author.[21] Otherwise, the system developed by De Buck for his publication of the Coffin Texts and later followed by Willems is used for references.[22] Texts personally seen by me and/or made available by the museums and collections through photographs are

---

[17] Cf. A. Schwab, *Die Sarkophage des Mittleren Reiches. Eine typologische Untersuchung für die 11. bis 13. Dynastie*, unpublished PhD Wien 1989, 84, 249 (Cat. no. 44), 129-130 (Cat. no. 107) and the anthropoid coffin of *Mrj.t* from the reign of Thutmose IV to Amenhotep III (S. Curto/M. Mancini, News of Khaᶜ and Meryt, *Journal of Egyptian Archaeology* 54 (1968), 77).

[18] The sarcophagus chamber KH1KH to be published by D. Silverman shows similar inscriptions written in black ink between the borders of several decorative and incised sections of the wall decoration. This fact was brought to my attention by D. Silvermann.

[19] The coffins from that region are prepared for publication by J.P. Allen. During a visit to the Metropolitan Museum of Art in New York I recognized at least one coffin on display bearing traces of such inscriptions on its mitres.

[20] The coffins MC 105, B6C, B9C, B13C may bear mitre inscriptions as well.

[21] Hannig, *Paläographie der Särge*. Willems, *Chests of Life* excluded coffins from that necropolis from his study and Lapp, *Typologie der Särge* studied only some published examples. The British Museum for example owns several unpublished (fragments of) coffins with mitre inscriptions from Asyut.

[22] Helpful lists of coffins are to be found in Willems, *Chests of Life*, 19-40 and Lapp, *Typologie der Särge*, 272-312; the latter uses a slightly different numbering system than De Buck and Willems but included the numbers of De Buck/Willems in his list. The reader may use these extensive lists as a source for the Egyptological publication(s) of any coffin. Due to lack of space only new publications of coffins or mitre inscriptions are mentioned in this study in order to avoid repeating these data.

indicated as "Seen: yes/no". Unfortunately, "yes" does not always mean that the texts were readable, but that inscriptions are existing. Other mitre inscriptions could be seen on the old photographs of the Adriaan de Buck Archive at Leiden University (AdB).

	Owner's name	Date after Willems	Date after Lapp	Inv-No	Seen
A1C	*Ḥqꜣ-ib-ʿꜣ/Ḥqꜣ-t(ꜣ)*	ca. Am I	type 11th dyn	CG 28127	yes
B1Bo	*Ḏḥwtj-nḫt*	late 11th – Am I	11th dyn – Am I	MfA 20.1822-27	yes[23]
B2Bo				MfA 21.962-963	no
B3Bo[24]	*Ḏḥwtj-nḫt* (f.)	late 11th – Am I	11th dyn – Am I	MfA 21.964-965	AdB
B4Bo				MfA 21.966-967	AdB
B6Bo[25]	*Sꜣ.t-mk.t* (f.)	late 11th dyn	11th dyn – Am I	MfA 21.810+21.968	no
B1C[26]	*Spj*	Sen II – Sen III	Am II – Sen III	CG 28083	yes
B3C	*Sꜣ.t-ḥḏ-htp* (f.)	Sen I	end of 11th dyn – Am I	CG 28085	yes
B4C				CG 28086	no
B5C[27]	*Ḏḥwtj-htp*	Sen II – Sen III	after Sen III	JE 37566	AdB
B6C?	*ʿḥꜣ-nḫt > Kꜣy*	late 11th – Am I	11th dyn – Am I	CG 28094	AdB
B7C	*Ḏḥwtj-htp*	Sen II – Sen III	after Sen III	JE 37567	AdB
B9C?	*Ỉmn-m-ḥꜣ.t*	Am II	Sen I	CG 28091	AdB
B10C				CG 28092	AdB
B12C	*Ỉhꜣ*	Sen II – Sen III	Am I – Sen II	CG 28089	no
B13C				CG 28090	AdB
B21C	*ʿnḫj.t* (f.)	late 11th – early 12th dyn	11th dyn – Am I	CG 28112	no
B1L	*Gwꜣ*	Sen II – Sen III	Am II – Sen III	EA 30840	yes
B2L				EA 30839	yes
B4L[28]	*Sn(j)*	Sen II – Sen III	Am I – Sen II	EA 30841	yes
B1Ph	*ʿḥꜣ-nḫt*	late 11th dyn	11th dyn – Am I	E 16218A-B	no[29]
Y2C	*Ḏḥwtj-nḫt* (f.)	late 11th – early 12th dyn	11th dyn – Am I	CG 28111	no

[23] Some mitre inscriptions are published anew by J.P. ALLEN, *The Egyptian Coffin Texts* VIII: *Middle Kingdom Copies of Pyramid Texts* (*Oriental Institute Publications* 132), Chicago 2006, 445 (B1Bo), 445-446 (B2Bo).

[24] I got information on the existence of mitre inscriptions on the coffin(s) of *Ḏḥwtj-nḫt* through the kindness of Dr. P. Der Manuelian whom I would like to thank for his assistance.

[25] The back cover of S. D'AURIA/P. LACOVARA/C.H. ROEHRIG (eds.), *Mummies & Magic. The Funerary Arts of Ancient Egypt*, reprint Dallas 1990, depicts the foot board of the coffin of *Sꜣ.t-mk.t*. The mitre inscriptions on both sides are clearly visible but not readable. Perhaps only the outer coffin B6Bo bears these texts, fragment Boston MfA 21.968 being a part of the lid of a coffin according to the museum's online database (http://www.mfa.org/collections). B6Bo is perhaps part of a coffin ensemble with B7Bo.

[26] The rectangular coffin of *Spj* contained an anthropoid coffin. Mitre inscriptions are clearly visible on the photograph published in H. SOUROUZIAN/M. SALEH, *Die Hauptwerke im Ägyptischen Museum Kairo herausgegeben vom Antikendienst der Arabischen Republik Ägypten*, Mainz 1986, no. 95.

[27] B5C may form an ensemble with B7C and perhaps B8C, WILLEMS, *Chests of Life*, 77-78; cf. LAPP, *Typologie der Särge*, 278 (B29a-b).

[28] B4L is the inner coffin of B3L.

[29] I thank Professor D.P. Silverman for bringing the existence of mitre inscriptions on this coffin to my knowledge (letter of August 9, 1994). The publication of this coffin is in preparation.

	Owner's name	Date after Willems	Date after Lapp	Inv-No	Seen
BH1Br[30]	*M3(j)*	Am II – Sen III	after Sen III	MRH E. 5037	yes
M2C	*H̱nm-ḥtp > Ḥnj*	Sen I – Am II	type 12th dyn	JE 42947	yes
M3C[31]	*Snbj* (f.)	Sen I – Am II	type 11th/12th dyn	JE 42825	AdB
M5C	*Nḫt-Ḥw.t-Ḥr.w* (f.)	Am I – Sen I	type 11th dyn	JE 42826	AdB
M8C[32]	*Wr=s-nfr*	> Sen II	type 12/13th dyn	CG 28038	no
M9C	unknown	Sen I	-	CG 28043	no
M37C	*Snbj*	Sen I	type 11th/12th dyn	CG 28041	no
M43C	unknown	Sen I	-	CG 28051	no
M47C	*Sn-ʿnḫ*	Sen I	-	CG 28057	no
M48C	unknown	Sen I	-	CG 28059	no
M50C	*Ḥw.t-Ḥr.w-ḥtp* (f.)	Sen I	-	CG 28062	no
M52C	*Wḫ-ʿ3*	Sen I	-	CG 28064	no
M53C	unknown	Sen I – Am II	-	CG 28065	no
M56C	unknown	early 12th dyn	-	CG 28082	no
M2NY[33]	*Ḥpj-ʿnḫ.tjfj*	Am II – Sen III	type 12th/13th dyn	MMA 12.183.11.A	no
M49	*Ḥnj-hr-ib*	Sen II?	type 12th/13th dyn	CG 28061	no
M1War[34]	*Šmsw-wḫ*	early 12th dyn	-	139937	no
M2War[35]	unknown	Sen I – Am II	-	139938A,B	no
M5War[36]	*Wḫ-ḥtp*	early 12th dyn	-	142114	no
M6War[37]	*Wḫ-ḥtp*	Am II	-	142141	no
M13War[38]	*H̱nmwj*	Sen I – Am II	-	142157	no
S1C	*Msḥtj*	-	type 11th dyn	CG 28118	no
S2C				CG 28119	no
S10C	*ʿnḫ=f > Ἰrj*	-	type 12th dyn	JE 44980	no
S14C?	*Ḥn.t-n=j* (f.)	-	Sen III – 13th dyn	JE 44981	AdB
S1Hil[39]	*Nḫt*	-	-	RPM 5999	yes

30 I am grateful to Dr. Luc Limme for providing me with infra-red photographs of this coffin and for allowing to publish them in this volume.

31 Old photographs of A.H. Gardiner are now published by MEYER-DIETRICH, *Senebi und Selbst*, pl. 1-3. Unfortunately the ink inscriptions are not readable on the plates.

32 M8C was placed as the middle coffin into M7C. It contained the inner coffin M42C, cf. LAPP, *Typologie der Särge*, 286 (M6a-c).

33 Mitre inscriptions are mentioned by W.C. HAYES, *The Scepter of Egypt. A Background for the Study of the Egyptian Antiquities in The Metropolitan Museum of Art.* Part I: *From the Earliest Times to the End of the Middle Kingdom*, New York 1953, 319-320. Professor J.P. Allen was so kind as to check the museum archive (personal letter of July 26, 1993). Unfortunately only one picture was taken during the short time when the coffin was dismantled. Inscriptions on other mitres were too faded for recording. M2NY forms a coffin ensemble with the rectangular coffin M56 without inner decoration.

34 Mentioned in E. DABROWSKA-SMEKTAŁA, *Studies on the Character of the Inscriptions Recorded on the Middle Kingdom Coffins from National Museum of Warsaw* (unpubl. PhD), Warsaw s.a., no. 2.

35 DABROWSKA-SMEKTAŁA, *Studies on MK Coffins*, no. 3.

36 DABROWSKA-SMEKTAŁA, *Studies on MK Coffins*, no. 6.

37 DABROWSKA-SMEKTAŁA, *Studies on MK Coffins*, no. 9.

38 DABROWSKA-SMEKTAŁA, *Studies on MK Coffins*, no. 21.

39 HANNIG, *Paläographie der Särge*, 565-575.

	Owner's name	Date after Willems	Date after Lapp	Inv-No	Seen
S3L[40]	*Nfr.w-iqr*	-	-	EA 46630	yes
S22L[41]	unknown	-	-	EA 47584-585	yes
S36L[42]	unknown	-	-	EA 47597	yes
S39L[43]	unknown	-	-	EA 46662	yes
S62L[44]	unknown	-	-	EA 47607	yes
S65L[45]	*Ỉnj-itj=f*	-	-	EA 46644	yes
S66L[46]	*S3.t-ipj*	-	-	EA 34259	yes
S67L[47]	*Sbk-ḥtp*	-	-	EA 41571	yes
Sq5Be[48]	*Ttj-S3-Sbk*	type I	-	7796 (B)	yes
Sq3C	*Nfr-smd.t* (f.)	early MK	type 11-12th dyn	JE 39014	no
Sq6C	*K3-rnni*	type I/2	type 11–12th dyn	JE 39054b	AdB
Sq12C	*Wsr-mw.t*	type I/1b	type 11–12th dyn	TN 18/1/27/2	AdB
Sq1X[49]	*Gm.n(=j)-m-ḥ3.t*	11th/12th dyn	type 11-12th dyn	-	no
Sq10X[50]	*Ỉpj-ʿnḫ.w*	type I?/1b?	type 11-12th dyn	-	no
T1Be[51]	*Mnṯw-ḥtp*	after Am II/Sen III	Sen III – 13th dyn	9	no
T9C	*Mnṯw-ḥtp > Bw3w*	Men II	Men II – Men III	CG 28027	yes
T1L[52]	*Ỉm3*	Men II – Men IV	Men II – Men III	EA 6654	no
MC105?	*Šdj* (f.) > *Didj*	11th dyn	-	JE 51875	AdB
X3War[53]	unknown	after Am II	-	142149	no

Out of the total of 67 coffins sixteen formed a part of a coffin ensemble consisting of two or three rectangular coffins (M8C). Only B1C was used as an outer coffin for an inner anthropoid coffin. Except for M49 all the coffins are decorated on both the outer and inner surfaces. Thus, it can be assumed that the coffin owners belonged not to the lowest strata of society, but that they had some wealthy background to order such coffins.

40 HANNIG, *Paläographie der Särge*, 595-598 = S42 of LAPP, *Typologie der Särge*, 294-295.

41 HANNIG, *Paläographie der Särge*, 645-646.

42 HANNIG, *Paläographie der Särge*, 672-673. He missed to mention the presence of mitre inscriptions in his publication.

43 HANNIG, *Paläographie der Särge*, 677-679 including three small pictures of mitre inscriptions.

44 HANNIG, *Paläographie der Särge*, 715-717 with two pictures of mitre inscriptions.

45 Not included in HANNIG, *Paläographie der Särge*.

46 Not included in HANNIG, *Paläographie der Särge*.

47 Not included in HANNIG, *Paläographie der Särge*.

48 Numbered by WILLEMS, *Chests of Life*, 39 as Sq14 and recorded as a coffin without inner decoration. The observation of the coffin in the Egyptian Museum at Berlin showed that it is completely decorated inside, although this decoration is very faint now. The coffin was not known to LAPP, *Typologie der Särge*. The new number is added by the present author in accordance with WILLEMS, *Chests of Life*; the coffin is mentioned and partly described in GENERALVERWALTUNG (Hrsg.), *Ausführliches Verzeichnis der aegyptischen Altertümer und Gipsabgüsse, zweite völlig umgearbeitete Auflage*, Berlin 1899, 74 and ID., *Ägyptische Inschriften aus den Königlichen Museen zu Berlin* I, Leipzig 1913, 133.

49 Sq1X is the outer coffin of Sq2X.

50 Only LAPP, *Typologie der Särge*, 298 (Sq3a-b) noticed that the inner coffin of *Ỉpj-ʿnḫ.w* is completely preserved, whereas of the outer coffin only the head and foot board survived. This is clearly mentioned by C.M. FIRTH/B. GUNN, *Teti Pyramid Cemeteries* I (*Excavations at Saqqara*), Cairo 1926, 50, 232. WILLEMS, *Chests of Life*, 31 numbered both coffins separately as Sq10X (outer coffin) and Sq5Sq (inner coffin).

51 It is unclear whether T1Be bears all the recorded inscriptions or whether they are shared with T2Be as well, the inner coffin of the ensemble, cf. G. STEINDORFF, *Grabfunde des Mittleren Reichs in den Königlichen Museen zu Berlin* I: *Das Grab des Mentuhotep* (*Mitteilungen aus den orientalischen Sammlungen* 8), Berlin 1896, 3, pl. 12-13.

52 The mitre inscriptions are published anew by ALLEN, *Egyptian Coffin Texts* VIII, 456.

53 DABROWSKA-SMEKTAŁA, *Studies on MK Coffins*, no. 15.

Since the mitre inscriptions usually contain no titles of the coffin owner, any conclusion on their social status must be based on the decorative bands of hieroglyphs on the inner and outer faces of the coffins. The number of titles is very limited there because of the lack of space; fragmentary coffin boards often show no traces of them, and even the proper name of the coffin owner may be lost or not given. Thus, in many cases this important information is lost for us. The following titles are known for some of the coffin owners:

B1-2Bo: *ḥ3.tj-ᶜ ḫrp ns.tj*; B3-4C: *nb.t pr*; B5C: *sš ᶜ nsw.t, sš hn*; B9-10C: *ḥ3.tj-ᶜ*; B12C: *wᶜb ᶜ3*; B1-2L: *wr swnw*; B3-4L: *wr swnw*; B1Ph: *ḥ3.tj-ᶜ*; BH1Br: *mr ᶜḥwt* (?); M2C: *mr pr*; M8C: *mr pr n ḫbs*; M2NY: *mr pr*; M5War: *mr pr*; M13War: *mr ḫtm.t*; Sq1X: [titles on his false door: *ḫtmw bj.tj, smr-wᶜ.tj, rḫ-nsw.t m3ᶜ, mr pr, mr šnw.tj, mtj n z3 Ḏd-s.wt-Ttj, mtj n z3 W3ḏ-s.wt Mrj-k3-Rᶜ.w*][54]; T1Be: *mr pr*; T9C: *ḫtmw bj.tj, mr pr, mr šnw.tj, mr ip.t nb.t m Šmᶜ.w Mḥw, mr ᶜb.w wḥm.w šw.w nšm.wt* (titles of the usurper); T1L: *ḫtmw bj.tj*

2.2 Arrangement of Inscriptions on Coffins and Style of Writing

The walls, bottom and lid of a coffin usually comprise several dowelled planks, sometimes of very irregular shape, demonstrating high standards of wood working in Egypt. Only the most expensive coffins are made of cedar and their walls are assembled of very few high quality planks. Theoretically, mitre joints inscriptions and images can be incised or painted on all of them. Actually, the vertical mitre joints of the four sidewalls (head, foot, front, back) are their favoured locations (cf. Pl. 1-2). In some instances they are placed on the top or on the thickness of the bottom (B1-2Bo, T9C) where the sidewalls are fixed to cover them (Fig. 1, Pl. 4) or they are found more often (B21C, M49, M53C, BH1Br, S22L, S36L, S62) inside the horizontal junctions of a sidewall (Fig. 2).

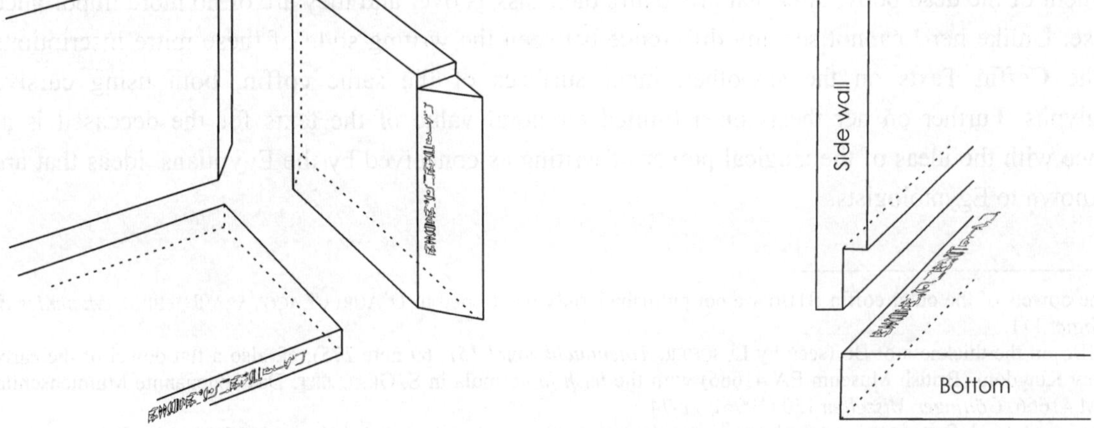

Fig. 1: Possible location of inscriptions on the vertical mitres and on bottom

54 FIRTH/GUNN, *Teti Pyramid Cemeteries* I, 52-54 (tomb HMK 30), II, pl. 27.

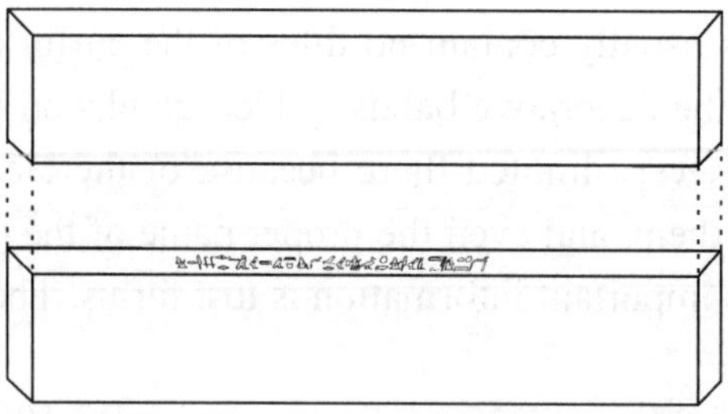

Fig. 2: Possible location of inscriptions between planks of a side wall

The same inscriptions as on the mitres of a coffin occur on the flat or rounded dowels of Middle Kingdom coffins and some published examples are included in this study (B2Bo[55], M53C).[56] More often the structure of such pegs/dowels limits the space for the text to the simple *imȝḫ ḫr GN PN* formula[57] or the name of the owner[58] or a god's name (Qebehsenuef[59]).

As far as the publications offer this information, the mitre inscriptions are written in cursive hieroglyphs, the same type of script that is used for the Coffin Texts. Only on M8C, M37C, T1Be, T1L, BH1Br and on the coffins from Asyut (S36L, S39L, S62L) the hieratic script is used, although it is not always easy to make a clear distinction between cursive hieroglyphs and hieratic. The mitres of Y2C and B1Bo bear hieroglyphic inscriptions, some signs even show inner details. Many texts were applied to the rough surfaces of the mitres in vertical columns after the construction of the whole sidewall had been finished. Nevertheless, when the walls and the bottom were mounted together, it often happened that the inscriptions were perforated by the holes for the rounded dowels. In some instances, it seems that these holes were prepared first and then the texts were carefully inscribed around them (S36L, S62L, M2NY?). On horizontal mitres the inscriptions can be also written in lines (S62L, BH1Br: Pl. 4). Normally black ink was used for writing or the inscriptions were incised in a somewhat careless manner. This writing style on the rough unprepared surfaces led Meyer-Dietrich[60] in the case of M3C to the thesis, that the spells′ contents were not settled for eternity but had to be effective only for a short time, like a note. Their purpose is to prepare the wooden boards for the placement of the dead body; after that procedure their task is over and they are of no more importance and use. Unlike her I cannot see any difference between the writing style of these mitre inscriptions and the Coffin Texts on the smoothed inner surfaces of the same coffin, both using cursive hieroglyphs. Further on her thesis on a limited temporal value of the texts for the deceased is at variance with the ideas of the magical power of writing as conceived by the Egyptians, ideas that are well known to Egyptologists.

---

55 The dowels of the outer coffin B1Bo are not published, only mentioned in D′AURIA/LACOVARA/ROEHRIG, *Mummies & Magic*, 111.

56 B4Bo on the thickness of Bo (seen by LÜSCHER, *Totenbuchkapitel 151*, 69 note 275); cf. also a flat dowel of the early New Kingdom (British Museum EA 41666) with the *imȝḫ ḫr* formula in S. GRALLERT, Das sogenannte Mumienschild BM 41666, *Göttinger Miszellen* 150 (1996), 71-74.

57 For example H. SCHAEFER, *Ausgrabungen der deutschen Orient-Gesellschaft in Abusir 1902-1904* II: *Priestergräber und andere Grabfunde vom Ende des Alten Reiches bis zur griechischen Zeit vom Totentempel des Ne-User-Rê* (*Wissenschaftliche Veröffentlichungen der Deutschen Orient-Gesellschaft* 8), Leipzig 1908, 36 fig. 36 (Hapi); a piece in the Metropolitan Museum of Art without number is mentioned by H.G. FISCHER, Marginalia II, *Göttinger Miszellen* 128 (1992), 76 note 3 (Hapi).

58 For example SCHAEFER, *Priestergräber vom Totentempel des Ne-User-Rê*, 33.

59 MMA 27.3.59 (Eleventh Dynasty) in FISCHER, *Göttinger Miszellen* 128 (1992), 76 note 4; cf. SCHAEFER, *Priestergräber vom Totentempel des Ne-User-Rê*, 33.

60 *Senebi und Selbst*, 31 and pl. 1-3.

2.3 The Content of the Mitre Inscriptions

The inscriptions painted or incised on the mitres consist of several different spells designated in my unpublished MA thesis and its short summary in "Studien zur Altägyptischen Kultur 23" by capital letters for easier quoting (texts A-S). Some texts are documented in several versions (Texts A-F, N, S), as concerns the remaining inscriptions, with the present state of coffin publications only a single version is available for study (texts G-M, O-R). This fact may be an excuse of the structure of this chapter being far from uniform. The chapter will first deal with texts of several versions, followed by the single versions of inscriptions. Some texts are not included into the present study. Text L is documented by Lesko[61] on Sq3C (Fr/F), but the hieroglyphic writing is not clear at all. The text is not attested in the Pyramid and Coffin Texts or the Book of the Dead. Text O can no longer be classified as a mitre inscription according to the new publication of Allen.[62] It is rather a label or heading of an image of an offering table.[63] Text S or CT spell 1186 of Willems[64] is known to me in three more fragmentary versions on coffins from Asyut but it needs more study (two times on S39L, S62L). Other texts not yet numbered are in a too fragmentary state for publication and need further collating on the original.

The mitre inscriptions are usually introduced by *ḏd mdw* "Saying words" if the deceased speaks, or by *ḏd mdw jn GN* "Saying words by God/Goddess N". Only texts I-K introduce the self identifications of the gods by *ḏd mdw*. Several spells are uttered by the deceased himself or by an anonymous speaker. In some instances the original version in the first person was changed to the third person by a text compiler. In general, we can assume that most of the mitre inscriptions are utterances of the deceased and are therefore formulated in the first person, or they are direct divine statements in the first person as well. This feature they share with the Coffin Texts.

Usually the two mitres of a coffin wall bear one spell each, and, thus, different spells are easily distinguished one from another by this feature. Some richly decorated coffins like B1Bo place several spells on a single mitre. Many mitre inscriptions (texts I-K, M) are attested only on an ensemble of coffins from el-Bersheh (B1-2Bo) that is famous for its great artistic paintings[65]. These two coffins show up to five columns of text on one mitre and bear the greatest variety of known mitre inscriptions. The same is true for BH1Br which offers the only version of texts Q and R.

2.3.1 Texts A-F

Texts A-F are very often combined on one coffin and seem to form a close unit. This is also confirmed by the usage of these texts as a group in the New Kingdom and the Late Period (see below). The closest relation can be detected between texts A-C.

Since the combinations of text A and text C or text B and text C are documented repeatedly on one coffin, it may be possible that the lack of text B or text A results from the poor documentation of the sources or from the loss of the text (cf. Fig. 3). The more mitres of a coffin are preserved and recorded, the greater seems to be the probability that the whole group of texts A-F was present on the coffin.

---

61 *Index of Spells*, 91.

62 To be corrected in my MA thesis and in *Studien zur Altägyptischen Kultur* 23 (1996).

63 ALLEN, *Egyptian Coffin Texts* VIII, 444 note 1: "Lines 861-862 are painted hieroglyphs. Under them 'probably a table with objects, but almost gone' (AdB)".

64 WILLEMS, *Coffin of Heqata*, 138-139.

65 E.L.B. TERRACE, *Egyptian Paintings of the Middle Kingdom*, London 1968.

Apart from T9C, BH1Br, B1-2Bo, and M3C only some of the possibly inscribed mitres of a coffin bear documented inscriptions today.

T9C	A	B	C		E	F		9 mitres (H+Fr+F+B+Bo)
T1L	A		C		E			3 mitres (H+B+F)
S1Hil	A	B	C				G	4 mitres (H+F)
S65L	A	B	C					3 mitres (H+F)
M2C				D			others	3 mitres +1? (Fr+F+B)
M3C		B	C	D		F		8 mitres (H+Fr+F+B)
M5C		B			E			2 mitres (H+B)
M9C				D				1 mitre (H)
M47C	A							2 mitres (F)
M53C	A						N	1 mitre (F), 2 dowels
M2NY	A?							5 mitres (H+Fr+F+B)
B1Bo	A	B	C		E	F	M, N, P	10 mitres (H+Fr+F+B+Bo)
B2Bo	A	B		D			I-K	8 mitres (H+Fr+F+B)
BH1Br	A	B	C		E	F	Q, R	7 mitres (H+Fr+F+Bo)
Sq3C	A		C		E?		L	5 mitres (H+F+B)
Sq1X				D				1 mitre (F)
Sq10X				D				2 mitres (F)

Fig. 3: Correlation of mitre inscriptions A-F on single coffins

Text A

Text A is written on the mitres of eleven coffins from the cemeteries of el-Bersheh, Meir, Asyut, Western Thebes and Saqqara. As the table demonstrates, this text is usually placed on the mitres of the F, and it is associated there with the Fr more often than the B. M47C and T9C use the text on both mitres of the F.

ḏd mdw Gb ˁ.wj=k ḥ3=j/PN sḥḏ=k ḥr=j/f wn=k ir.tj=j/f

"Saying words: O Geb, may your arms be (turned) around me/PN, may you illuminate my/his face, may you open my/his eyes".

In seven instances the dead person himself appeals to the god Geb, in four cases an anonymous speaker addresses to him. Thus, on four coffins the spell is transformed from the first person to the third person. Geb must protect the dead from any harm and to do it he embraces the latter. As a god of the earth Geb hides every dead body and, accordingly, he can remove himself from it. This action enables the dead person to get in contact with daylight and to use his eyes again. In his role of the earth Geb is literally placed under the feet of the deceased, the footboard of the coffin being identified in mythological terms with the earth that is under the feet of a walking man. At the same time it is the earth that covers any corpse after burial in the western desert. The stable location of the inscriptions on F shows the predominance of that idea over the connection of the eyes with the H.

T9C	T9C	T1L	S65L	S1Hil	B1Bo	B2Bo	BH1Br	M2NY	M47C	M47C	M53C	Sq3C

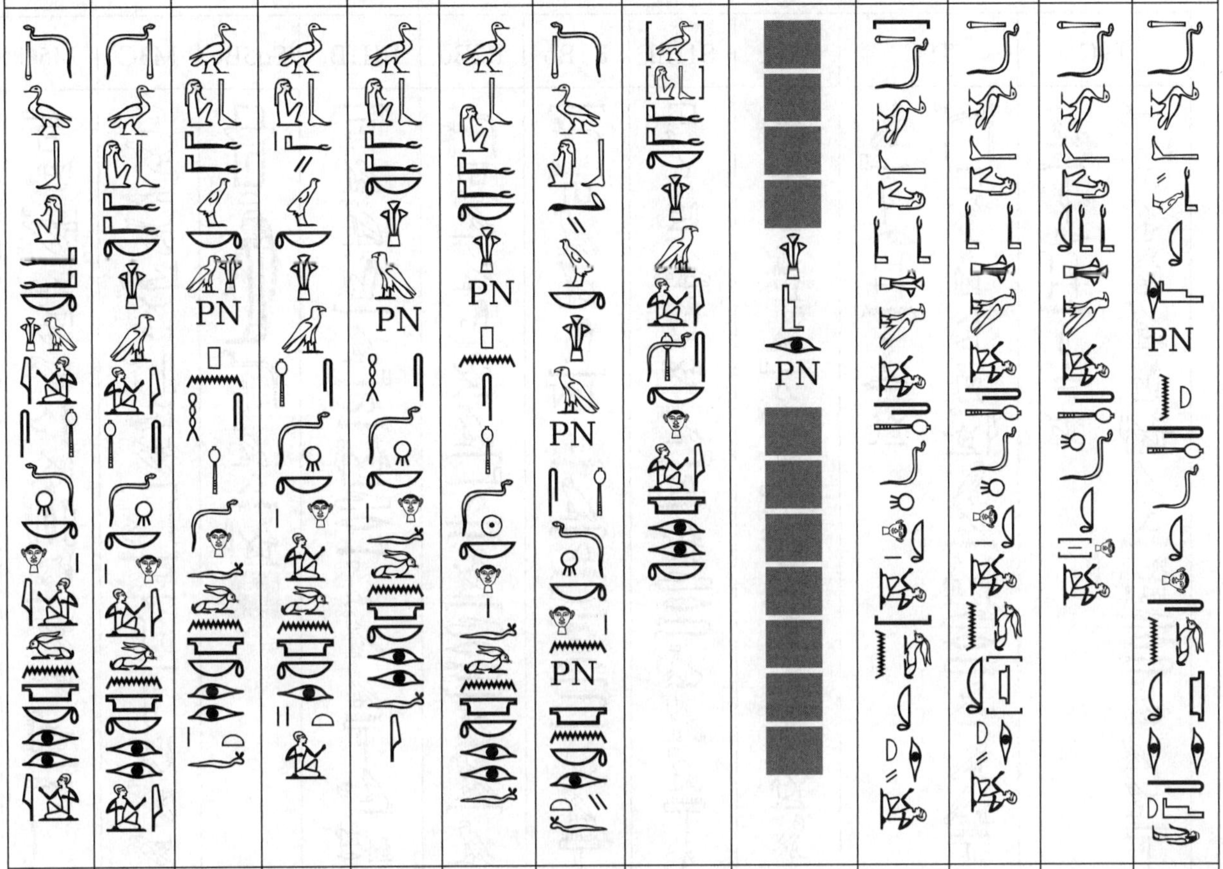

F/Fr	F/B	F/Fr	F/Fr	F/Fr	F/B	F/Fr	F/Fr	F/Fr	F/Fr	F/B	F/L?	F/Fr

Commentary on versions:
B1Bo: *ḥ3* needs further verification, sufficient space is available; BH1Br: cf. Pl. 1; very few traces of the beginning of the text, enough space available for restoration; *wn(=j?) ỉr.tj=k* is a scribal error for *wn=k ỉr.tj=j*; M2NY: remains of the text are most likely to be identified as a part of spell A because of their location on F/Fr; M47C: text restored in accordance with the second version on the same coffin; M53C: the end of the text is missing, but is to be restored after other versions; the determinative of *wn* is restored after other versions; S65L: cf. Pl. 3; Sq3C: *ḥ3* is omitted by scribal error; T1L: newly published by ALLEN, *Egyptian Coffin Texts* VIII, 456; old publication of S. Birch has two strokes after *ỉr.tj*.

Text B

Text B is known from nine coffins from Western Thebes, Meir, el-Bersheh, Asyut and Beni Hasan. Perhaps a much destroyed text on Sq5Be attests to the existence of this text also in the Memphite area, then it is as widely spread over Egypt as text A. Text B seems to be associated with the head end of the coffin; only two coffins place it on the opposite end (BH1Br, T9C). The arrangement at BH1Br may be a mistake because the inscriptions are to be read upside down on the mitres of the front board. It is possible that the mitre inscriptions were written on their usual location (H), but then the carpenter or painter turned the coffin wall over by mistake when painting the wall or building up the box. Text B is present on either mitre of Fr on T9C.

T9C	T9C	S65L	S1Hil	B1Bo	B2Bo	BH1Br	Sq5Be	M3C	M5C
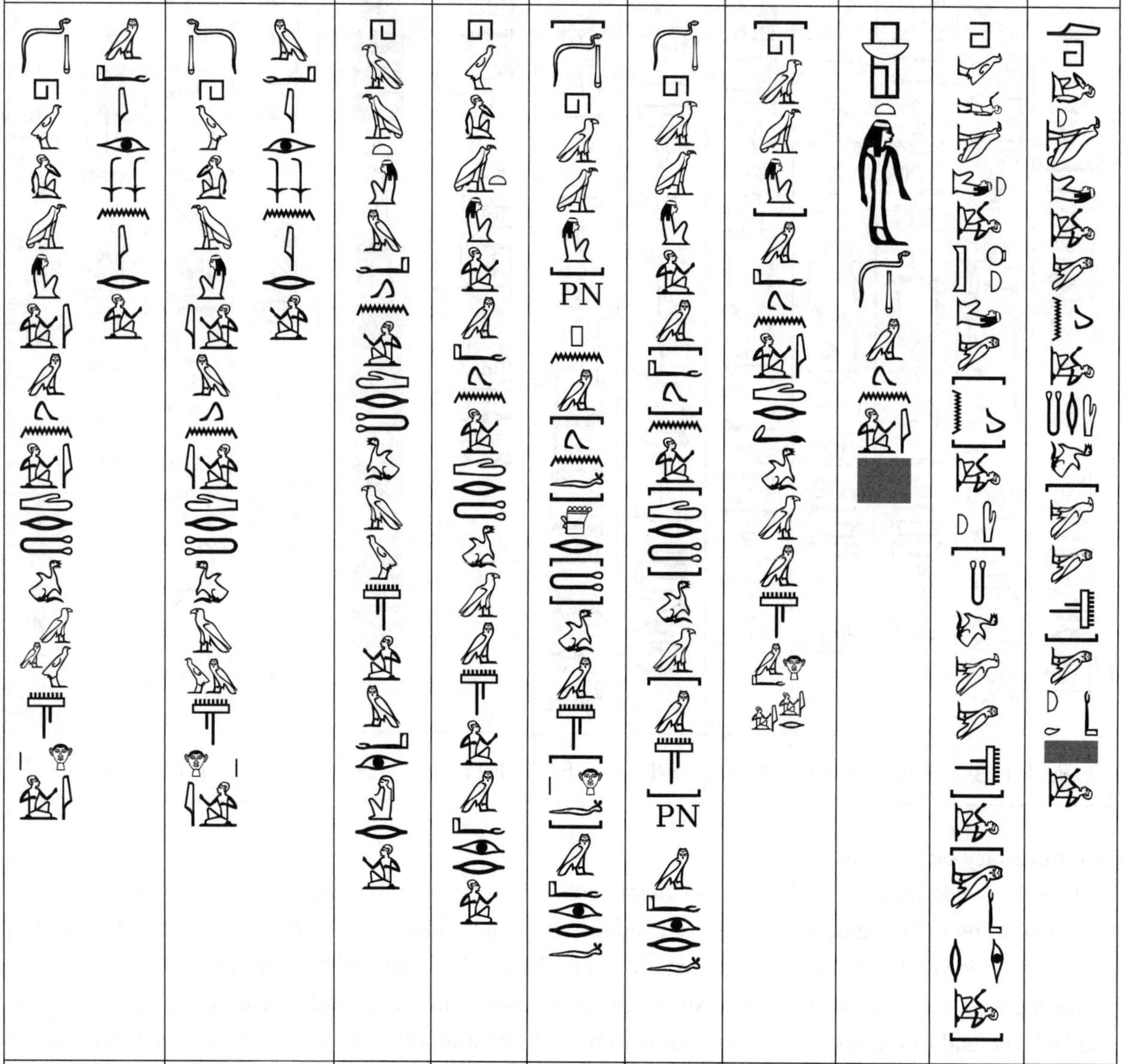									
Fr/H	Fr/F	H/Fr	H/Fr	Fr/H	H/Fr	Fr/F	H/B	Fr/H	B/H

Commentary on versions:

For *ṯ3m* "Schleier" in Middle Kingdom texts see now R. HANNIG, *Ägyptisches Wörterbuch* II: *Mittleres Reich und Zweite Zwischenzeit* (*Hannig-Lexica* 5), Mainz 2006, 2724, the determinative of BH1Br shows the unusual shape ; B1Bo: beginning of the text is restored after the version of B2Bo from the same coffin ensemble; *m[j n=f]* too few traces for certain reading, but enough space is available; *ḏr* instead of correct *dr*; very few uncertain traces of [*ḥr=f*], but the space is sufficient for the preposition and suffix; the text is completely reworked into the third person; B2Bo: unexpected change from the first person to the third person, a scribal error when copying from *Vorlage* to coffin mitre?; BH1Br: cf. Pl. 1; ink too faded to verify the beginning of the text, space is sufficient for this restoration; *=ṯ* after *dr* and *irj* after *m-ꜥ* omitted by scribe, an interpretation as imperative *dr* is also possible; S65L: cf. Pl. 3; Sq5Be: remains of text, most probably the initial part of spell B, the end of text is lost; M3C: *t* after *d* in *dr=ṯ* may be misreading of LESKO, *Index of Spells*, 60, to be corrected to *r*; M5C: restoration in accordance with LESKO, *Index of Spells*, 61 who places two quadrants after the beginning of *ṯꜣm*; after *ꜥ.t* plural strokes may be added before the suffix, the text version is different from those on other coffins.

> *(ḏd mdw) hꜣ mw.t(=j)/PN Nw.t mj n=j/f dr=ṯ ṯꜣm(.w)=j/PN/ḥr=j m-ꜥ irj (nn) r=j/f*
>
> "(Saying words:) O[a] (my) mother/of PN (Nut), come to me/him! You might remove[b] the/my mummy bandages of PN/upon me[c] by the hand of him who did (this) against me!"
>
> a M. VON FALCK, Text- und Bildprogramm ägyptischer Särge und Sarkophage der 18. Dynastie: Genese und Weiterleben, *Studien zur Altägyptischen Kultur* 34 (2006), 130 reads *hꜣj* "descend" instead of a vocative particle *hꜣ* "o, he" (A. ERMAN/H. GRAPOW (eds.), *Wörterbuch der ägyptischen Sprache* II, Berlin-Leipzig 2nd 1957, 471). The two sarcophagi produced under Thutmose III (E and F of HAYES, *Royal Sarcophagi*) determine *hꜣ* with Gardiner-Sign D54 (walking legs), whereas several Middle Kingdom versions clearly show a sitting man with a hand to mouth (Gardiner-Sign A2) as a determinative. This contradicts the view of von Falck.
>
> b Formerly inadequately interpreted by me as an imperative: *Studien zur Altägyptischen Kultur* 23 (1996), 152.
>
> c VON FALCK, *Studien zur Altägyptischen Kultur* 34 (2006), 130 translates *ṯꜣm(.w) ḥr=j* as "... entferne die Bandagen meines Gesichts ...".[66] He understands *ḥr* not as a preposition but as a substantive "face". The Egyptian writing conventions can not help to choose between the two options. The parallel texts (unknown to von Falck) with suffix after *ṯꜣm(.w)* and especially the text version M5C (see below) denote *ḥr* as a preposition. No version gives any hint that the facial bandages alone shall be removed. Further on, Middle Kingdom mummies often bear masks or are equipped with painted facial details on their bandages. In my opinion this attention to the face demonstrates that the face was not thought to be covered by bandages, and therefore it was singled out of the rest of the body that was wrapped in linen.
>
> *ih mw.t=j mj n=j dr=ṯ ṯꜣ[m] m ꜥ.[w]t=j* (M5C)
>
> "O my mother, come to me! You might remove the mummy [bandages] from my limbs".

Text B is an invocation of the deceased addressed to his mother explicitly identified as the sky goddess Nut only on M3C. She is expected to meet the dead person and to free him from the mummy bandages. These are obviously an unpleasant covering for the body that was applied to it by an anonymous enemy, perhaps an embalmer. Their negative connotation indirectly expresses the wish of the deceased to walk freely in the netherworld.[67] The sky goddess and the wife of Geb, Nut, is an important deity well known from the Pyramid Texts where she cares for the dead king. Her record at the head end of a coffin is due to her role of the sky in Egyptian mythology. Thus, the divine couple mentioned in texts A and B is placed above and beneath the deceased as sky and earth creating a cosmos with the dead in his role of Osiris in its centre.

66 Cf. also M. VON FALCK, *Textgeschichtliche Untersuchungen zu Götterreden und verwandten Texten auf ägyptischen Särgen und Sarkophagen von der 3. Zwischenzeit bis zur Ptolemäerzeit. Teil 1: Nut-Texte, ausgewählte Götterreden und Pyramidentextspruchauszüge* II, Münster 2001, 314. This PhD is available at http://nbn-resolving.de/urn:nbn:de:hbz:6-79699585534.

67 This viewpoint is especially well stated in the later texts of the Amduat and the Book of the Gates, cf. E. HORNUNG, *Das Buch von den Pforten des Jenseits* I (*Aegyptiaca Helvetica* 7), Genève 1979, 235-239; ID., *Das Amduat. Die Schrift des verborgenen Raumes* I (*Ägyptologische Abhandlungen* 7), München 1963, 40-41, II, 56, 77, 122.

Text C

Text C is attested on eight coffins from six Middle Kingdom cemeteries in eleven versions that slightly differ one from another. Although spread over a great part of the country (el-Bersheh, Beni Hasan, Meir, Asyut, Saqqara, Western Thebes), it is concentrated mainly in Middle Egypt. All coffins date to the end of the Eleventh Dynasty or the beginning of the Twelfth Dynasty except BH1Br that was produced in the end of the reign of Amenemhet II or under Senusret III. Text C is related with the B of the coffin with the exception of BH1Br. It can be placed there either on the foot or on the head end.

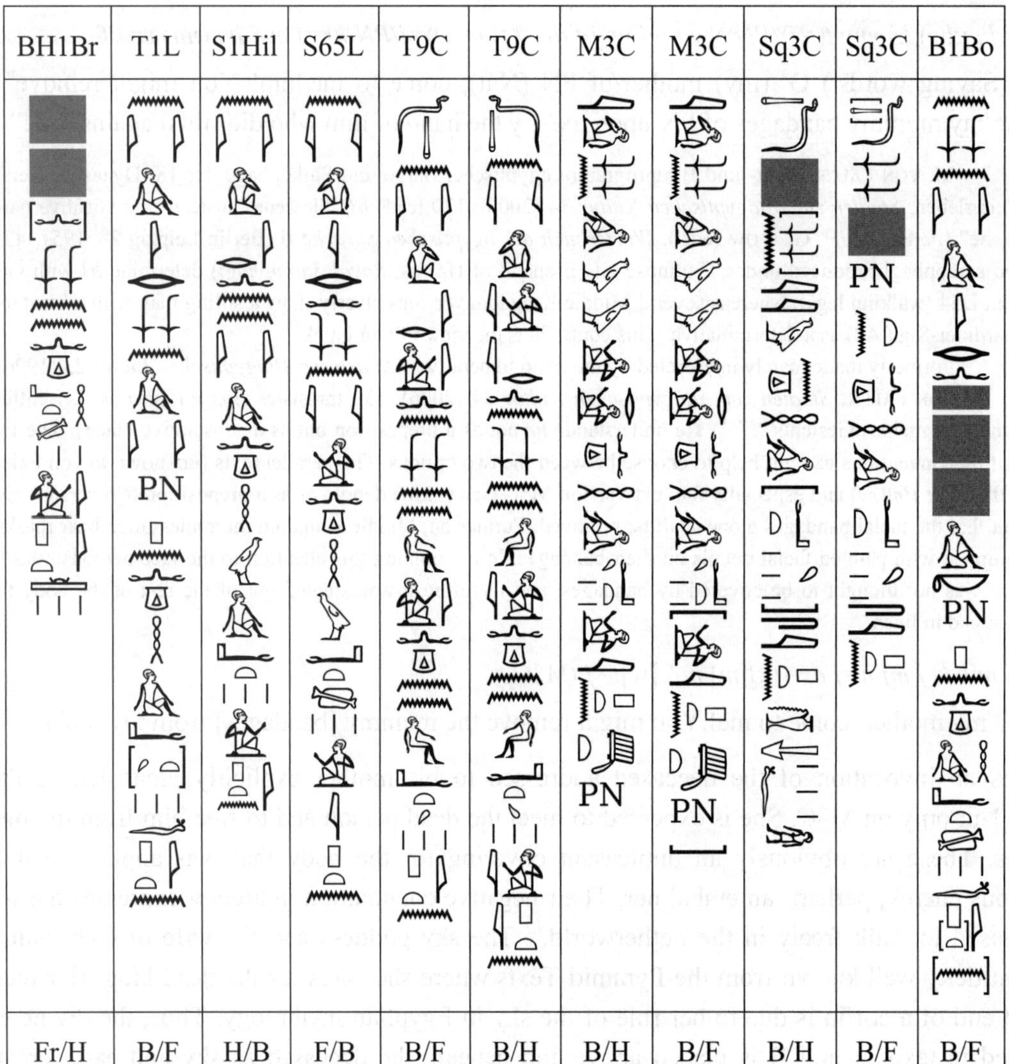
BH1Br
T1L
S1Hil
S65L
T9C
T9C
M3C
M3C
Sq3C
Sq3C
B1Bo
PN
Fr/H
B/F
H/B
F/B
B/F
B/H
B/H
B/F
B/H
B/F
B/F

Commentary on versions:

BH1Br: cf. Pl. 2; very few traces of ink that cannot be restored with any certainty in approximately 2 to 2,5 quadrants at the beginning; *n* is erroneously replaced by the book roll in *iptn*; T1L: newly published by ALLEN, *Egyptian Coffin Texts* VIII, 456; negation *n* (Gardiner-Sign D35) is missed by the scribe before *nnj*; ʿ.*wt* is restored after other versions; an unexpected change from the first person to the third person; M3C: LESKO, *Index of spell* has  and  after *w wj*, perhaps misread; *t* is replaced by *r* by the present author; S65L: cf. Pl. 3; T9C: the suffix *=j* of *ny=j ir* perhaps a metathesis of *ny ir=j* as in the second version on the same coffin; B1Bo: Suffix *=k* after Gardiner-Sign A7 unclear in the context may be a scribal error; *ip*[*tn*] restored after other versions.

Five versions of spell C of the coffins from Asyut and Thebes show the greatest similarities. The text is a speech of the deceased himself who utters the sound *ny* and assures that his extremities are not in the state of weariness.

S1Hil: *ny ir(=j) n nny(=j) n gḥ ʿ.wt=j iptn*
S65L: *ny ir(=j) n nny=j n gḥ ʿ.wt=j iptn*

"*ny* belongs to (me). (I) will not be tired. These my limbs will not be weary".

T9C: *ny ir=j n{n} nnj=j n gnn ʿ.wt(=j) iptn*
T9C: *ny{=j} ir[=j] n{n} nnj=j n gnn ʿ.wt–j iptn*

"*ny* belongs to[a] me. I will not be tired[b]. These my limbs will not be weak".

a Unique variant reading *ir=j* on T9C, different from LESKO, *Index of Spells*, 103, who gives for both versions , followed by VON FALCK, *Textgeschichtliche Untersuchungen* II, 205. The second version shows most probably a metathesis of the suffix pronoun first person singular that is fixed to *ny* instead of *ir*.

b Originally perhaps a verbal sentence, then a sentence of non-existence as it looks here. Thus, the negation *nn* should be corrected to *n*.

T1L: *ny ir(=j) <n> nny PN pn n gḥ* [ʿ].*w*[*t*]*=f iptn*

"*ny* belongs to (me). This PN will not be tired, these his [limbs] will not be weary".

BH1Br: [*ny(=j) n*] *nnj(=j) n gḥ ʿ.wt=j iptn*

"[I say *ny*].[a] (I) will [not] be tired. These my limbs will not be weary".

a BH1Br as the youngest source of text C in the Middle Kingdom may already have misunderstood the sentence and corrected it. The lacuna at the beginning would be sufficient to restore *ny n* , a writing that is attested on the royal sarcophagi of early Thutmoside age.[68] Cf. the reconstructed version (δ1') for this text by VON FALCK, *Textgeschichtliche Untersuchungen* II, 208. Another (less plausible?) restoration may be *ḏd mdw* that would suggest some similarity with the version of B1Bo that starts clearly with the negation *n* + verbal *nnj*. Another beginning can not be excluded as well.

Other versions of text C on coffins from el-Bersheh, Meir and Saqqara start with another beginning (not *ny* but *nnj*) and are not as similar as the first group.

B1Bo: *n nny(=j) ir(=j) n ///=k PN pn n gḥ ʿ.wt=f ip*[*tn*]

"(I) then will not be tired. Your [tiredness] will not exist, this PN. The[se] his limbs will not be weary".

a Perhaps restoration *nnj* or *gnn* as noun is possible, then the negation *n* should be restored to *nn*. A sentence of non-existence is though very unusual. Nevertheless, the change from the first person to the second and then the third person is unexpected and its reason is unclear.

Sq3C: *ḏd mdw* [*n?*] *nny(=j) w n gḥ* [*ʿ.wt*]*=s iptn – Qbḥ-sn.w=f*
Sq3C: *ḏd* [*mdw*] <*n*> *nn*[*j?*] *PN tn n gḥ ʿ.wt=s iptn*

68 W.C. HAYES, *Royal Sarcophagi of the XVIII Dynasty*, Princeton 1935, 199 (text 40 on the four sarcophagi C-F of the time of Hatshepsut and Thutmose III).

"Saying (words):[a] I/this PN[b] <will> not be tired. These her limbs will not be weary (– Qebehsenuef)".

a The beginning of the spell is quite unclear to me. The lacuna of one version may have contained the negation *n*, then the text would remind the version of B1Bo. The scribe would have missed it then in the second version. Or we restore an invocation particle like *ỉ* of M3C. Then we can opt for the same beginning as on M3C, [*ỉ*] *nnjw* "O fatigue ones" for both versions of Sq3C. *w* should be a part of the ending of the participle then.

b The record of the name of PN after the lacuna remains unclear to me. Its size seems to be a reason for understanding *nnj* as part of suffix conjugation and PN as a subject – "this PN will not be tired". Then for reason of parallelism we can interpret *nnj* as verbal *nnj(=j)* in the other version of Sq3C. There, we have to recognize a transformation of first person to third person again as in other texts. Thus, only one version of Sq3C was completely transferred into the third person by the scribe or text compiler.

M3C: *ỉ nnjw wj r=j n gḥ ꜥ.wt[=j ỉptn] [ỉmꜣḫ.t PN?]*

M3C: *ỉ nnjw wj r=j n gḥ ꜥ.wt=j ỉptn ỉmꜣḫ.t PN*

"O fatigue ones[a], *wj* belongs to me[b]." or "O sluggish[b] fatigue ones against me." "These my limbs will not be weary, revered one PN".

a For the enigmatic beginning, I can give no satisfactory translation. Perhaps we must consider some misreading of the source Lesko used for his publication (*Index of Spells*, 60). The spell starts clearly with an invocation. Invocations to abstract nouns are seldom, so *nnj* may be here a plural participle "fatigue ones" (Erman/Grapow, *Wörterbuch der ägyptischen Sprache* II 275). It is referring usually to a group of "gespenstische elende Tote", cf. D. Bidoli, *Die Sprüche der Fangnetze in den altägyptischen Sargtexten* (*Abhandlungen des Deutschen Archäologischen Instituts Kairo* 9), Glückstadt 1976, 50-52. The context of their appearing is still unclear to me.

b Can  be the ending of the participle *nnj*? That is a solution proposed by von Falck, *Textgeschichtliche Untersuchungen* II, 205 note 310 who reads and translates: *ỉ nnww (ỉ)r.j n(j) g(ꜣ)ḥ ꜥwt.j ỉptn ỉmꜣḫyt N* "Oh (ihr), die ihr Müdigkeit wider mich macht …" and refers to Erman/Grapow, *Wörterbuch der ägyptischen Sprache* II 275.8 for a transitive meaning of *nnj*. It is attested only in Graeco-Roman time according to Erman/Grapow, *Wörterbuch der ägyptischen Sprache*.
Or may it be a parallel to the above sentence *ny ir(=j)*, a hitherto unknown word comparable with *ny* "sound of a newborn baby" (Erman/Grapow, *Wörterbuch der ägyptischen Sprache* II 201.9)? Then it can be translated "*wj* belongs to me". A determinative Gardiner-Sign A2 nevertheless would fit better than A1. Perhaps another faint possibility is the 6-rad. adjective *wj(ꜣ)wj(ꜣ)* "sluggish" (R.A. Caminos, Papyrus Berlin 10463, *Journal of Egyptian Archaeology* 49 (1963), 35) used as attributive of *nnj* and translated "O sluggish fatigue ones"?[69] The determinative of *wj(ꜣ)wj(ꜣ)* does not conform with *wwj*, of course. The reading and translation of Meyer-Dietrich, *Senebi und Selbst*, 37 for *wy wj r=j* as "Wehe mir!" is not quite clear to me. Obviously she reads simple *w* for 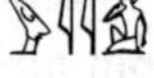 *wy* as the interjection "woe" Erman/Grapow, *Wörterbuch der ägyptischen Sprache* I 272.

From the very beginning of the history of text C, it was less stable than the texts A and B. It is corrupt and its meaning is obscure even in the Middle Kingdom. The deceased addresses to an unknown person, and states that he and especially his limbs are not fainted. The word *ny* is known from Papyrus Ebers as the first sound made by a newborn baby and interpreted as a positive sign for its survival.[70] Thus, the dead perhaps shows his ability to speak uttering this noise. The beginning of M3C, Sq3C and B1Bo seems to be more corrupt. Only on M3C the spell starts with an invocation particle that can be followed only by a reference to a creature. So the proposed "(sluggish?) fatigue ones" may refer to somebody who is tired but who is dangerous and can transfer his own undesirable condition to other

69 I am grateful to S. Bojowald, Bonn for this suggestion.

70 Erman/Grapow, *Wörterbuch der ägyptischen Sprache* II 201.9 and H. von Deines/H. Grapow, *Wörterbuch der medizinischen Texte* I (*Grundriß der Medizin der alten Ägypter* 7.1), Berlin 1961, 445.

persons like the dead. Either he is asked to stay away from the deceased (*r=j*) or the dead assures him that he can utter sounds and must therefore not fear him (*wj r=j*). In any case, the understanding of the beginning of text C is more than difficult. Since it is often related to texts A, B and E, it should be used in the same context like these spells.

Text D

Text D is present on six coffins from Meir, el-Bersheh and Saqqara. Its content relates it in every case to the H or F of a coffin. This correlation is so close that the mentioned placement of Isis or Nephthys at the head or feet of the deceased corresponds with the location of the spell on the mitres. Only on B2Bo its two versions are placed on the Fr instead the H or F themselves.

> *dd mdw in Nw.t/Rꜥ.w rdj<.n>(=j) n=k/ṯ ꜣs.t ẖr tp=k/ṯ*
>
> "Saying words by Nut/Ra: (Hereby[a] I) place Isis under[b] your head".
>
> *ḏd mdw in Nw.t/Rꜥ.w inj<.n>(=j) n=k/ṯ Nb.t-Ḥw.t ẖr rd.wj=k/ṯ*
>
> "Saying words by Nut/Ra: (Hereby I) bring Nephthys[c] under both your feet".

a Performative *sḏm.n=f*, cf. P. VERNUS, "Ritual" *sḏm.n.f* and some values of the "Accompli" in the Bible and in the Koran, in: S. ISRAELIT-GROLL (ed.), *Pharaonic Egypt, the Bible and Christianity*, Jerusalem 1985, 307-316. The second *n* is omitted by mistake of the scribe (haplography).

b M9C adds a redundant pseudo participle *rdj.t(j)* before the usual *ẖr tp=k*.

c Isis is located at the feet of the deceased only on Sq10X. Perhaps a mistake of Quibell, who published these texts?

On B2Bo the sky goddess Nut as a speaker is replaced by the solar god Ra, a peculiar situation otherwise typical of the necropolis of Meir and not el-Bersheh. Thus, the same replacement is to be found also on M2C. The basic sentence can be followed by additional statements that specify the actions of the goddesses in particular.

> ... *stp=s sꜣ=s PN* (M3C); *irj=s sꜣ=ṯ PN tn* [71] (M3C); *rmj=s ṯw sꜣḫ=s ṯw* (*pr.t-ḫrw n.t PN*) (B2Bo, M2C); *sꜣq=s n=k rd.wj=k n mt=k* (Sq10X); *nḏrj=s ꜥ=k PN dj=s n=k ib=k n ḏ.t<=k> ///* (Sq1X)
>
> "... May she protect PN; May she give protection to this PN; May she mourn you, may she glorify you (an invocation offering of PN); May she assemble for you your legs, may you not die; May she grasp your arm, PN, may she give you your heart of <your> body ///."

The actions of the sisters Isis and Nephthys may be transposed, both goddesses being responsible for the same urgent help to the dead person. They first mourn for the dead, thus simultaneously glorifying him by that their action, then they protect him against dangers, and reunite the legs and the heart with the body of the deceased that he shall not die. Thus, their deeds reproduce their mythological actions over the murdered Osiris. The deceased is recognized in his role of Osiris, which is necessary to come to life again as Osiris PN in the underworld.

---

71 Misread on M3C by MEYER-DIETRICH, *Senebi und Selbst*, 35 as "*ir.s mt.ṯ Snbj tn*". The sign is obviously a common writing of *sꜣ* "protection" and not a "... Durchstreichen des Zeichens für 'sterben' ..." (37). Unfortunately she builds up some conclusions on liminality on this spelling.

B2Bo
B2Bo
M2C
M3C
M3C
M3C
M3C
M9C
Sq1X
Sq10X
Sq10X
PN
Fr/H
Fr/F
F/B
H/Fr
H/B
F/B
F/Fr
H/Fr
F/Fr
F/Fr
F/B

Commentary on versions:
B2Bo: the version on Fr/F has some scribal errors, a suffix of the second person is missing after the preposition *n* and after *rd.wj*, a suffix of the third person is absent after the verb *rmj*; M3C: the preposition *n* is missing in both cases after *rdj.n(=j)* as a haplography; Sq1X: restored according to other versions; Sq10X: version on F/Fr misses a determinative of *Nw.t*.

Text E

Text E is recorded on six coffins from Western Thebes, Meir, el-Bersheh and Beni Hasan. The spell shows an obvious connection with the H.

Commentary on versions: T1L: newly published by ALLEN, *Egyptian Coffin Texts* VIII, 456; BH1Br: cf, Pl. 2; B1Bo: perhaps plural strokes must be added after *sn.w,* but traces are too faint for a dependable conclusion; M5C: LESKO, *Index of Spells*, 61 starts the text with *ḥ3*, but *pḥr* must certainly be restored before – perhaps ink was too faded for recognition; *ˁ.t* without *t* by scribal error; Sq3C: text restored according to other versions.

(*ḏd mdw*) *pḥr ḥ3=j/ PN pn sn.w=j/f n gḥ ˁ.wt=j/f iptn*

"(Saying words:) Surround me/this PN, my/his brothers! These my/his limbs will not be weary."[72]

T1L	BH1Br	B1Bo	T9C	T9C	M5C	Sq3C
		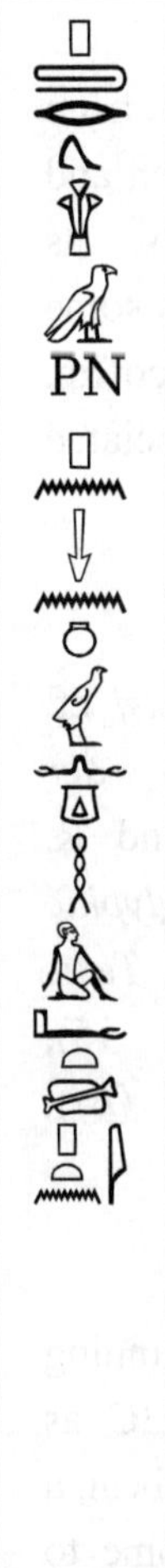				
H/B	H/Fr	H/B	H/B	H/Fr	H/B	H/B

The versions of text E show no great changes during the period of its existence. The speaker is identified with the deceased, only T1L and B1Bo transformed the first person to the third. Who are the brothers is nowhere explained. The determinatives of *sn.w* on T1L and M5C (Gardiner-Sign A1 and B1) suggest a group existing of female and male members. Therefore, we can only deduce that these are mythological brothers and sisters of Osiris: Isis, Nephthys, and Seth. Meyer-Dietrich includes Thoth into this group.[73] The circle created by these creatures constitutes an area of protection around the deceased. Very often a group of four or eight deities gather around the dead as his protection in

[72] The translation of MEYER-DIETRICH, *Nechet und Nil*, 128 "O wären doch meine Geschwister da, auf daß diese Glieder nicht matt seien!" (M3C) neglects the nature of the verbal form *n g(3)ḥ ˁ.wt=f* that is not a final clause. A better literal translation of the action of the *sn.w* may be "surround someone".

[73] *Nechet und Nil*, 128 with note 489.

Egyptian funerary texts. Most common are four Children of Horus that are mentioned in the hieroglyphic inscriptions on the Fr and B of Middle Kingdom coffins or are depicted as squatting divine figures, mainly on the H and F of the coffins from Asyut.[74] Von Falck thinks of a bigger group of protective deities, since they are depicted as images from the New Kingdom onwards.[75]

Text F

Text F is recorded on four coffins from Western Thebes, Meir, el-Bersheh and Beni Hasan. According to its arrangement on the coffins it has some affinity with the bottom of the coffin, and there it is more often associated with the Fr.

B1Bo	M3C	T9C	BH1Br
	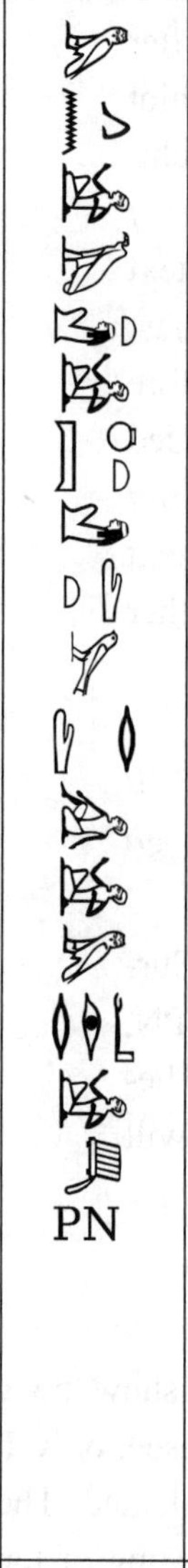	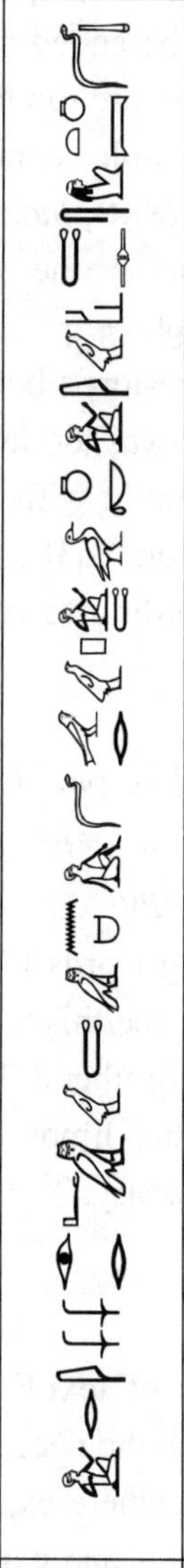	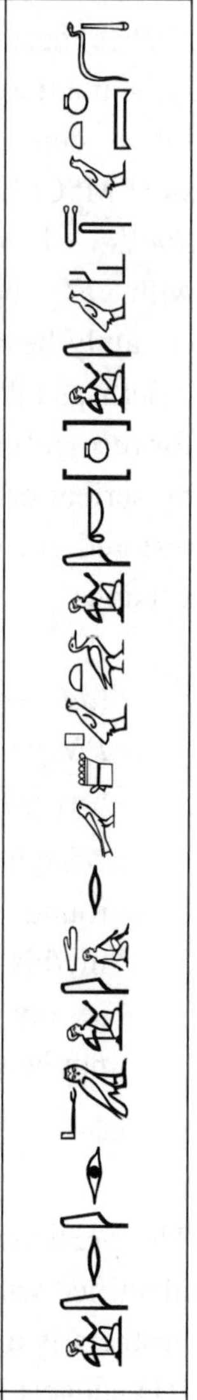
Bo/B	Fr/F	Bo/Fr	Bo/Fr

Commentary on versions:
For ʿpr-like determinatives of *sṯsj* cf. ERMAN/GRAPOW, *Wörterbuch der ägyptischen Sprache* V 405 and R. VAN DER MOLEN, *A Hieroglyphic Dictionary of Egyptian Coffin Texts* (*Probleme der Ägyptologie* 15), Leiden-Boston-Köln 2000, 773 (*tsj*); BH1Br: cf. Pl. 4.

The synopsis shows that the beginning of the spell is different on M3C as compared to other coffins that bear a similar text. Here, Nut must come to the dead instead of raising him according to other versions. The expected action of the sky goddess who must remove the weakness of the deceased caused by an unknown enemy is the same in all the versions. On T9C she is also asked for a protection against that enemy. The inscriptions on coffins from el-Bersheh, Beni Hasan and Thebes explicitly identify the deceased with her son Osiris.

[74] WILLEMS, *Chests of Life*, 138-141; HANNIG, *Paläographie der Särge*, passim.
[75] VON FALCK, *Studien zur Altägyptischen Kultur* 34 (2006) 128.

ḏd mdw Nw.t sṯs wj ỉnk sꜣ=ṯ pw <*dr*> *wrḏ(=j) nḥm=ṯ wj m-ꜥ ỉrj nn ỉr=j* (T9C)

"Saying words: Nut, raise me up! I am this your son. <Remove> (my) weariness! May you protect me against him who did this against me!"

mj n=j mw.t(=j) Nw.t d<*r*>*=ṯ wrḏ=j m-ꜥ ỉrj (ỉ)r=j imꜣẖ.t PN* (M3C)

"Come to me, (my) mother Nut! May you remove my weariness by the hand of him who did (it) against me, revered PN."

ḏd mdw Nw.t sṯs PN pn sꜣ=ṯ pw dr=ṯ wrḏ=f m-ꜥ ỉrj (ỉ)r=f (B1Bo)

ḏd mdw Nw.t sṯs wj [ỉn]k sꜣ=ṯ pw dr<*=ṯ*> *wrḏ=j m-ꜥ ỉrj ỉr=j* (BH1Br)

"Saying words: Nut, raise me/this PN! I am/he is (this) your son! May you expel my/his weariness by the hand of him who did (it) against me!"

Interpretation and Summary of Texts A-F

The main focus of the texts A-F is the well-being of the deceased laid into the coffin. This body in the coffin is already more than a dead corpse, it had been mummified and had passed through the ritual of embalming before it found its final resting place there. After the ritual treatment the body becomes a living being again that can communicate with gods as described in the mitre inscriptions. He is a god himself, or rather a certain Osiris PN, he takes over the role and the fate of Osiris. Only that mythological role enables him to overcome the death, to come to life again in the underworld and then, in a second step, to contact with the world of the living. Although he has reached this stage of his transformation, he is tired, his limbs are weary, his eyes are closed and his face is not illuminated according to the mitre inscriptions. His senses do not work and he urgently needs a divine assistance to change that unpleasant and unwilled condition. The person or enemy who acted against him is not mentioned directly but this may be an embalmer who harmed the body, or Seth who murdered Osiris in the mythological sphere.

Thus, the deceased as Osiris asks the sky goddess Nut, the earth god Geb and an unspecified group of creatures to help him. Nut takes off his mummy bandages, removes his tiredness and lifts him up. She places Isis and Nephthys at his disposal at his head and feet that they may mourn him, protect him and glorify him. The god Geb embraces him, illuminates his face and opens his eyes that he can see the sun. The deceased wants to be surrounded by his sisters and brothers. He himself can only utter some sounds (*ny* and *wj*?).

From the Pyramid[76] and Coffin Texts[77] the goddess Nut is known as a personification of the night sky and of a coffin or sarcophagus. As the sky she comes down or bends over the deceased to lift him up to the sky. Thus, he is placed under or among the stars that exist inside their mother Nut. As a coffin she embraces the deceased, who literally lies in her body and can be reborn every day like the

---

[76] A. RUSCH, Die Entwicklung der Himmelsgöttin Nut zu einer Totengottheit, *Mitteilungen der Vorderasiatisch-Aegyptischen Gesellschaft* 27 (1922), 1-14; S. KÖTHEN-WELPOT, *Theogonie und Genealogie im Pantheon der Pyramidentexte* (*Habelts Dissertationsdrucke Reihe Ägyptologie* 6), Bonn 2003, 199-207.

[77] B. ALTENMÜLLER, *Synkretismus in den Sargtexten* (*Göttinger Orientforschungen IV.Reihe Ägypten* 7), Wiesbaden 1975, 86-88.

sun. Since Nut is announced as mother by the deceased, he is identical with her firstborn son, the god Osiris. While in the Pyramid Texts Nut mourns over her dead son, gathers his bones, reunites them and brings him to life again, these are in our texts the tasks of her two daughters, Isis and Nephthys. Here the growing influence of the Osirian religion drove back the older conceptions of the mother Nut who helped her dead son and committed her functions to the sisters of Osiris who are prominently featured in the Osirian myth.[78] The removal of the mummy bandages and the healing of the weariness is a new idea introduced by the mitre inscriptions and not well attested in the former Pyramid Texts.[79] Perhaps this theme became more important with the increase of mummification at the end of the Old Kingdom, when the bandages were felt as a cover that prevents free movement. In the New Kingdom at least, when the mummification of the upper classes is a normal procedure and a well developed technical process, it is a prominent theme in the Amduat and the Book of Gates.[80]

Geb, the father of Osiris and the husband of Nut, plays a prominent role in the Pyramid[81] and Coffin Texts[82] as well and he is present also in the mitre inscriptions. As the earth that surrounds any dead body he contributes to the resurrection when he removes himself from above the deceased. As a result, the face of the dead is illuminated, his eyes are opened again and he can orientate himself in the world. Besides his parents and his sisters, a group of people whose names are not mentioned in the mitre inscriptions is asked to surround the deceased. The grammatical masculine genus and the determinatives of T1L and M5C (Gardiner-Sign A1 and B1)[83] point to a group of female and male persons. The Heliopolitan genealogy of the gods would indicate Isis, Nephthys, and Seth as the sisters and brother of the deceased in his role of Osiris, whereas Meyer-Dietrich[84] adds Thoth to this group in the case of M5C. Since their actions result in a positive change of the condition of Osiris (loss of weakness), it would be surprising to find Seth in this group. Therefore, I would prefer to see here a group of protective deities like the Children of Horus who are mentioned on the mitres of some coffins (Sq3C, B3C, M9C?[85]) or other deities involved in the nightly wakes of the embalming ritual.[86] All the deeds mentioned in the mitre inscriptions A-F and committed by several deities for the welfare of the deceased in his role of Osiris can belong to the sphere of the embalming ritual, especially of the hour vigils performed therein. This is substantiated by the younger sources, such as chapter 151 of the Book of the Dead and the Ptolemaic Hour Vigil (see below).

---

78 RUSCH, *Himmelsgöttin Nut*, 60.

79 RUSCH, *Himmelsgöttin Nut*, 33-34; cf. PT §§ 349b, 593b, 1363a-b.

80 E. HORNUNG, Vom Sinn der Mumifizierung, *Welt des Orients. Wissenschaftliche Beiträge zur Kunde des Morgenlandes* 14 (1983), 167-175.

81 Cf. PT §§ 9d, 99a, 583b, 643a, 1673a, 1722c, 1727a; KÖTHEN-WELPOT, *Theogonie und Genealogie*, 142-143.

82 ALTENMÜLLER, *Synkretismus in den Sargtexten*, 226-229.

83 ALLEN, *Egyptian Coffin Texts* VIII, 456.

84 *Nechet und Nil*, 128 with note 489. PT § 163d, quoted by her, mentions a negative behaviour of Seth and Thoth, who do not mourn over Osiris.

85 The text is an address of Nut to Amset (*ḏd mdw in Nw.t Ỉms.t n///*), in P. LACAU, *Catalogue général des antiquités égyptiennes du Musée du Caire Nos 28001-28086, Sarcophages antérieurs au Nouvel Empire* I, Le Caire 1904, 137 (CG 28043).

86 Cf. W. WAITKUS, Zur Deutung einiger apotropäischer Götter in den Gräbern im Tal der Königinnen und im Grab Ramses III., *Göttinger Miszellen* 99 (1987), 51-82; J. ASSMANN, Harfnerlied und Horussöhne. Zwei Blöcke aus dem verschollenen Grab des Bürgermeisters Amenemhet (Theben Nr. 163) im Britischen Museum, *Journal of Egyptian Archaeology* 65 (1979), 54-77. M. von Falck seems to see all the deities assembled during the night of embalming in the hour vigils as the group of *sn.w* (*Textgeschichtliche Untersuchungen* II, 199 and *Studien zur Altägyptischen Kultur* 34 (2006), 128).

2.3.2 Text N

Text N is known at present on two coffins from the cemeteries of el-Bersheh and Meir. At Meir it is written not on the coffin boards but on two big flat dowels (M53C). At B1Bo it is found on the front side of H and F:

> *ḏd mdw in Nw.t/ꜣs.t dj.n(=j) n=k tp=k nb ḏ.t – ꜣs.t/ Nb.t-Ḥw.t*
>
> "Saying words by Nut/Isis: (Hereby I) give (back) to you your head, Lord of eternity. – Isis/Nephthys".

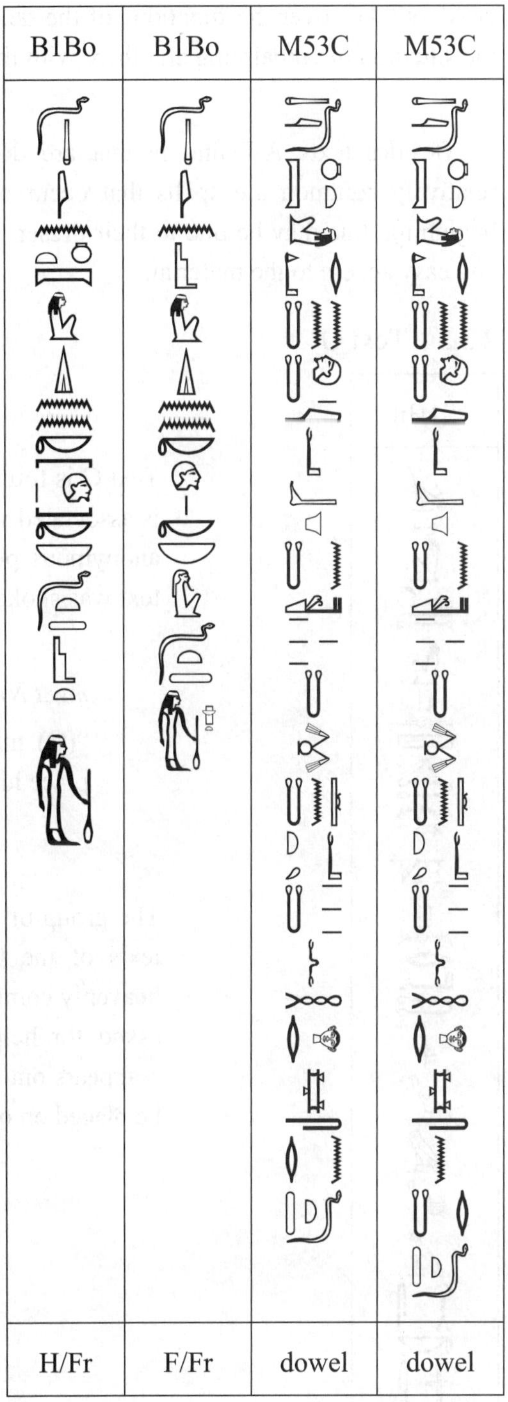

The spell consists of a speech of Nut or Isis who gives back the head to the deceased. On B1Bo the spells are followed by depictions of the goddesses Isis and Nephthys as standing women with long sceptres in their front hands. On the dowels of M53C the basic text is extended by descriptions of some more actions of the goddess Nut.

> *ḏd mdw in Nw.t rdj.n(=j) n=ṯ tp=ṯ iꜥb(=j) n=ṯ qs.w=ṯ dmḏ(=j) n=ṯ ꜥ.wt=ṯ n hrj=sn r=ṯ ḏ.t*
>
> "Saying words by Nut: (Hereby I) give (back) to you your head, (I) reassemble your bones for you, (I) reunite your limbs for you. May they not be far from you eternally".

The activities of Nut or Isis are well known from the Pyramid Texts where similar sequences are attested in spells that may be the original source for the text N (PT §§ 828a-b, 840b, 639b (for Geb)). All the actions call the deceased back to being. The sky goddess acts in the same manner as it is known in the (younger) Osirian sources for Isis and/or Nephthys. A modernizing tendency is perhaps the reason for substituting Nut by Isis on B1Bo. This could be done all the more easier as Isis (or

Nephthys) is identified with the head or the foot end of a coffin (CT spells 229, 236).[87] Since the goddess takes over the functions of the deities of texts A-F, they may be also originally related with the situation of embalming and there with the hour vigils.

Besides texts A-F and N that are documented on several coffins from different cemeteries, relatively common are spells that occur only once in the mitre inscriptions. As mentioned at the beginning, this may be due to their preservation and even more to their hidden location that prevents any easy access to the material.

2.3.3 Text G

S1Hil

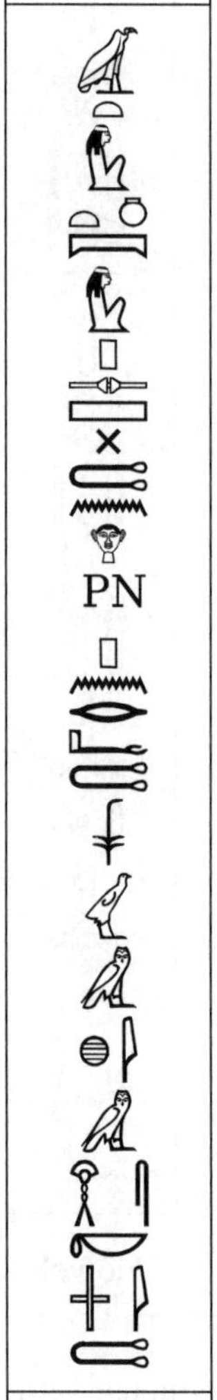

F/B

Text G is found on a coffin from Asyut (S1Hil)[88] and is placed on F/B. It is associated with the texts A-C on that coffin. The text is a speech of an anonymous person addressed to the sky goddess Nut. Most likely this text was spoken originally by the deceased himself as spells A-F.

mw.t Nw.t psš ṯn ḥr PN pn rdj=ṯ sw m iḫm.w-sk jmj=ṯ

"(O) mother Nut, spread yourself over this PN! May you place him under the imperishable (stars) that are in you."

The group of the imperishable stars is well known in the royal funerary texts of the Old Kingdom describing the king's wish to enter their heavenly community. Here, Nut as a nocturnal sky goddess is reasonably asked for help because the stars are in her womb and the sun daily reappears out of it. The stars, and the deceased with them, are thought to be placed on or in her body and are therefore her children.

87 M. MÜNSTER, *Untersuchungen zur Göttin Isis vom Alten Reich bis zum Ende des Neuen Reiches* (*Münchner Ägyptologische Studien* 11), Berlin 1968, 24-31; WILLEMS, *Coffin of Heqata*, 92-101, 131-137.

88 HANNIG, *Paläographie der Särge*, 565-575; R. SCHULZ, *Coffin of Nakht*, in: A. EGGEBRECHT (ed.), *Pelizaeus Museum Hildesheim, The Egyptian Collection Guidebook*, Mainz 1996, 41-43. The mitre inscriptions on F and H can be recognized on the photographs.

2.3.4 Text H

Text H is placed on the mitres of the Fr and B of B3C (Fr/H, Fr/F, B/H, B/F) and is supplemented by two slightly different texts on the H and F panel. They follow an image of a falcon-headed mummified god and, thus, are a label to this image.

B3C	B3C	B3C	B3C
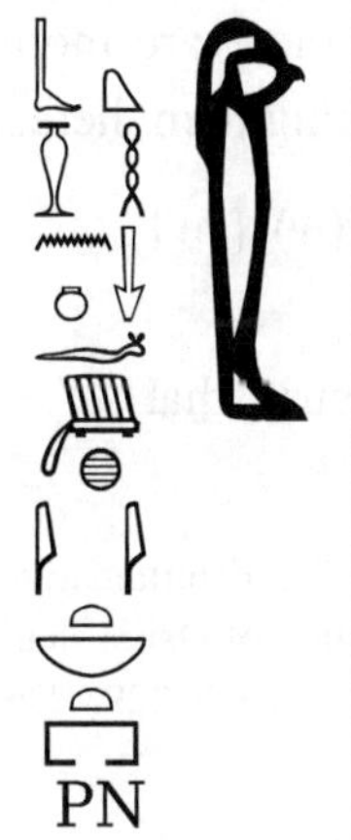	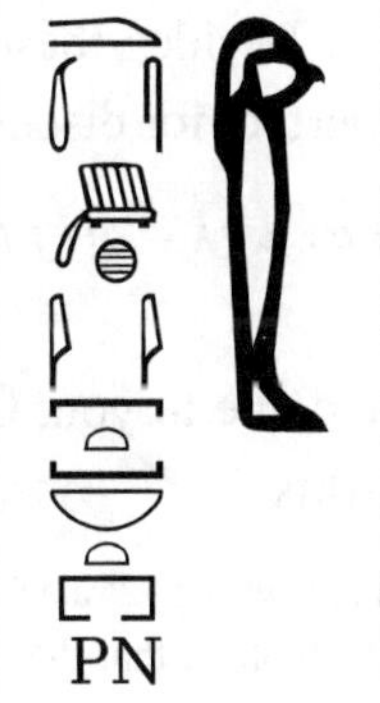	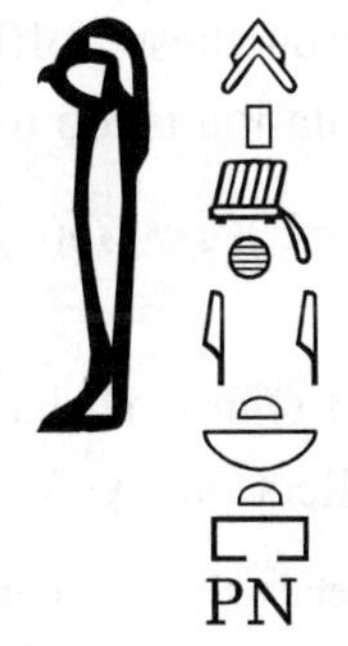	
B/F	Fr/H	B/H	Fr/F

jm3ḫy.t Ḥpj nb.t pr PN
im3ḫy.t Dw3-mw.t=f nb.t pr PN
jm3ḫy.t (I)m(s).t nb.t pr PN
jm3ḫy.t Qbḥ-sn.w=*f nb.t pr PN*

"Revered of Hapi/Duamutef/ Imset/Qebehsenuef, mistress of the house PN".

ḏd mdw [im3ḫy.t? 3s.t] nb.t pr PN (H/B); *ḏd mdw Nb.t-Ḥw.t* (F/B)
"Saying words: [Revered? of Isis], mistress of the house PN". – "Saying words. Nephthys".

The deceased inside the coffin is surrounded by four Children of Horus, his helpers in the afterlife. Representations with falcon heads are attested for some canopic boxes from el-Bersheh as well.[89] Human shaped squatting male images (Gardiner-Sign A40) can be found in the external decoration of the coffins from Asyut in the Middle Kingdom.[90] Hapy and Imsety are placed on the H of the deceased together with Isis, Qebehsenuef and Duamutef are arranged on the F with Nephthys. What other protective goddess should be expected on the other mitres is difficult to decide. On three canopic chests from el-Bersheh (B18C, London British Museum EA 30838 and EA 34272) Isis and Nephthys are combined with the well known goddesses Neith and Serqet[91], so this may be a likely restoration for our coffin. Nevertheless a certain preference of these two goddesses with the head or feet is unknown in the Middle Kingdom. Thus, it seems that the whole circle of protective deities is assembled around the dead. Two canopic chests from the same necropolis (B2C, B18C) document CT spells 520-523, four spells of the Children of Horus.

---

[89] B. LÜSCHER, *Untersuchungen zu ägyptischen Kanopenkästen vom Alten Reich bis zum Ende der Zweiten Zwischenzeit* (*Hildesheimer Ägyptologische Beiträge* 31), Hildesheim 1990, 15-17, 35-44.
[90] HANNIG, *Paläographie der Särge*, passim; LÜSCHER, *Kanopenkästen*, 16.
[91] LÜSCHER, *Kanopenkästen*, 18.

2.3.5 Texts I, J, K, M, and P Attested on the Coffins B1Bo and B2Bo

The coffin ensemble of *Ḏḥwtj-nḫt* (B1-2Bo) shows an unusually great quantity of mitre inscriptions that shall be discussed together. The well preserved outer coffin B1Bo is famous for its fine paintings published by Terrace.[92] It is displayed in the Museum of Fine Arts, Boston disassembled to separate walls, which lightens the work on the mitre inscriptions. The inner coffin B2Bo is still assembled, but the location of its several mitre inscriptions is recorded by Allen for the first time now.[93] Besides the texts A-F and N that are included in the above list of those inscriptions, B1Bo and B2Bo are inscribed with five more published texts that are known only on these coffins. Besides these there are more inscriptions on at least B1Bo, but my current documentation is too imperfect for discussing them here.

Text I: *ḏd mdw ink Nb.t-Ḥw.t sn.t Wsjr iy.n(=j) ḥr=k Wsjr s3q(=j) qs.w=k – ḏj=j ṯz(w) {sw} rḏ.w=k pn*

"Saying words: I am Nephthys, the sister of Osiris. (I) have come to you, Osiris, that (I) may assemble your bones, that I may collect[a] this your efflux."

a The reflexive personal pronoun after *ṯz* "rejoin, collect" may be mixed with *ṯsj* "raise". The determinative given by ALLEN, *Egyptian Coffin Texts* VIII, 445 may belong to *ṯsj*. Nevertheless, that the efflux of Osiris shall raise itself, makes no sense at all, whereas it is the task of Nephthys to collect it, cf. CT spell 229, 236 (MÜNSTER, *Isis*, 24-31).

Text J: *ḏd mdw ink Ptḥ nb ḥmw.wt iy.n=j srwḏ=j pr Wsjr PN – n nḥḥ{ḥ} ḏ.t im3ḫy PN*

"Saying words: I am Ptah, lord of the craftsmen. I have come (to you) that I may strengthen the house of Osiris PN for all eternity, revered PN."

Text K: *ḏd mdw ink Ḥr.w iy.n(=j) ḥr=k itj=j Wsjr PN pn ṯz(=j) n=k qs.w=k srwḏ=j ꜥ.wj=k – /// m pr=k n nḥḥ*

"Saying words: I am Horus. I have come to you, my father, Osiris PN, that (I) may rejoin your bones for you, that I may strengthen your two arms /// in your house of eternity."

Text M: *ḏd mdw in Gb z3=j pw mry rdj.n(=j) n=f wsr m t3 3ḫ m p.t ḥr nṯr.w jmj.w p.t*

"Saying words by Geb: He is my beloved son. (Hereby I) give to him strength on the earth, glory in the sky among the gods who are in the sky."

Text P: *ḏd mdw in Nw.t 3ḫ.t wr.t z3(=j) <pw> PN pn [s]msw/smsj(=j) wpj{t} ẖ.t=j mry=j pw ḥtp.kw <ḥr=f>*

"Saying words by Nut, the effective one, the great one: (My) son <is> this PN, the eldest[a] who opened[b] my belly. He is my beloved[c]. I am content[d] <with him>."

a PT §1a has *z3 pw smsw Ttj*. Cf. ALLEN, *Egyptian Pyramid Texts*, 67 who translates now "whom I caused to be born" and reads therefore *smsj=j*.

b *t* perhaps misreading of LESKO, *Index of Spells*, 19 for book roll (Gardiner-Sign Y1).

c Metathesis of the suffix of the first person (Gardiner-Sign B1) with the determinative A1.

d PT §1b reads *ḥtp.n(=j) ḥr=f*, and is replaced by Old perfective on the coffin.

92 L.B. TERRACE, *Egyptian Paintings of the Middle Kingdom*, London 1968.

93 *Egyptian Coffin Texts* VIII, 445-446.

B2Bo	B2Bo	B2Bo	B1Bo	B1Bo
Text I	Text J	Text K	Text M	Text P

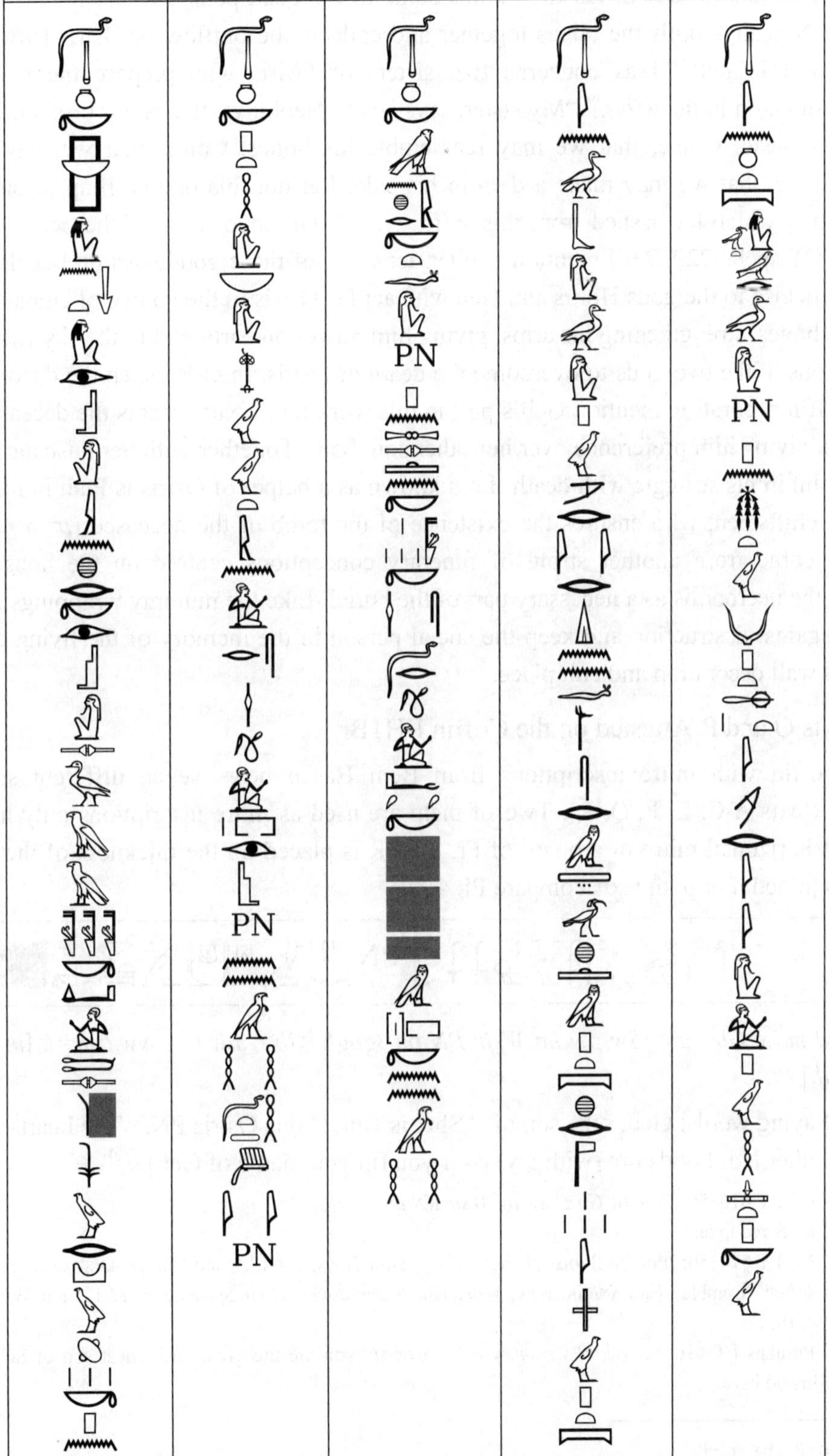

F/B	B/F	H/B	Bo/Fr	Bo/B

The content of most of the spells has to do with the resurrection of the deceased in his role of Osiris. In texts I, J, K the speaking deity identifies himself or herself by *ink* + name. Such self-presentations are typical for ritual situations, when priests act as gods or goddesses. Nephthys is even called a sister of the deceased. All the deities come to the dead person to act for his survival in the underworld. Nephthys pulls the bones together and collects the outflow of Osiris (*rḏw*). This is also mentioned in CT spell 74 as concerns two sisters of Osiris who prepare the body during the embalming situation in the *wꜥb.t*.[94] "My sister, says Isis to Nephthys, this is our brother. Come, that we may raise his head. Come, that we may reassemble his bones. Come, that we may rearrange his members. Come, that we may make a dam in his side. Let not this one be limp in our hands; there drips the efflux which has issued from this spirit. … ".[95] The invocation of the personified head and foot board (CT spells 229, 236) mention similar activities of these goddesses on behalf of Osiris. CT spell 74 refers also to the gods Horus and Geb who act for Osiris in the course of embalming. Knitting together his bones, strengthening his arms, giving him power on earth and in the sky (*wsr, ꜣḫ*) are well attested actions of the two gods to overcome the death of Osiris. In el-Bersheh the decorative bands of the outer coffin decoration mention Geb's part in this work too.[96] Nut accepts the deceased as her own firstborn son giving him preference over her other son, Seth. Together with her husband and daughters she assists him in his struggle with death. Less known as a helper of Osiris is Ptah in his aspect of the Lord of the craftsmen, who ensures the existence of the tomb of the deceased (*pr n nḥḥ*). This idea might have come from another string of funerary conceptions centred on the house/tomb of the deceased in the necropolis as a necessary part of the burial. Like the mummy wrappings it must protect the corpse against destruction and keep the social person in the memory of the living community by means of its wall decoration and cult place.

2.3.6 Texts Q and R Attested on the Coffin BH1Br

The only coffin with mitre inscriptions from Beni Hasan bears seven different spells of mitre inscriptions (texts A-C, E, F, Q, R). Two of them are used as mitre inscriptions only here. Text Q is written on a horizontal mitre of a board of Fr. Text R is placed on the thickness of the Bo where the back wall is joined. For both texts compare Pl. 4.

BH1Br	

Text Q: *ḏd mdw Gb <zꜣ> Šw pw nn Wsjr PN pn ꜣgbgb <ib> mw.t=k Nw.t ḥr=k* [*m rn=k n Gb*] ///

"Saying words: Geb, <the son of>[a] Shu, is {this}[b] this Osiris PN. <The heart> of your mother Nut floods up[c] (with joy) over you [in your name of Geb] ///[d].

a Cf. PT §1615a: *ḏd mdw Gb zꜣ Šw pw Wsjr KN pn.*

b *nn* is redundant.

c Cf. PT §1615b: *ꜣgbj* "to flood" cf. ALLEN, *Pyramid Texts*, 214 (52) and MEYER-DIETRICH, *Nechet und Nil*, 91; or *ꜣgbgb* "tremble" ERMAN/GRAPOW, *Wörterbuch der ägyptischen Sprache* II 22.17 and WILLEMS, *Chests of Life*, 195.

d Perhaps PT §1615c: *ṯwt zꜣ wr smsw n Šw wṯw=f* "you are the great and eldest son of Schu, his firstborn" followed here.

94 Cf. MÜNSTER, *Isis*, 42-46.

95 R.O. FAULKNER, *The Ancient Egyptian Coffin Texts* I, Warminster 1973, 69 (= CT I 306d-307c).

96 Cf. partly with some modifications e.g. B6C, B10C, B12C, B15C, B17C. WILLEMS, *Chests of Life*, 196.

BH1Br	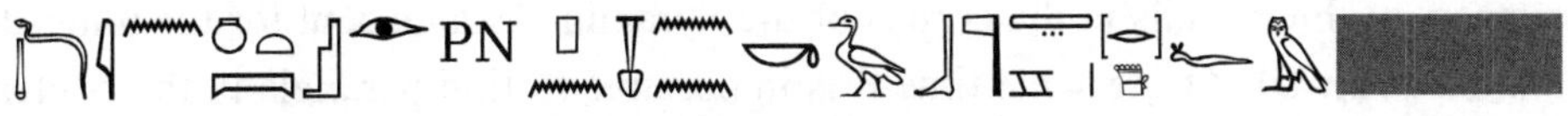

Text R: *dd mdw in Nw.t PN pn sm3.n n=k Gb t3 [r] ḏr=f m [bw nb n t3 pn m ḏnj=k m Gb rpꜥ.t nṯr.w]*

"Saying words by Nut: This PN, Geb has united for you the whole earth in [every place[a] of this country while you restrained[b] Geb, the *rpꜥ.t* of the gods][c]".

a Cf. PT §783b.

b Cf. CT 453c.

c Cf. WILLEMS, *Chests of Life*, 195 = M1Be and S1C, Da1C, Da2-4X, or M5C with a longer version *m ḏnj=ṯ m Gb m rn=ṯ pw n p.t ḥrj=ṯ r t3 m rn=ṯ n ḥr.t* (female coffin owner; MEYER-DIETRICH, *Necheb und Nil*, 101, 327). Willems reads *m dr.t n.t Gb* "by the hand of Geb" instead of *m ḏnj=ṯ m Gb* of Meyer-Dietrich. Her interpretation seems to be preferable, because all of the coffin owners except S1C are females. The original length of the text is unknown.

Both texts are present already in the corpus of Pyramid Texts. On the Middle Kingdom coffins PT §§ 1615a-b (= text Q) and PT §§ 783a-b (= text R) appear close together as a part of the decoration of the outer or inner walls of the coffins from Meir, el-Bersheh and Asyut, but not from Beni Hasan. Text Q is usually a speech of Nut, only at el-Bersheh Geb utters the same words. Perhaps there was a common tradition of the coffin decoration between el-Bersheh and Beni Hasan. Text Q appears also on the inner decorative bands (Fr, B) of some coffins from Meir (M5C) and Asyut (S1C, S14C). Here the invocation to Geb from the Pyramid Texts is reinterpreted as *ḏd mdw in Gb Šw pw Wsjr PN*. Thus, the deceased is identified with the father of Geb, the god Shu. The version on the mitre is placed in between the version of the Pyramid Texts and the version of the hieroglyphic inscription of the outer decoration. Therefore, it is difficult to make an emendation of the text. Either the dead is identified with the god of the earth, Geb, or with the god of the air, Shu. The three gods are associated with the structure of the cosmos, Nut as the sky, Shu as the air separating her from the earth, that is Geb.[97] As a complement to text Q, text R is interpreted as a speech of his wife, the sky goddess Nut on those coffins. Both take care of Osiris as his parents, which is a well-known constellation from other mitre inscriptions (texts A, B, D, F, G, N). The longer version of M5C is clearly connected with the Nut spells from the Pyramid Texts although there is no direct forerunner. Thus, this text identifies the coffin owner with the sky goddess who separates herself from the earth god Geb. This connection is especially easy to establish when the deceased is a woman as in the case of M1Be, M5C, Da1C, Da2-4X. BH1Br and S1C are the only coffins of men with this text.

2.4 The Mitre Inscriptions: a New Textual Design for Coffins?

The corpus of the mitre inscriptions consists of separate spells that are documented either in several versions (A-F, N, S) or in a single one (G-M, P-R). The absence of thorough and detailed studies on Middle Kingdom coffins from all cemeteries makes it impossible to compose a coherent picture of these texts and their importance as well as that of their influence on the textual and figurative decoration of the rectangular coffins of that period. Most surprising is the fact that there are no

97 MEYER-DIETRICH, *Nechet und Nil*, 137-138.

forerunners of these spells in the corpus of the Pyramid Texts except for the minority of texts (N, P-R and parts of text D). At the same time it is impossible to find parallels in the contemporary corpus of the Coffin Texts as well. Thus, the two most substantial collections of funerary texts that were in use in the Middle Kingdom provided no close formulations for the spells of the mitre inscriptions. The kind of spells, short utterances of gods and the deceased, seem to correspond more with the hieroglyphic decorative texts of the coffins than with the Coffin Texts, since some of the spells can also appear as ornamental hieroglyphic texts.[98] In the New Kingdom some texts will show up as part of the standardised outer (and inner) coffin decoration (see below). This will become more obvious if we shall trace the tradition of these texts in the New Kingdom and the Late Period as well. First, we must direct our attention to the following questions.

1 – Can we define a certain conceptual base common for all of the spells of the mitre inscriptions?

2 – Is there any relation with the Coffin Texts and how can it be revealed?

3 – Does the arrangement of the inscriptions on the mitres of the rectangular coffins offer some extra-textual information?

4 – Can we propose a certain sequence of reading of the mitre inscriptions on a single coffin?

Can We Define a Certain Conceptual Base Common for All of the Texts of the Mitre Inscriptions?

A general positive answer can, of course, not be given at this stage of research. The spells are of a too different kind and character, several are not identified yet and perhaps are unknown to Egyptology at the moment. Nevertheless, the focus and therefore the basic idea of all mitre inscriptions is the mummified deceased lying in the coffin on his left side, with the head to the north and looking eastwards. In this position the dead is imitating the position of a sleeping person, thus already showing that the deceased is not dead but ready to wake up (in the new habitat of the underworld). The mitre inscriptions describe his condition as that of Osiris killed by his brother Seth. His state is far from desirable: he fears that he cannot move freely anymore because of the mummy bandages wrapped around him by an embalmer. He fears that he cannot speak and see, that he is permanently tired and weak, that his bones and limbs are not fixed (in their correct position) but are scattered and dismembered, and that he has lost all his social relations on the earth. The undesirable condition is changed with the help of several gods who assemble around the deceased. The deities involved are the goddess of the nocturnal sky Nut (replaced by Ra on B2Bo), the earth god Geb, the sisters Isis and Nephthys, the falcon god Horus and his four sons Imset, Hapi, Duamutef, Qebehsenuef (text H), and the Lord of the craftsmen Ptah (text J). All of them communicate with the deceased. Their association with the dead person is defined as a genealogical relation. Nut is called his mother (text B: M3C, F: M3C, G: S1Hil) and she accepts him as her firstborn son (text P). Geb, the husband of Nut, addresses the deceased as his son as well (text M), but in text Q he is identified with him in his aspect of the son of Shu. Here his mother is mentioned indirectly as rejoicing over him. Nephthys denotes herself as a sister of Osiris (text I), and Horus comes to his father Osiris (text K). A group of female and male creatures is invoked by the deceased as *sn.w* "sisters and brothers" (text E). The sisters Isis and Nephthys are placed by Nut or Ra (B2Bo) to the head and feet of the deceased, although their kinship

---

98 WILLEMS, *Chests of Life*, 134 (head and foot end: text D), 195 (text Q, R) and the endless number of *im3ḫ ḫr* formula (text H).

with him is not specified (text D). The deities belong either to the Osirian mythological constellation (Isis, Nephthys, Horus, Children of Horus) or play their role in the older conceptions built around Nut (Geb). Only Ptah is not associated with both these important ideas.

Most of the actions of Nut and Isis or Nephthys on behalf of the dead are well known from other contemporary sources on coffins. The outer decoration of many coffins show decorative bands with hieroglyphic inscriptions on the H and F that are parallel to text D. Also here, Nut or Ra (in el-Bersheh) place the sisters Isis and Nephthys on the H and F that they mourn over the dead, that they reassemble his bones and give him back his heart. The same actions are described as performed by Nephthys in text I that occurs only as a mitre inscription. The result of their assistance is the triumph over the death and the attainment of the quality of an *ꜣḫ*-spirit by the deceased.[99] The manifestation of Isis and/or Nephthys as the F or H end of a coffin was established by Müller and attributed to the hieroglyphic inscriptions of the outer decoration.[100] These invocations contain the only explicit reference to the location where all these acts are performed. CT III 297i speaks of her as the goddess who mourns over Osiris in the *wꜥb.t*. The explicit placement of the two goddesses at the H and F may have been taken over rather from the actual performance of the embalming ritual than from the mythical prototype, and then it was successfully reproduced on the coffin with all its four sides related with the cardinal points. In the later Middle Kingdom images of the two goddesses are added to the F and H decoration showing them sometimes with upraised arms, a gesture of sadness and grief.[101] The gathering of bones and the strengthening of the limbs recorded in text K as done by Horus may be thus located in the embalming hall as well, since Horus in his mythical role of the son and heir of Osiris is predestined to help during the embalming period and the hour vigils. During the vigils the four Children of Horus also play a prominent part as well (text H). Besides text D the Children of Horus are often present in the hieroglyphic decoration of the coffins from el-Bersheh and Asyut. They are depicted as squatting mummified gods with their names recorded in the labels.[102] From the Ptolemaic ritual of the hour vigils it is known that the participating deities surround Osiris and communicate with him.[103] The same arrangement seems to be realized by the mitre inscriptions that surround the dead from every quarter and guarantee a protection of the powerful gods. These gods or another group may be identical with the *sn.w* gathering around the deceased in text E. In this situation he may utter his first sounds of a new life (*ny*) and state that his members will not be weary and tired (text C).

Spell C, further, has a strong association with texts A and B that occur regularly together on the same coffin (see above). All of them are attested only as mitre inscriptions. Texts A and B belong to the group of texts related with the concepts of the goddess Nut. She is invoked by the deceased in the

99 Cf. the outer decoration of M9C, M38C, M41C, M47C, M14C, M48C, B1C, B3C, B4C, B17C, B16C, B12C, S1C, S2C, Da1C. Cf. MÜLLER, *Isis*, 47-51; WILLEMS, *Chests of Life*, 134-135. M5C has the texts on the inner side (MEYER-DIETRICH, *Necheb und Nil*, 327).

100 MÜLLER, *Isis*, 24-59.

101 B. DOMINICUS, *Gesten und Gebärden in Darstellungen des Alten und Mittleren Reiches* (*Studien zur Archäologie und Geschichte Altägyptens* 10), Heidelberg 1994, 58-61.

102 Cf. HANNIG, *Paläographie der Särge*, passim.

103 H. JUNKER, *Die Stundenwachen in den Osirismysterien nach den Inschriften von Dendera, Edfu und Philae* (*Denkschriften der Kaiserlichen Akademie der Wissenschaften in Wien Philosophisch-Historische Klasse* 54), Wien 1910; on the lid of the sarcophagus of king Merneptah, J. ASSMANN recognized in a long speech of the goddess Neith the placement of several deities around the dead king during the embalming situation already for the time of the New Kingdom (Neith spricht als Mutter und Sarg, *Mitteilungen des Deutschen Archäologischen Instituts Kairo* 28 (1973), 125-131). There seem to be even archaistic tendencies reaching back to the assembly of gods on Middle Kingdom coffins. Cf. J. ASSMANN, *Altägyptische Totenliturgien* I: *Totenliturgien in den Sargtexten des Mittleren Reiches* (*Supplemente zu den Schriften der Heidelberger Akademie der Wissenschaften Philosophisch-Historische Klasse* 14), Heidelberg 2002, 52-53, 121-164, 266-276.

role of Osiris and frees him from his mummy bandages (Text A). In text B Geb embraces him from behind, illuminates his face and opens his eyes. Both parents care for their dead child Osiris in a similar way as we are aware of Isis and Nephthys in the Osirian tradition of that event. The older Nut/Geb tradition well documented in the Pyramid Texts of the Old Kingdom[104] was modernized under the influence of the newer Osirian ideas as it can be exemplified in text D. There, Nut as the physical mother of Osiris places his sisters Isis and Nephthys at his head and feet to act for him. Their actions in the process of resurrection of Osiris are the same as in the Pyramid texts where the sky goddess herself executes them.[105] That older corpus of funerary texts allocates a more prominent role in the mythological assumptions about the dead Osiris to Geb (and Nut). This idea is obviously expressed on the royal sarcophagus of Teti from the Sixth Dynasty with its inner walls and the lid uniquely inscribed with the speeches of Nut and Geb (PT spell 1-6).[106] No other royal sarcophagus of the Old Kingdom was ever inscribed in the same manner before or afterwards. But already here, Nut puts Isis and Nephthys on their places by the body of Osiris to help him. Thus, the older and the newer traditions are already mixed at that time. Besides text D that combines the Nut/Geb and Osirian tradition the mitre inscriptions include some more spells with these deities as actors. Text G speaks of the arrangements by Nut that are typical for a sky goddess. She raises the dead and places him among the imperishable stars inside her own body. These celestial conceptions have nothing to do with the Osirian myth but they got in close contact with them through the conception of the daily birth of the sun by Nut. Text F instead refers to the weak and helpless condition of a dead corpse that finally must be raised up to become alive again – a concept that already approved itself in the Pyramid Texts and was often assigned to the presentation of offerings.[107] The proven physical relation of text F with the group A-D on the Middle Kingdom coffins (see above) is paralleled by the tenor of the speeches. They all deal with the expulsion of some bodily infirmities of the dead. They all feature Nut and Geb as the physical parents of Osiris in the genealogical system of Heliopolis. Text N is also associated with the reuniting of the dismembered body. Nut returns the head of Osiris to him to complete the restitution of the body, since the loss of a head was a horrible idea for the Egyptians of any period. Like text N, text P being part of the corpus of the Pyramid Texts and even written on the sarcophagus of king Teti (PT §§ 1a-b) proclaims the deceased her eldest beloved son. Texts Q and R are recorded on the coffins both as mitre inscriptions and as a part of the hieroglyphic decoration[108] and display the actions performed for Osiris by his father. Geb either unites the whole earth on his behalf (R) or is his manifestation over which his mother rejoices (Q). Here the deceased belongs to the same generation of the Heliopolitan genealogy as Geb and Nut who are his parents in other spells. Then his mother is Tefnut, the first female being of the time of the creation of the world. The character of the goddess Nut as the nocturnal sky relates her as a mother both to the stars and to Osiris. She and Geb form the first pair of gods who created the next generation in a normal human way through sexual intercourse and, thus, introduced the phenomena of birth and death. It is only natural that both of them must assist their son Osiris in the case of his own death. Being the sky, Nut descends or bends over him and covers him

[104] RUSCH, *Himmelsgöttin Nut*; N. BILLING, *Nut the Goddess of Life in Text and Iconography* (*Uppsala Studies in Egyptology* 5), Uppsala 2002.

[105] Cf. RUSCH, *Himmelsgöttin Nut*, 60.

[106] DONADONI ROVERI, *Sarcofagi dell'Antico Regno*, 107 (A 11).

[107] Cf. PT §§ 654a, 734a, 960a, 1002b, 1003b, 1012a, 1167c, 1292b, 1503a-b, 1878c; cf. CT I 221d-e, 299d, VII 35e; MÜNSTER, *Isis*, 35-37; ASSMANN, *Journal of Egyptian Archaeology* 65 (1979), 58-59.

[108] S1C, M5C (both texts), S14C, B1Bo, M1Be, M6C, M13C, M28C, M37C, M1NY, M1War, M4Ann, Da1C, Da2-4X.

as a lid of a sarcophagus or coffin, or, being a manifestation of a coffin or sarcophagus box, she embeds him in her body like a star. Both conceptions are already known in the Pyramid Texts.[109]

In general it seems that two primarily different traditions of mythical explanations of the death and the triumph over it are mixed in the mitre inscriptions (Nut/Geb and Osirian constellation). Since this phenomenon is already present in the Pyramid Texts, the mitre inscriptions add nothing new to the general perspective of funerary texts apart from their ingenious wording. From the viewpoint of the coffin decoration they are a big and important new invention with a long term influence after the Middle Kingdom. Their merit is not only the exposure of the former royal conceptions to private persons, but also an introduction of a set of spells that can perpetuate the most complicated situation of the hour vigils during the embalming ritual and, thus, assemble an everlasting divine company around Osiris PN. At the end of the Old Kingdom it was felt necessary to rework the coffin decoration under the influence of the new Osirian conceptions. Now, when it was promised that every deceased would come to life again in the role of a king or of a god, the coffin was the closest surrounding of the mummified body and therefore an ideal object for expressing this new concept. Political instability and decay of tomb construction in the First Intermediate Period certainly contributed to the quick development of the coffin decoration. Coffins were large enough to bear extensive pictorial and textual programmes and were widely available. As a result, both older but still influential ideas reflected in the decorations of the elite tombs (i.e. food offerings, images of ritual equipment) and the new Osirian concepts could be combined and recorded on a single object in addition to the former parts of the coffin decoration like, for example, the offering formulae on B and Fr and the pair of eyes. The coffin's rectangular shape kept the very old idea of dwelling in the tomb alive, via the false door and palace façade panels the desired and necessary contact with the outside world of the living ones was guaranteed. Perhaps the mitre inscriptions, although they obtained input from the temporary Pyramid Texts and Coffin Texts, form a newly assembled and created set of texts for the decoration of a coffin.

Is There Any Relation with the Coffin Texts and How Can it Be Revealed?

As far as the mitre inscriptions are concerned, there seems to be no direct connection of formulations between them and the Coffin Texts. The correlation is based on the content of both groups of texts. The Coffin Texts are mainly just copies of papyri, which is manifest in the light yellow or white background used for their cursive hieroglyphs. The mitre inscriptions are on the contrary not related to a certain background colouring, but are written either in hieroglyphs like those of the outer and inner ornamental decoration or in cursive hieroglyphs, perhaps as a result of an adaptation to the rough surface or as a due to the traditions of writing religious texts. However, the survival of several spells of the mitre inscriptions into the New Kingdom as part of the outer decoration of coffins and sarcophagi demonstrates that they are more intimately connected with the ornamental hieroglyphic decoration than with the Coffin Texts (for details see below). Therefore, they seem to be a group of texts that was invented for decorating coffins in the Middle Kingdom or somewhat earlier in the First Intermediate Period. Together with the older hieroglyphic bands of inscriptions already known in the Old Kingdom, these texts are perhaps the "genuine" design for coffins, later completed by representations of gods uttering some of the texts.

109 RUSCH, *Himmelsgöttin Nut*, 1-22; BILLING, *Nut*, passim.

Does the Arrangement of the Inscriptions on the Mitres of the Rectangular Coffins Offer Some Extra-textual Information?

The content of the mitre inscriptions is purely religious and it gives no direct hint why they were placed on the mitres. The mitres are, of course, the most endangered parts of a coffin since something evil may penetrate through the small joints into the coffin to harm the mummy. Thus, it would be but natural for the Egyptians to fill them with a special "virtual glue" by writing magical spells on them. But only text S terminates with such an invocation to a harmful snake named Rerek[110], which recalls in some way the position of anti-snake spells of the Pyramid Texts, where they are directly attached to the doorways of the burial chambers and, thus, protect the inner part of the resting places of the kings.[111] Since the spells A-E are obviously related to a certain part of the coffin, their appearance together seems to form a circle around the dead person. This is even more highlighted by their appearance on the early New Kingdom royal sarcophagi. These four quartzite sarcophagi produced under the reigns of Hatshepsut and Thutmose III bear texts A-C and E in sunk relief on the upper surface of the walls of the sarcophagus box.[112] The texts "seal" the sarcophagi and protect them from penetration of the evil.[113] The protective circle created by these spells may reflect at the same time the reality of the embalming ritual: priests performing gods gathered around the deceased in the centre. Von Falck even regards text E ("(Saying words:) Surround me/PN, my/his brothers! These my/his limbs will not be weary.") as a textual explanation of this situation – tutelary gods assembled around the dead.[114]

Can We Propose a Certain Reading Sequence of the Mitre Inscriptions on a Single Coffin?

According to Meyer-Dietrich who studied two coffins of females from Meir (M3C, M5C) in detail, the inner decoration of a coffin can be read with regard to the position of the mummified body laid into it. She starts to read and interpret first the East wall (Fr), followed by the South wall (F), the West wall (B) and then the North wall (H). After them the lid and then the bottom follow in her interpretation.[115] Since both coffins bear mitre inscriptions and since they are a part of the inner decoration, she includes them into her reading sequence as well. Coffin M3C contains texts B, C, D and F, whereas text D appears in four variants occupying all the mitres of the H and F. M5C bears only texts B and E extended by the names of Nephthys and Isis placed on one mitre of both H and F. Four mitres seem to bear no texts, but this may be a problem of preservation and documentation. As demonstrated above, I suggest that coffin M5C originally bore also texts A and C, and perhaps also D, on its mitres, but today they are lost on account of adverse circumstances.[116] This suggestion would, of course, lead to an interpretation different from that offered by Meyer-Dietrich. The chart (Fig. 4) shows that no rules of arrangement of spells on a single coffin can be established with certainty yet. But it is obvious that

110 WILLEMS, *Coffin of Heqata*, 138-139 and pl. 18.

111 J. OSING, Zur Disposition der Pyramidentexte des Unas, *Mitteilungen des Deutschen Archäologischen Instituts Kairo* 42 (1986), 132-136; a wooden board-walk that was placed under a wooden coffin bears similar spells against snakes, cf. ID., Sprüche gegen die *jbh3tj*-Schlange, *Mitteilungen des Deutschen Archäologischen Instituts Kairo* 43 (1987), 205-211. The piece may be dated to the First Intermediate Period.

112 HAYES, *Royal Sarcophagi*, 97-98 (texts 50-53).

113 Accordingly M. von Falck calls these texts "Versiegelungstexte" in his PhD *Textgeschichtliche Untersuchungen* to differentiate them from the "Fugeninschriften" of the Middle Kingdom.

114 VON FALCK, *Studien zur Altägyptischen Kultur* 34 (2006), 128.

115 MEYER-DIETRICH, *Senebi und Selbst*, 33; *Nechet und Nil*, 88-89.

116 On the photographs in the Adriaan De Buck Archive at Leiden University I could recognize mitre inscriptions on the head and foot end of the front wall, that are not recorded yet. This observation may confirm the above suggestion.

some texts show a preference for a certain coffin wall by its content. Text A is associated with the foot wall via the earth god Geb, text B with the front wall, text C with the back wall and text D either with the foot or head board via Isis and Nephthys with a preference for the former one. Text E appears almost solely on the head end. In the New Kingdom the same correlation between texts A-E and their position can be established (see below). Other spells are still too few to speculate on meaning of their position. Text F may have a affinity to the front side and bottom, whereas on several royal sarcophagi from Hatshepsut until Amenhotep III it is placed on the underside of the lid (see below). The difficulties of finding and documenting the mitre inscriptions or simply the physical loss of a coffin wall may be a reason of the absence of one or the other spell of group A-F on a single coffin. Therefore, I would suppose the original existence of more mitre inscriptions for some coffins.

	Fr/H	Fr/F	F/Fr	F/B	B/F	B/H	H/B	H/Fr	other mitres
T9C	B	B	A	A	C	C	E	E	Bo/Fr: F
T1L			A		C		E		
S1Hil			A	G			C	B	
S65L			A	C			?	B	Bo/H: mark
M3C	B	F	D	D	C	C	D	D	
M5C				god		B	E	god	
M9C				D					
M47C	A								
M53C									F/L: A; 2 dowels: N
M2NY	?		A?	?		?	?		
B1Bo	B		N	A	C		E	N	L/B: F, P; L/Fr: M
B2Bo	D	D	A	I	J	?	K	B	
B3C	H	H		H	H	H	H		
BH1Br	C	B	A					E	Fr/inside: Q, Bo/Fr: F, Bo/B: R
Sq3C	?	L	A		C	C	E?		
Sq1X	?	?	D		?				
Sq10X			D	D			?	?	
	A = 1 **B = 5** C = 1 D = 2 E = 0 **F = 1 (+2)**		**A = 10** B = 0 C = 1 **D = 6 (+2)** E = 0 F = 0 (+1)		A = 0 B = 1 **C = 8** D = 0 E = 1 F = 0		A = 0 B = 3 C = 1 D = 2 **E = 7** F = 0		

Fig. 4: Arrangement of mitre inscriptions on mitre joints of single coffins

A fundamental hypothesis was offered by Meyer-Dietrich for explaining and interpreting the inner decoration of a Middle Kingdom coffin. Her starting point is that the inner decoration has the purpose to change the status of the mummified dead, to transform him for a new existence. Therefore, all the decoration must be read as a certain sequence to make this process of ritualization a success.[117] By means of ritualization the dead must be transformed from his inactive helpless physical situation into an active living person. In agreement with the ideal orientation of the coffin within the burial chamber (head in the north, face looking to the east and the body lying on its left side), the decoration of the inner sides of the coffin must be read in strict succession transforming the dead step by step: Front, Foot, Back, Head, Lid and Bottom wall.[118] Such a linear reading of decoration has already been applied to the Pyramid Texts placed on the walls of the inner rooms of royal pyramids. In her study of coffin M3C, Meyer-Dietrich supposes that the mitre inscriptions (texts B, C, D and F) are representing an earlier stage of ritualization than the inner decoration. Thus, they are not meant to function eternally but only for a short period.[119] This interpretation is proven according to her by the writing style of the inscriptions on the rough wooden surfaces (see above). Since the inscriptions are added to the wooden walls before the coffin is assembled, she associates this situation with the dismembered state of Osiris known from the myth, and explains the parts of the coffin as the members of Osiris. If the carpenter or another person assembles the walls of a coffin, a ritual is performed that overcomes this unwilled state of Osiris to prepare him for resurrection.[120] The function of the coffin in the role of Osiris is "den Mumienzustand den die Person beseitigen will zu verkörpern und mittels dieser Verkörperung den Zustand der Verstorbenen als herzustellende Einheit, Liminalität, erlahmte Aktivität und nicht eingetretenen Tod darzustellen. Die Verstorbene bietet das Bild des müden Osiris".[121] In a further step, the weak Osiris must be provided with a protective casing, the mummy bandages. This casing is created by placing the lid on the coffin and closing the container. According to Egyptian funerary beliefs, the dead wants to be freed of these bandages to become an active deceased again. The necessary ritualization process is realised with the help of the inner wall decoration analysed by Meyer-Dietrich. A weak spot of her reasoning is the attempt to equate the coffin with Osiris by a far fetched association of coffin parts and body parts of Osiris. From other elements of the coffin decoration we know that the mummified corpse laid into it is understood as Osiris, the coffin as a whole or its lid may be a representation of the sky goddess Nut, the coffin may also be the resting place (palace) of the Lord of the Underworld, and a microcosm – but Osiris himself? At least, I know no hints in texts speaking of a rectangular coffin as Osiris. Moreover, the whole coffin decoration seems to avoid mentioning the god Osiris except for the offering formula on Front, because the deceased placed as a mummy into the coffin takes his part as Osiris PN.

---

117 MEYER-DIETRICH, *Nechet und Nil*, 11-40; EAD., *Senebi und Selbst*, 4-25.

118 MEYER-DIETRICH, *Nechet und Nil*, 88; EAD.,*Senebi und Selbst*, 33.

119 MEYER-DIETRICH, *Senebi und Selbst*, 31.

120 MEYER-DIETRICH, *Senebi und Selbst*, 38: "Da die Herstellung der Fugeninschriften zeitlich vor der Fertigstellung des Sarges liegt, befindet sich dieser noch in einzelnen Teilen. Dieser Umstand macht es möglich die aus dem Mythos bekannte Verstreuung von Osiris' Gliedern auf den Textträger selbst zu übertragen. Die einzelnen Seiten des noch nicht verfugten Sarges verkörpern Osiris bevor Isis und Nephthys seine Körperteile aufgefunden und versammelt haben. Mittels der Inschriften wird die körperliche Osirisverfassung der Toten auf die Holzteile des Sarges übertragen. Das Zusammensetzen der Sargwände vollzieht dann symbolisch die Vereinigung von Osiris' Körperteilen durch Isis und Nephthys (die Personifikationen der Schmalseiten). Diese Maßnahme charakterisiert den Zustand, der vor dem Zusammensetzen besteht, als vorübergehend".

121 MEYER-DIETRICH, *Senebi und Selbst*, 39.

Another way to interpret a coffin expounded in detail by Willems[122] and favoured by the present author does not offer a linear reading sequence for the whole decoration. Instead of it, after the time of Senusret I "the ornamentation of a coffin as a whole can now be 'read' as an account of the ceremonies on the day of burial".[123] These ceremonies (mainly the object ritual, the offering ritual, and the embalming ritual) are represented on the coffin in a definite place caused by the circumstances and conditions of a mythological prototype and influenced also by the rituals performed by priests in reality. The coffin with its decoration is not a ritual instrument (after Meyer-Dietrich), but a funerary object recalling all the rituals performed during the time of preparing the corpse for the burial. In this way these positive actions on behalf of the dead can be perpetuated for eternity and ensure the well being of the Osiris NN. Thus, "the decoration as a whole served to regenerate the reality of the funerary ritual".[124] As shown above, the mitre inscriptions seem to fit perfectly into this view of a coffin decoration, since several spells can be located in the nightly wakes of the embalming ritual. Thus, the results presented here may support the view of Willems more than that of Meyer-Dietrich in this respect.

3. The Introduction of the Anthropoid Coffin: The Use of Mitre Inscriptions in the New Kingdom and Late Period

The creation of a new coffin type in the Twelfth Dynasty shaped as a mummified body gives a new prominence to another aspect of the older funerary beliefs. Until that moment the rectangular coffin embodied the idea of the house or tomb where the deceased was supposed to live. When the anthropoid shape was used solely as an inner coffin of a coffin ensemble, it was obviously introduced as a replacement of the mummified body of the deceased lying in it. If the latter would be destroyed over time by animals or tomb robbers, the anthropoid coffin would substitute it by means of the same shape. The shape of the new coffin type is generalized so much that the wrapped arms are completely hidden and the legs and feet form a single mass. Perhaps this specific shape was occasionally or intentionally developed as a typical iconography for depicting the divine. Several deities often related with the beyond, especially Osiris, are usually represented with a mummified body that is their stable characteristic. Since every deceased wanted to become Osiris PN from the late Old Kingdom onwards, the anthropoid shape of the coffin offered a second and additional way to ascertain this virtual identity through the power of an image. Thus, a coffin ensemble consisting of an outer rectangular and an inner anthropoid coffin could incorporate and express many different aspects of the funerary beliefs for the benefit of the deceased. Later in the Middle Kingdom the anthropoid coffin was used sometimes as the only repository for a mummy. This tendency intensified in the Second Intermediate Period and the New Kingdom, when bit by bit the human shape became most typical of coffins and sarcophagi. Thus, the idea of the coffin/tomb as a living house expressed from earliest time by the rectangular shape of the coffin and by architectural designs as a part of its decoration, lost its importance and was diminished in favour of the identity of every deceased with the Lord of the Beyond, the god Osiris. Only few anthropoid coffins and sarcophagi show a small false door or palace façade on the East side (Fr) in the New Kingdom.

122 WILLEMS, *Chests of Life*; ID., *Coffin of Heqata*.
123 WILLEMS, *Chests of Life*, 240.
124 WILLEMS, *Chests of Life*, 239.

Since the mitre inscriptions were conceived for rectangular coffins with their at last eight vertical mitres – two for every four sidewalls –, their very existence was called into question by the introduction of the new coffin type. The only remaining junction of an anthropoid coffin is the one between lid and box, but this is usually not inscribed in the Middle Kingdom and later.[125] Although we know no mitre inscriptions on coffins from the Thirteenth to Seventeenth Dynasties, several spells of this group survived into the New Kingdom (see below), whereas spells I, K, P-S were no longer used in the coffin decoration. Especially the royal and private materials from the early Eighteenth Dynasty (Amenhotep I – Thutmose III) indicate that the designers of the decoration of coffins and sarcophagi knew the mitre inscriptions well and considered them important enough to incorporate them into the new standardised decoration of rectangular and anthropoid repositories that was created at that time. As demonstrated recently by Grajetzki[126], the sarcophagus of Hatshepsut as god's wife (Cairo CG 6024, JE 47032)[127] was designed similar to a coffin of a princess of the late Middle Kingdom and imitated the "court style" of that period. This decorative program is very limited compared with her two later sarcophagi as a king (the first was reworked by her for her father Thutmose I).[128] Four quartzite royal sarcophagi from the time of Hatshepsut and Thutmose III form a distinctive group well studied by Hayes already in 1935.[129] At his time, he could not establish forerunners of several texts inscribed on these sarcophagi, but now we know that some of them are already attested among the mitre inscriptions, and such cases may become more numerous in future.

The anthropoid coffins of private individuals of the early Eighteenth Dynasty belong to the "white type", since the background colour is white.[130] They are contemporary with the "black type" of anthropoid coffins that started to replace them in the time of Thutmose III. Both types took over the pattern of bands of hieroglyphic inscriptions covering Middle Kingdom rectangular coffins and spreading out over their lid as well. The compartments between the text bands were step by step filled with the images of deities, most often by the four Children of Horus and two forms of Anubis (*imj-w.t* and *ḫntj-sḥ-nṯr*) on the long sides (Fr, B), complemented sometimes by figures of Geb, Thoth and the pair of eyes (on the façade). The head and foot end were occupied by the depictions of Nephthys and Isis, the top of the lid bore a standing or, later, squatting figure of the sky goddess Nut with or without winged arms spread out.

The layout of the decoration of the royal sarcophagi is the same in general, but the underside of the lid and the bottom can bear figures of Nut and inscriptions as well, as all the inner wall surfaces of the sarcophagi of Hatshepsut.[131] Thus, royal and private coffins/sarcophagi show the same layout, they differ only in material and shape, and some parts of the textual decoration. The variability of the

125 There are only very few exceptions, e.g., the coffin of *Pwjꜣ* of Seventeenth/Eighteenth Dynasty, Turin Museo Egizio 718 (R. MOND, Report of Work in the Necropolis of Thebes during the winter of 1903-1904, *Annales du service des antiquités* 6 (1906), 89-90; A. ROCCATI, *Sarcofago di Puia*, in: A.M. DONADONI ROVERI, *Dal Museo al museo. Passato e futuro del Museo Egizio di Torino*, Torino 1989, 53-55).

126 W. GRAJETZKI, The Coffin of the "King's Daughter" Neferuptah and the Sarcophagus of the "Great King's Wife" Hatshepsut, *Göttinger Miszellen* 205 (2005), 55-65.

127 Sarcophagus A of HAYES, *Royal Sarcophagi.*

128 Sarcophagi C and D of HAYES, *Royal Sarcophagi.*

129 Sarcophagi C-F of HAYES, *Royal Sarcophagi.* His system of text references is quoted here as "Hayes' texts 1-57". The new publication of the sarcophagus of Hatshepsut, Boston MFA 04.378, offers some corrections of Hayes' readings: P. DER MANUELIAN/C.E. LOEBEN, New Light on the Recarved Sarcophagus of Hatshepsut and Thutmose I in the Museum of Fine Arts, Boston, *Journal of Egyptian Archaeology* 79 (1993), 121-155.

130 Cf. the recent study of M. BARWIK, Typology and Dating of the "White"-Type Anthropoid Coffins of the Early XVIIIth Dynasty, *Études et Travaux* 18 (1999), 7-33.

131 Sarcophagi C and D of HAYES, *Royal Sarcophagi.*

arrangement of the figures shows that the system is still not stable on the private anthropoid coffins; thus, they may be dated slightly before the work on the royal sarcophagi that bear the standard layout.[132]

Texts A-C and E were distinguished from other spells of the mitre inscriptions since they often appeared together on a single coffin. This rule is taken over by the four royal sarcophagi that bear these spells on the thickness of the sarcophagus' box imitating obviously the hidden nature of the mitre inscriptions. The texts are almost identical with the older versions from the Middle Kingdom except for text C (Hayes' texts 53 and 57). The corrupt beginning of the versions of M3C, Sq3C, B1Bo was no more intelligible; thus it was eliminated there, and only the text versions of T9C, T1L, S65L, S1Hil and BH1Br starting with *ny* remained for reworking. Even this emendation could not solve the problems, and the text was modified more than others.[133] If my suggested restoring of the version on BH1Br ([*ny(=j) n*] *nnj(=j) n gḥ ˁ.wt=j iptn*) is correct, then this version can be taken as the direct Middle Kingdom forerunner of the versions on the royal sarcophagi.

The sarcophagus C of Hayes that contained the mummy of Thutmose III (still placed in his tomb in Western Thebes)[134] repeats texts A-C for the second time on the bottom where they are grouped along two long sides and the head end around a standing figure of Nut (Hayes' texts 55-57). Von Falck[135] has recently proved that these "bottom versions" of texts A-C belong to an earlier tradition than the texts on the upper thickness, and, thus, the sarcophagus used two different text traditions at the same time (see below). Both on the four aforementioned and later royal sarcophagi (Amenhotep II, Thutmose IV, Tutankhamun, Horemhab, Ramesses I, Sety I), texts A-C and E are part of the standardized decorative program that is also the basis of the decorative program of the coffins and sarcophagi of private individuals. They are never again used as a virtual sealing.

As an element of this standardized decoration layout text A (Hayes' text 22) is located on the foot end, text B (Hayes' text 31) on the back, text C (Hayes' text 40) on the front and text E (Hayes' text 15) on the head end.[136] Irregularities to this arrangement can be detected sometimes during the early New Kingdom, when some motifs had no fixed places yet.[137] Text A as part of the outer decoration of the foot end is related now with a representation of Isis squatting on a *nbw*-sign or standing with raised arms. Accordingly the beginning of the mitre inscription was changed in the early New Kingdom to *ḏd mdw jn 3s.t*. Now Isis asks the earth god Geb to help the deceased as follows:

> *ḏd mdw in 3s.t Gb ˁ.wj=k ḥ3 KN sḥḏ=k ḥr=f wn=k n=f ir.tj=f*
>
> "Saying words by Isis: O Geb, may your arms be behind KN. May you illuminate his face. May you open his eyes for him".

Text B is now correlated with a representation of Anubis *imj-w.t*, it is located on the back side, and therefore is marked as his speech:

---

[132] VON FALCK, *Studien zur Altägyptischen Kultur* 34 (2006) 129-131.

[133] Cf. VON FALCK, *Textgeschichtliche Untersuchungen* II, 204-208.

[134] Sarcophagus F of HAYES, *Royal Sarcophagi*.

[135] VON FALCK, *Studien zur Altägyptischen Kultur* 34 (2006), 135.

[136] Cf. HAYES, *Royal Sarcophagi*, pl. XXII-XXV.

[137] For example, the positions of the sisters Isis and Nephthys are not prescribed. Isis who is usually seen on the F can be depicted on the H instead, and Nephthys vice versa. Two images of Anubis in his aspects of *ḫntj sḥ nṯr* and *imj-w.t* are positioned on the B and Fr sides in the standard program but are transposed at that time on some coffins and sarcophagi. Cf. VON FALCK, *Studien zur Altägyptischen Kultur* 34 (2006), 130-131.

ḏd mdw in ʾInpw imj-w.t h3 mw.t=j[138] *3s.t mj dr=ṯ ṯ3m.w ḥr=j m-ʿ irj r=j*

"Saying words by Anubis Imiut: O (my) mother Isis. Come! May you remove the mummy bandages upon me by the hand of him who acted against me".

The goddess Nut who originally acted for the deceased in this spell was replaced by Isis whose relation with Anubis is not obvious, but both are common actors during the embalming situation.

The corrupt text C (Hayes' text 40) is now related to the image of Anubis *ḫntj sḥ-nṯr* and functions as his speech (*ḏd mdw in ʾInpw ḫntj sḥ-nṯr*). The early New Kingdom text *ny(=j) n nny nsw.t KN m3ʿ-ḫrw n gḥ ʿ.wt=f/=s iptn* reproduced on the top of the box and on the bottom followed clearly the version on BH1Br, but became not more intelligible.[139] The main problem is the change from the first to the third person singular that became necessary due to the combination with the image of Anubis on the front side of the sarcophagus. The scribes forgot to add the suffix *=f* after *ny*:

MK (BH1Br): *[ny(=j) n] nny=j n gḥ ʿ.wt=j iptn*

> NK δ1′ (= Hayes' texts 53/57)[140]: *ny(=j) n nny(=j) n gḥ ʿ.wt=j iptn*

> NK (Hayes' text 40): *ḏd mdw in ʾInpw ny<=f> ?*[141] *n nny KN n gḥ ʿ.wt=f iptn.*

A possible translation of the text as it appears with Anubis may be "Saying words by Anubis Imiut: <He> says *ny*. KN will not be tired. These his limbs will not be weary". Thus, until the time of Thutmose III the mysterious *ny* was still present in the Anubis version on front side. Only under his successor Amenhotep II it was deleted from the Anubis spell, making its understanding easier afterwards. Since this reign the spells A-C and E used on the top of the box and on the bottom were eliminated from the royal sarcophagi as well and only the Anubis spell remained as part of the standard decoration.

Text E of the standard decoration in the New Kingdom is related with an image of the squatting or standing figure of Nephthys and therefore is placed on the H end. Accordingly it became a speech of that goddess and was transformed from an invocation to a performative *sḏm.n=f* in the first person singular (Hayes' text 15):

ḏd mdw jn Nb.t-Ḥw.t pḫr.n(=j) ḥ3 sn=j KN n gḥ ʿ.wt=f iptn

"Saying words by Nephthys: (Hereby I) surround[142] my brother KN. These his limbs will not be weary".

---

138 Some versions write suffix *=j*.

139 This is also true for some Egyptological translations (cf. HAYES, *Royal Sarcophagi*, 88 (text 40) or similarly DER MANUELIAN/LOEBEN, *Journal of Egyptian Archaeology* 79 (1993), 142 (Hayes' text 40)). They therefore usually replace the determinative Gardiner-Sign A7 by D41, refer to ERMAN/GRAPOW, *Wörterbuch der ägyptischen Sprache* II 201.4-6 "zurückweisen, abwehren", and translate "I have thrust down the weariness of King KN, the justified, and these his limbs are not tired". The *n* before *nn* (Gardiner-Sign M22) must be interpreted as a phonetic complement in that case and not the negation *n* as it was in the Middle Kingdom. The omitted suffix *=j* is required as well.

140 According to VON FALCK, *Textgeschichtliche Untersuchungen* II, 204-208 this version goes back to δ1′ established under Thutmose III. It seems to me a reliable attempt of interpreting the spell in accordance with the Middle Kingdom version of the mitre inscriptions as it was done in older translations. Nevertheless, the transfer of the text to the sarcophagus obviously caused some more changes: the replacement of the first person by the third person in the speech of Anubis. Thus, *ny* lost its function and was no more comprehensible as its complete omission on the sarcophagus of Amenhotep II and some later sarcophagi shows. The versions on the upper thickness of the four royal sarcophagi give the δ1′version and better reading (see above).

141 The transformation from the first person to the third person singular makes this emendation necessary. Thus, this text version makes sense in accordance with the "bottom versions" on the royal sarcophagi and the Middle Kingdom text versions.

142 Performative *sḏm.n=f* according to C. Eyre.

Thus, the group of female and male persons surrounding the deceased in the mitre inscription disappeared completely leaving only his sister Nephthys. Her encircling is perfectly in agreement with her actual and virtual position on the sarcophagus or coffin: standing in the rear of the deceased she places her arms around him from behind (*ḥ3*). Isis as the more important of the two sisters stands at the foot of the deceased, who is Osiris KN/PN, to face him. And it should not be forgotten that Isis still must beget his son and heir Horus after their physical reunion. This idea could be of more interest in the New Kingdom than in the Middle Kingdom when Isis was placed regularly on the head end as well, and Nephthys on the foot. The coffins and sarcophagi of private persons show sometimes more reworkings of these texts. The relation of Isis and Geb in text A was not understood anymore in many cases. Therefore Geb was just eliminated (*ḏd mdw in 3s.t ʿ.wj(=j) ḥ3 PN/=k …*) and an explanation of the actual situation was added (*ḏd mdw in 3s.t iy.n(=j) ḫr PN ʿ.wj(=j) ḥ3 PN/=k …*).[143] The positive actions are thus all done by Isis. Texts C and E are known only in the Anubis and Nephthys version of the standard decoration on the outer walls of private repositories. The general tendency during the New Kingdom consists in the elimination of the physical parents of the deceased in his role of Osiris, the deities Nut and Geb, from the coffin and sarcophagus decoration. The decoration concentrates now on the Osirian circle of events and actors, leaving to Nut only the lid spells.

In the early New Kingdom there appears another funerary context for the spells A and E, and perhaps for other spells.[144] From that time onwards spell 151 of the Book of the Dead contains a compilation of several spells concentrated around the mummified Osiris on the bier. Some manuscripts even show the standing jackal god Anubis bent over the bier with the mummy of Osiris in the centre of the composition that is flanked at the head and foot by the kneeling goddesses Nephthys and Isis. This centre is surrounded by depictions of four Children of Horus, four magical bricks, two ushabtis and two *b3* birds. All the images are accompanied by their own texts or spells that can be used separately on the real objects of the burial equipment depicted there. Parts of the speeches of Isis and Nephthys (BD 151 b,c) show similar formulations as the mitre inscriptions A and E, parts of the speeches of the Children of Horus may eventually remind spells D, J and N. The figure of Anubis besides the bier shows him bent over the mummy uttering a speech that invokes the mummy mask (BD 151 a), after he had placed his hands on the coffin (called *nb-ʿnḫ* "Lord of Life") and equipped it with necessary things. On the coffins and sarcophagi of the same time, his two figures are combined with the mitre spells B and C. Perhaps his bent position in the tableau scene was a hint clear enough for the Egyptians that he is taking off the mummy bandages, so that Osiris PN can move freely and utter sounds again. In general the composition of BD 151 seems to be loaned from the coffin decoration of that time, and added to the corpus of the Book of the Dead in order to develop the same function as on the rectangular and anthropoid coffins and sarcophagi: guaranteeing a successful transformation of PN to Osiris PN during the last ritual night wake of the embalming process.

Besides texts A-C and E, no other spells show such a long and consistent tradition during the New Kingdom and later times. Parts of text J, a speech of Ptah attested only on the coffin B2Bo, seem to be incorporated into the utterance of Amset (Hayes' text 29) that belongs to the standard decorative program of the royal and private coffins and sarcophagi of the New Kingdom. The text is changed

---

143 So called "Situationserklärungen" of K. JANSEN-WINKELN, *Text und Sprache in der 3. Zwischenzeit. Vorarbeiten zu einer spätmittelägyptischen Grammatik* (*Ägypten und Altes Testament* 26), Wiesbaden 1994, 180-187.

144 Cf. a detailed study by LÜSCHER, *Totenbuch Spruch 151*, passim and especially 57-71, 108-110, 123-128.

from a direct speech of Ptah to that of Amset, who is now responsible for the strengthening of the house of the deceased:

B2Bo: *ḏd mdw ink Ptḥ nb ḥmw.wt iy.n=j srwḏ=j pr PN n nḥḥ ḏ.t jmꜣḫy PN*

> NK: *ḏd mdw jn ꞽIms.t sꜣ KN iy.n(=j) wn(=j) m sꜣ=k srwḏ=j pr=k mj wḏ.t.n Ptḥ mj wḏ.t.n Rꜥ.w ḏs=f.*

Of importance may be the command of Ptah who made this action himself in the Middle Kingdom. Perhaps a hypothetical text redactor of the early New Kingdom text was commissioned to place all Children of Horus on the coffin or sarcophagus walls around the mummy in its centre. As the sisters Isis and Nephthys on the head and foot ends (texts A and E > Hayes' texts 22 and 15), these deities had to be supplied with speeches as well, and he felt it necessary to reuse the spells of the mitre inscriptions too. Thus, he reworked text J for Amset adding the phrase *wn=j m sꜣ=k* and *wḏ.t.n Ptḥ* to show who is the original initiator as in the case of Nut (text D). The mention of the house of the deceased may be a revival of the idea that a coffin or sarcophagus is a resting place of the dead, or it may refer to the tomb. *srwḏ=j pr=k m-ḫt=k ꜥnḫ.tj ḏ.t* is also part of the speech of Qebehsenuef (Hayes' text 41) and it may also derive from the text J. But there it is connected with the reuniting of the limbs and the heart of the deceased.

Another group of texts among the mitre inscriptions centres around the sky goddess Nut and her husband, the earth god Geb (texts D, F, G, M, N, P). Of them only text G has a long tradition as texts A-C and E although coming from a different background. From the New Kingdom onwards it is related with the top of the lid. There it appears on the four royal sarcophagi and on the later ones (Hayes' text 1) as well as on private coffins and sarcophagi. In many cases the text is associated with a figure of the goddess Nut with outstretched wings as the sole image on the lid. The text and the image identify the cover of the coffin or sarcophagus box with the sky goddess who is spread over the deceased. Text F, another Nut spell that appears together with text G, is also related with the lid of the royal sarcophagi, but is attached to its underside near by a standing figure of the goddess (Hayes' text 44). In contrast to text G, it is not used for the decoration of private coffins and sarcophagi, since they bear no image of Nut on the underside of the lid.[145]

The younger tradition of the texts D, N and P as part of the Nut spells attested from the Pyramid Texts onwards is not as clear as that of texts F and G. The version of text D of the coffin Sq1X can partly be correlated with Hayes' text 23:

Sq1X: *ḏd mdw in [Nw.t rdj.n(=j) ꜣs.t] ḫr tp=k nḏr=s [n=k] ꜥ=k Wsjr PN ḏj=s n=k ib=k n ḏ.t[=k]*

> NK (Hayes' text 23): *ḏd mdw KN iy.n(=j) nḏr=j im=k/ṯ*[146]

Since the foot end is occupied by Isis, text 23 must be her utterance, perhaps to be read like text 21 after text 20 (*ḏd mdw KN ink sn.t=k/ṯ ꜣs.t*) that identifies the speaker as the sister of Osiris.[147] These three texts are supplementary marked as forming a certain unit by the cartouche frames surrounding them on sarcophagus C, D and F. Since the version of Sq1X is known only from the sarcophagus of

---

145 An exception is the coffin of *Ywjꜣ* J.E. QUIBELL, *Catalogue général des antiquités du Musée du Caire N°s 51001-51191. The Tomb of Yuaa and Thuiu*, Le Caire 1908, 14 (CG 51004).

146 Text 23 of Hayes is now in the version of the New Kingdom also attested on the coffin of the princess Neferuptah, daughter of Amenemhat III, cf. GRAJETZKI, *Göttinger Miszellen* 205 (2005), 60, pl. 3.

147 HAYES, *Royal Sarcophagi*, 189-190 and pl. XXII.

pharaoh Teti (= PT §§ 3b-e), it may have survived as a mitre inscription and transferred to the royal sarcophagi in the early New Kingdom. A revival of *ḏj=s n=k ỉb=k n ḏ.t*[=*k*] may perhaps be recognized in a part of the speech of Qebehsenuef (Hayes' text 41) … *ỉnj.n=j n=k/ṯ ỉb=k/ṯ ḏj.n*(=*j*) *n=k/ṯ sw ḥr s.t=f m ẖ.t=k/ṯ*. Like text D, text N refers to the actions of Nut during the restitution of the corporal integrity of the deceased. She gives his own head back to him (Hayes' text 19: *ḏd mdw ỉn Nw.t KN rḏj.n*(=*j*) *n=k/ṯ tp=k/ṯ* <*n*> *ḏ.t=k/ṯ n gḥ ꜥ.wt=k/ṯ ỉptn*). The same does Hapi in Hayes' text 39 (… *ḏj.n*(=*j*) *n=k/ṯ tp=k/ṯ ḏ.t*) that may be inspired by the older spells of the Middle Kingdom. However, these are only assumptions that may be revised through the study of new mitre inscriptions in the future. Both spells D and N are not used for the decoration of the private coffins and sarcophagi during the New Kingdom and Late Period. Text M, a speech of Geb, is found on Middle Kingdom coffins from el-Bersheh on the mitres (B1Bo) as well as on the inner surface of Fr (B9C, B10C, B15C). A variant on B6C and B12C contains a similar text as the royal sarcophagi of the early New Kingdom on the front side of Bo (Hayes' text 54[148]) where *wsr* is replaced by *wꜥb*. Private coffins and sarcophagi however make no use of this spell during the New Kingdom and the Late Period. Text P of the mitre inscriptions is not attested as coffin/sarcophagus decoration in the Middle and New Kingdom either.

The transmission of some spells of the mitre inscriptions reaches well into the Late Period but shall not be included in detail here. All late text versions are documented on sarcophagi as well as in the New Kingdom. Besides the sarcophagi of Nectanebos I[149] and Nectanebos II[150] of the Thirtieth Dynasty, all remaining sources are contemporary with the Twenty-sixth Saite Dynasty. The Napatan sarcophagus of Anlamani (Boston MfA 23.729) and of Aspelta (Khartoum 1868) are the only royal examples of the Sixth century.[151] Four private persons had also access to this old text material and used it on their anthropoid or rectangular sarcophagi. Three of them, Bakenrenef (Turin Museo Egizio 2182)[152] and Nes-Thoth (Cairo CG 29312)[153] in Saqqara and Nes-Ptah[154] in Thebes, lived under the reign of Psametik I at the beginning of the Twenty-sixth Dynasty, whereas Hapimen, to whom the sarcophagus box London British Museum EA. 23[155] belongs, is not precisely dated in this period.

The basic source for the long life of some spells is the group of early Thutmoside sarcophagi (C-F of Hayes) that was obviously well appreciated by that time for their artistic values and their important text program. And it was easily available in an archive situated most probably at Thebes. Among these New Kingdom containers the sarcophagus of Thutmose III that was produced as the last one and as the peak of this series seems to be the preferred and main source for the compilers of the late attestations.

---

148 The reading of HAYES, *Royal Sarcophagi*, 204 No. 54 must be corrected according to DER MANUELIAN/LOEBEN, *Journal of Egyptian Archaeology* 79 (1993), 147 with note 74.

149 This sarcophagus survived only in some fragments published by G. DARESSY, Inscriptions hiéroglyphiques trouvées dans le Caire, *Annales du service des antiquités de l'Égypte* 4 (1903), 105-109.

150 British Museum EA 10, published by H. JENNI, *Das Dekorationsprogramm des Sarkophages Nektanebos' II.* (*Aegyptiaca Helvetica* 12), Genève 1986.

151 Both published by S.K. DOLL, *Texts and Decoration on the Napatan Sarcophagi of Anlamani and Aspelta* (PhD Brandeis University), Ann Abor 1978.

152 E. SCHIAPARELLI, *Museo Egizio di Firenze. Antichità Egizie* (*Catalogo Generale dei Musei di Antichità e degli Oggetti d'Arte raccolti nelle Gallerie e biblioteche del regno. Edito per cura del Ministero della Pubblica istruzione. Serie Sesta: Toscana ed Umbria* I), Roma 1887, 440-453.

153 G. MASPERO/H. GAUTHIER, *Catalogue générale des antiquités égyptiennes du Musée du Caire Nos 29301-29323. Sarcophages des époques persane et ptolémaïque* II, Le Caire 1939, 60-66.

154 A. AWADALLA/A. EL-SAWY, Un sarcophage de Nsi-Ptah dans la tombe de Montouemhat, *Bulletin de l'Institut français d'archéologie orientale du Caire* 90 (1990), 29-39.

155 COMMISSION DES MONUMENTS D'ÉGYPTE, *Description de l'Égypte ou recueil des observations et des recherches qui ont été faites en Égypte pendant l'expédition de l'armée française* V, Paris 1823, pl. 24-25.

Since they are all based on the New Kingdom royal versions they transmit the same Middle Kingdom spells of the mitre inscriptions: texts A, B, C, E, F and G. For a detailed analysis of the text situation in the Late Period compare now M. VON FALCK, *Textgeschichtliche Untersuchungen* I-II.

4. Summary

On Middle Kingdom coffins a new group of short texts – spells uttered by the deceased or various deities – appeared throughout the whole country. Rectangular coffins with these inscriptions were produced already in the Eleventh Dynasty and continued until the very late Twelfth or even early Thirteenth Dynasties. They are incised or inscribed in ink mainly on the vertical joints of the four coffin's walls, but may be present also on the horizontal joints of the walls and of single planks forming a wall. For reference purposes single texts are designated by characters from A to S, and most of them are presented in this paper. Some already identified spells need further study and comprehension of new versions; other texts are known to the author but were not definitely decoded and/or identified at the moment and therefore they are excluded here. 67 coffins, all of them of the type with inner decoration, are recorded currently to bear mitre inscriptions. Since these texts can be detected only when a coffin is dismantled, the probability of existence of more inscriptions seems to be very high.

Separate spells are mostly not included in the contemporary corpus of the Pyramid and Coffin Texts, but form a group of texts deriving from another source. Unlike other elements of the coffin decoration in the Middle Kingdom, the mitre inscriptions seem to be composed especially for coffins.[156] A single coffin usually bears several spells on its mitres but it is still impossible to formulate the rules of their arrangement. Nevertheless, Texts A-E regularly appear together on a single coffin in the Middle Kingdom as well as in the later tradition. Too few versions of other spells are known to make any certain statement. Moreover, some spells show a certain affinity with certain walls of a coffin. Text A is associated with the foot end, text E with the opposite head end, whereas text D is always applied to the head and/or foot end in accordance with the record of the respective protective goddess in the text. Text B is related to the back or West wall and text C to the front wall. Some of these amalgamations between the text and its disposition on the coffin walls are still consistent in the New Kingdom and Late Period and determine the arrangement of the inscriptions on the coffins and sarcophagi of rectangular and anthropoid shape.

Several texts are connected with the Osirian myth and can be related with the hour vigils of the last night in the embalming hall (texts A-C, E-F, I-K, N). Others prominently feature the parents of Osiris, Nut and Geb, and are partly known from the Pyramid Texts (texts D, F, G, M-N, P-R), where several Nut spells are attested only on the sarcophagus of pharaoh Teti of the Sixth Dynasty. Thus, the well known duality of the younger Osirian ideas and the older conceptions centred around the sky goddess Nut are combined in the mitre inscriptions as well as in the other elements of the coffin decoration. The older ideas loose their importance only in the New Kingdom when the Osirian tradition dominates the coffin and sarcophagus decoration. Although the number of coffins with mitre inscriptions is still very limited, the importance of these spells, especially of texts A-E, cannot be underestimated due to their later tradition in the New Kingdom and Late Period where they are part of the standard decoration pattern.

156 VON FALCK, *Textgeschichtliche Untersuchungen* II, 794.

Remarks on the Temple of Heqet and a Sarcastic Letter from el-Lahun

Zoltán Horváth

Through granting access to hundreds of surviving letters and letter-fragments, the first full presentation of the University College London's hieratic papyri from el-Lahun clearly demonstrates the extent to which letter-writing was central to interpersonal communication for the inhabitants of a Middle Kingdom settlement.[1] Indeed, this great mass of papyri, especially when appended with another large group of business papers once pertaining to the official archive of the royal mortuary temple,[2] not only urges one to revise the current estimates of literacy for the Middle Kingdom,[3] but draws attention to the strong generative connections of letters with other literary genres. The recurrence of epistolary terms, idioms, even full formulae in text types, which cannot be accepted readily by the modern reader as "real" letters, underlines the importance of intertextuality in approaching ancient correspondence. Sometimes the line of division between "letters" and "non-letters" is quite fluid, and the distinction itself is artificial and arbitrary, reflecting the rigidity of our system of classification which is based on modern preconceptions of what an ancient letter should look like.[4] The state of affairs may be illustrated with a papyrus of modest size from el-Lahun which makes use of terms and idioms familiar to us from contemporary private correspondence, yet it has no address, and it is characterised by an exceedingly unusual adaptation of epistolary formulae – never attested elsewhere in the corpus. The present paper reconsiders the circumstances which have serious bearings on the proper interpretation of this text, and discusses features that went apparently unnoticed in previous scholarly literature but could be used effectively to have a more detailed view of the nature of the document.

Papyrus UC 32204 is a well-preserved, small, rectangular piece of papyrus, inscribed on both sides (Pl. 5a-b).[5] Black as well as red ink have been applied to jot a short text down that contains "angry perversions of the ordinary formulae" – to quote its first editor.[6] As it was mentioned above, neither the sender, nor the recipient is explicitly given and no folding lines were detected confirming that the

1 The whole set of Middle Kingdom hieratic papyri in the University College London has been published in three consecutive volumes: M. COLLIER/S. QUIRKE, *The UCL Lahun Papyri: Letters* (*British Archaeological Reports International Series* 1083), Oxford 2002; ID., *The UCL Lahun Papyri: Religious, Literary, Legal, Mathematical and Medical* (*British Archaeological Reports International Series* 1209), Oxford 2004; ID., *The UCL Lahun Papyri: Accounts* (*British Archaeological Reports International Series* 1471), Oxford 2006.

2 For the catalogue of the temple files now in the Egyptian Museum Berlin, see U. KAPLONY-HECKEL, *Ägyptische Handschriften* I (*Verzeichnis der orientalischen Handschriften in Deutschland* XIX.1), Wiesbaden 1971. Choice letters from the corpus were published in A. SCHARFF, Briefe aus Illahun, *Zeitschrift für ägyptische Sprache und Altertumskunde* 59 (1924), 20-51; more recently, forty dated letters, selected on the basis of their contribution to chronology, were edited by U. LUFT, *Das Archiv von Illahun: Briefe* 1 (*Hieratische Papyri aus den Staatlichen Museen zu Berlin – Preußischer Kulturbesitz Lieferung* 1), Berlin 1992, followed by *Urkunden zur Chronologie der späten 12. Dynastie: Briefe aus Illahun* (*Contributions to the Chronology of the Eastern Mediterranean* VII), Wien 2006.

3 The generally accepted and often cited low average rate of literacy, less than 1%, proposed by J. BAINES/C. EYRE, Four Notes on Literacy, *Göttinger Miszellen* 61 (1983) 65-72, has been challenged by L.H. LESKO, s.v. *Literacy*, in: D.B. REDFORD (ed.), *The Oxford Encyclopedia of Ancient Egypt* II, Oxford 2001, 297-299.

4 Problems with the definition of "letter" and its various subtypes will be discussed at length in the author's doctoral dissertation on private correspondence in the Old and Middle Kingdoms, which is in preparation.

5 Former Lot VI.8. The papyrus measures 8.5 x 17 cm. COLLIER/QUIRKE, *Lahun Letters*, 118-119, CD files UC32204-f, UC32204-b.

6 The papyrus was first published in F.L. GRIFFITH, *The Petrie Papyri. Hieratic Papyri from Kahun and Gurob* (*Principally of the Middle Kingdom*), London 1898, 76-77, pl. XXXII.

writing had been actually sent. Albeit the sheet is practically intact and the script is clear enough to be deciphered, the text as a whole possesses a series of difficulties, translators of ancient Egyptian letters are generally faced with. In my rendering, the text goes as follows:

Recto
(1) *s:wḏꜣ-jb r-nt.t ḏd n bꜣk-jm jw nb ꜥ.w.s. spr r Sḫm-S-n-wsr.t-mꜣꜥ-ḫrw m*
(2) *IIII šmw 10 bjn.wj jj=k ꜥḏ.tj wḏꜣ.tj*
(3) *ḏd=k m bjn.t nb.t m ḥs.t n.t Sbk nb Rꜣ-sḥ.wj*
(4) *rdj.t(j)=fj tw n wḥꜣ.tjw(?) m ḥs.t n.t kꜣ=f jr.n kꜣ n*
(5) *jmj-rꜣ ḥw.t-nṯr n ḥq.t*[sic] *Ppj r=k r mn r wꜣḥ*
(6) *nḥḥ ḏt bjn sḏm=k sqr.t(j)*

Verso
(1) *mj r-k mꜣ=j*
(2) *tw m-k šsp=n*
(3) *wnw.t bjn.t*

Recto:

Verso:

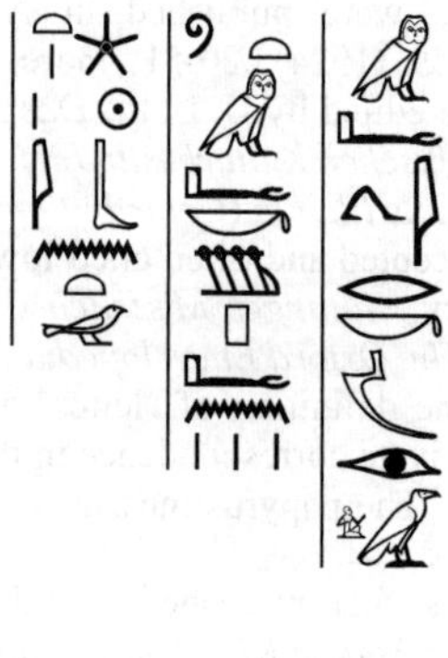

Recto

(1) A communication to the effect that the humble servant has been told: "The Lord, l.p.h., has arrived at Sekhem-Senusret-true-of-voice in

(2) IIII shemu 10." How bad it is that you have come safe and sound!

(3) It is utter viciousness that you say. In the favour of Sobek, Lord of Ra-sehuy,

(4) who will forward you to the quarrymen(?), and in the favour of his *ka*! – the *ka* of

(5) the manager of the temple of *ḥq.t*, Pepi has acted against you until the enduring of

(6) eternity. Ill may be if you take note. May you be smitten!

Verso

(1) Come that I may see

(2) you! Behold, we may have

(3) an evil hour.

I argued elsewhere that Sekhem-Senusret-true-of-voice was a place name employed for the unit incorporating the pyramid-enclosure, the valley temple with its subsidiary installations, and the western strip of houses once accommodating the temple personnel.[7] For the dubious reading *wḥꜣ.tjw* translated as "quarrymen" instead of "cauldron"[8] or "oasis(-dwellers)"[9], see Luft's remarks in his study on the pyramid town at el-Lahun.[10] Whether the same word occurs on P UC 32302 frame 3 recto (x+2) in a desperately damaged context, is difficult to say.[11] I have taken *sqr.t(j)* at the end of recto (6) as a stative without a preceding subject employed in main clauses to command or request a state.[12] This view may be supported by the fact that, unlike the more formal and elevated *nfr sḏm nb ꜥ.w.s.* terminal formula, the *nfr sḏm=k* variant seems to be never followed by the stative as a polite wish to soften a request – the explanation of this should obviously be sought in the social context of correspondence, where forms and patterns employed seem to have been heavily dependent on the parties' relative status in social or institutional hierarchy.

Despite Petrie's loose way of recording individual find-spots at Kahun, P UC 32204 is known to have been found together with a larger group of miscellaneous manuscripts (Lot VI in Griffith's edition).[13] Of the altogether twenty-four documents, ten were dated letters and accounts[14], all but one written during a very limited period of time: between year 41 of Amenemhat III and year 9 of

---

7 Z. HORVÁTH, Temple(s) and Town at El-Lahun. A Study of Ancient Toponyms in the El-Lahun Papyri, in: J. WEGNER/D. SILVERMAN (eds.), *Archaism and Innovation. Studies in the Culture of Middle Kingdom Egypt*, New Haven-Philadelphia (forthcoming). See, however, U. LUFT, The Ancient Town of El-Lâhûn, in: S. QUIRKE (ed.), *Lahun Studies*, New Malden 1998, 1-41 for a different interpretation.

8 So E.F. WENTE, *Letters from Ancient Egypt*, Atlanta 1990, 85.

9 As suggested in COLLIER/QUIRKE, *Lahun Letters*, 119.

10 LUFT, *Ancient Town of El-Lâhûn*, 15 with note 103.

11 COLLIER/QUIRKE, *Lahun Letters*, 173.

12 Cf. J.P. ALLEN, *Middle Egyptian. An Introduction to the Language and Culture of Hieroglyphs*, Cambridge 2000, 214, §17.17.2.

13 The "vast heap" of papyri was found on week 28 April - 4 May 1889, when Petrie's workers were excavating Rank N, i.e. the blocks of houses alongside the thick partition wall separating the large eastern section of the settlement from the western enclosure; see C. GALLORINI, A Reconstruction of Petrie's Excavation at the Middle Kingdom Settlement of Kahun, in: QUIRKE (ed.), *Lahun Studies*, 48-49 with fig. 3. On the limitations of identifying individual find-spots at Kahun, see COLLIER/QUIRKE, *Lahun Letters*, v-vii, esp. vii. Based on the find circumstances, I prefer seeing this mass of miscellaneous papyri as discarded papers deposited all at once.

14 An overview of the content of Lot VI was given in S. QUIRKE, *The Administration of Egypt in the Late Middle Kingdom. The Hieratic Documents*, New Malden 1990, 165, and in C. GALLORINI, *Reconstruction of Petries Excavation*, 57, note 53.

Amenemhat IV.[15] Such an overt clustering of documents lends some sort of homogeneity to the group as a whole, and assigns a similar date to the small manuscript as well.[16]

Griffith considered the text as a genuine letter, and primarily on the choice of ink, divided the text into three parts: letter written in black ink – reply thereto, written in red – postscript to the reply or a further letter in red.[17] His view of the content has found its way into more recent scholarly literature as well, citing the manuscript on account of its unique character.[18] This widely held concept of the papyrus has just been challenged by M. Collier and S. Quirke, editors of the UCL Lahun papyri, pointing at the lack of address and the highly sarcastic tone pervading the composition at its full length[19]; the letter admittedly breaking through the norms of letter-writing, and implying a mastery of scribal skills on the part of the author. It may be assumed that the text, *pro forma* a letter, acquired the status of a literary genre, and was intended to entertain a wider reading public, as fictional letters normally do. Nevertheless, its elliptic character strongly contradicts this assumption. Unlike literary letters which tend to provide their non-specific reading public with a sufficient amount of background information, the author of a genuine letter can refer to matters in his message only elliptically, appealing to the knowledge he shares with the addressee. In missive letters, ellipsis is in fact a means of focusing attention to the new material communicated.[20] Furthermore, the nomination of the sender and/or the addressee is a typical but no way an essential criterion of genuine letters, as substantiated by

---

15 Amenemhat III: year 29 – P UC 32057 (former Lot VI.1) verso; year 41 – P UC 32168 (Lot VI.21) recto; year 43 – P UC 32182 (Lot VI.15), P UC 32174 (Lot VI.13), P UC 32178 (Lot VI.20) recto; year 44 – P UC 32180 (Lot VI.22); year 46 – P UC 32177 (Lot VI.19); Amenemhat IV: year 1 – P UC 32158 (Lot VI.12) verso; year 2 – P UC 32201 (Lot VI.4); year 9 – P UC 32168 (Lot VI.21) verso. Most of the dated accounts are concerned either with constructional works or with the man-power employed, perhaps at the royal cemetery at Hawara. As to the length of time between the two regnal years, cf. with the list of sources for Amenemhat IV's short coregency with his father, in W. GRAJETZKI, *The Middle Kingdom of Ancient Egypt. History, Archaeology and Society*, London 2006, 61 with note 251.

16 A later date within the inner chronology of el-Lahun papyri may be corroborated with palaeographical similarities between the *ductus* of our papyrus and that of the religious composition inscribed onto the outside of two pottery vessels from Harageh (Tomb 290), dated to Thirteenth-Seventeenth Dynasties on palaeographical grounds – in itself a weak evidence, however, due to the brevity of the text and the difference in the writing surface. For the pottery vessels, see B. GUNN, *Hieroglyphic and Hieratic Inscriptions*, in: R. ENGELBACH, *Harageh* (*British School of Archaeology in Egypt* 28), London 1923, 30-32; W. GRAJETZKI, *Harageh. An Egyptian Burial Ground for the Rich around 1800 BC*, London 2004, 49-53. Note, furthermore, the orthographical similarity between *ḥq.t* in P UC 32204, 5 and the goddess *ḥs.t* on the religious pot UC 16129, 5 from Harageh as well as the goddess *ḥq.t* in P Westcar (P Berlin 3033) 9,23; 10,8; 10,15 and 10,23. The analogy provided by P Westcar has already been noted in LUFT, *Ancient Town of El-Lâhûn*, 15, note 104.

17 GRIFFITH, *Petrie Papyri*, 76.

18 Long before the *editio princeps*, Griffith referred to a specific papyrus in his summing chapter "The Hieratic Papyri", in: W.M.F. PETRIE, *Illahun, Kahun, and Gurob 1889-90*, London 1891, 48 with the words: "Some quaint notes are scribbled on small squares of papyrus: one contains both the note and the reply, the latter in red ink", which fits the key features of UC 32204. Passages of this brief letter were also quoted in R. DAVID, *The Pyramid Builders of Ancient Egypt. A Modern Investigation of Pharaoh's Workforce*, London-New York 1986, 121, since it was found to be "especially interesting" by the author. English translations were provided in two anthologies of substantial importance: WENTE, *Letters from Ancient Egypt*, 85, and R. B. PARKINSON, *Voices from Ancient Egypt. An Anthology of Middle Kingdom Writings*, London 1991, 93. Partial translation was given by LUFT, *Ancient Town of El-Lâhûn*, 15, owing to the implications of the content on spatial organization of the site.

19 COLLIER/QUIRKE, *Lahun Letters*, 119.

20 The new piece of information emphasised in P UC 32204 by ellipsis is the temple official Pepi, who was claimed to have acted against an unknown person. Otherwise, even the nature of the conflict that provoked such hostile response remains hidden before us. The difference between literary and non-literary letters as well as the relevance of ellipsis has been explored in D. SWEENEY, *Correspondence and Dialogue. Pragmatic Factors in Late Ramesside Letter-Writing* (*Ägypten und Altes Testament* 49), Wiesbaden 2001, 4. My argumentation does not exclude the possibility that the letter as it is may have been kept and re-used later on for didactic purposes or for entertainment, since missive letters are known to have been included into the *Miscellanies* to serve as models for the apprentice scribes. It is, however, irrelevant to the question, if the text was originally intended as a genuine letter, or not.

short messages on small scraps of papyri, quite often found without an address.[21] Such texts, rarely termed as "communications"[22], are attested among the el-Lahun manuscripts but are also known virtually from all periods of dynastic history. The bulk of them were exchanged between bureaucrats, and could be delivered from hand to hand, making the address superfluous in situations when correspondence was generated primarily by the necessity of recording matters in writing and not by the need to communicate over great distances. The omission of the correspondents' names may also be explained by the fact that, as D. Sweeney aptly remarks, letters of this kind were intended not for specific individuals but for representatives of the same or other institutions, thus the identity of the parties was not a salient factor in successful communication.[23]

The chief argument against regarding the writing as a single composition – and thence against assigning literary merits to it – is the difference in the *ductus* on the recto. Despite the brevity of the text, two distinct hands can be securely detected:

– hand producing a fine, tightly-spaced inscription in black made up of large and slender signs, slanting slightly to the left (first scribe);
– another hand characterised by a less elegant and loose handwriting in red, composed of crudely-fashioned and more angular signs (second scribe).

I consider these differences too profound to be the result of one scribe changing pens, as it was proposed by R. Parkinson.[24] The text on the verso is hard to compare with that of the recto, since a shift in the arrangement brings forth essential changes in the shaping of signs. It can be concluded then that at least two turns of letter have been recorded on the sheet (first scribe → second scribe → first scribe again): the black lines of the original message are followed immediately by those of the rubricized reply. However, this way of answering a letter was fairly old-fashioned, and only

---

21 A number of them with dimensions comparable with those of P UC 32204. See, e.g. P UC 32211 – letter addressed to a superior mentioning daily rations (7.3 x 19.8 cm, no address): COLLIER/QUIRKE, *Lahun Letters*, 136-137, CD files; P UC 32180 – including a protocol of land-inspection, also from Lot VI (7.5 x 14+x cm, no address): IBID., CD files UC32180-f, UC32180-b; P Berlin 10081 A – letter from a superior (certainly the mayor) to the steward Horemsaf concerning the release of a singer (10.4 x 21.2+x cm, addressee in rubrics attached to the end of the message): LUFT, *Urkunden zur Chronologie*, 101-102, pl. 31.

22 J.J. JANSSEN, *Late Ramesside Letters and Communications* (*Hieratic Papyri in the British Museum* 6), London 1991, 8; ID., Literacy and Letters at Deir el-Medîna, in: R.J. DEMARÉE/A. EGBERTS (eds.), *Village Voices. Proceedings of the Symposium "Texts from Deir el-Medîna and their Interpretation" Leiden, May* 31-June 1, 1991 (*Centre of Non-Western Studies Publications* 13), Leiden 1992, 88.

23 SWEENEY, *Correspondence and Dialogue*, 3. Perhaps letters, in which the sender is indicated only with his title, should be explained on similar grounds. An early example is the short inner address formula (*jmj-rꜣ mšꜥ ḏd*) of the so-called "Saqqara-letter" (P Cairo JE 49623) from the late Sixth Dynasty, sent by the commander of the expedition to the office of the archivist situated within the enclosure of the Step Pyramid: B. GUNN, A Sixth Dynasty Letter from Saqqara, *Annales du service des antiquités de l'Égypte* 25 (1925), 242-255, pl. 1, 1a; for a convenient translation, see WENTE, *Letters from Ancient Egypt*, 42. This attitude of Egyptian administration that title and not the title-holder needs to be registered, evinces in extracts from the journal of Senusret II's mortuary temple, e.g. in P Cairo JE 71580 (former P Berlin 10005 B) recto II 10-22, a record of allowances paid for the crew, where temple-titles are listed in strict hierarchy without the denomination of the actual title-holders. For the papyrus, see L. BORCHARDT, Der Zweite Papyrusfund von Kahun und die zeitliche Festlegung des Mittleren Reiches der ägyptischen Geschichte, *Zeitschrift für Ägyptische Sprache und Altertumskunde* 37 (1899), 94; KAPLONY-HECKEL, *Ägyptische Handschriften* I, 266 (Anhang I,1) and pl. II.

24 PARKINSON, *Voices from Ancient Egypt*, 93. Furthermore, I cannot follow Parkinson's idea that the scribe who composed the whole text was the temple manager Pepi, whose *ka* is stated to have acted against the anonym sender. As early as in letters from the Dakhla oasis, the *ka* occurs in formulae denoting the authority of a particular person. A similar usage may also be evidenced the private correspondence of the Middle Kingdom; however, the term is never used as a self-reference. For the *ka*-formula in letters from Ayn Asil, see L. PANTALACCI, La documentation épistolaire du palais des gouverneurs à Balat-'Ayn Asil, *Bulletin de l'Institut français d'archéologie orientale* 98 (1998), 308-309. For instances of *ka* in the el-Lahun correspondence, see P UC 32199 recto (13) and P UC 32213 recto (17), (22): COLLIER/QUIRKE, *Lahun Letters*, 97, 143, 145.

exceptionally employed in letters contemporary with P UC 32204.[25] The gradual shift in letter-writing from vertical to horizontal lines during the long reign of Amenemhat III allowed a much more economical use of the writing surface and at the same time left hardly any space for taking additional notes, except in the margin.[26] Yet, the reason for adopting this method in our case is likely to be found in another formal characteristic of the papyrus.

A series of neatly arranged black spots, evidently the tips of imperfectly erased signs are visible on the right hand side of the sheet, immediately below and parallel with the last black line (Pl. 6a).[27] These traces reveal that the first message did continue over the point we are able to follow now, but the concluding section has been wiped off and superscribed by the second scribe. How much of the message has been lost, is impossible to say, however, the second scribe certainly kept only the relevant passage of the letter to which he was responding. The strategy is possibly a later counterpart of the practice attested in the early business letters from el-Lahun written in vertical lines: to save quoting at length from a previous message, the recipient put his comment in red immediately beside the passage it refers to, and returned the same sheet to the sender.[28] There are further indications that the second scribe not merely erased parts of the original letter, but the papyrus itself has undergone major changes in his hands. First of all, the reply, which is undoubtedly complete as it closes with the perverted terminal formula attesting the scribe's intention to finish off his words at that point, covers the entire surface of the recto, and leaves no room for any further lines. There is not a single trace, however, like e.g. a shift to smaller-scale signs or distorted forms, that the scribe was running out of available blank spaces. Such a full and optimal exploitation of the writing surface coupled with the fact that a narrow margin was left for the rubricized text only, while the bevelled right edge cut into the initial signs of the inscription in black, makes it plausible that the first message was originally written onto a larger sheet of papyrus, and it was the second scribe who, having completed his reply, cut the piece to size. What lends some credit to this theory is a dated record of the "Lord's" coming to Sekhem-Senusret-true-of-voice – obviously, a type of note which was made fun of by the first scribe of our satirical papyrus – written across the large blank spaces on the verso of P UC 32205, another letter from Lot VI (Pl. 6b)[29]:

rnp.t-sp 6 ꜣbd I prj[*.t*] *2*	*Regnal year 6, month I of peri[t], day 2.*
ḏd.tw n bꜣk-jm [*jw*] *nb ʿ.w.s.*	*It is reported to the humble servant: The Lord, l.p.h.,*
jw.t r Sẖm-S-n-w⸢*sr.t*] *mꜣʿ-ẖrw*	*is coming to Sekhem-Senusret-true-of-voice.*

25 Early letters of the temple archive, i.e. dated to the reign of Senusret III or to the first half of Amenemhat III's reign, reveal that the mayor of Hotep-Senusret-true-of-voice regularly responded to letters by inserting his rubricized comments between the vertical lines of the original message; see e.g. P Berlin 10018 (year 10 of Amenemhat III): LUFT, *Urkunden zur Chronologie*, 35-42, pl. 4-9; and P Berlin 10023B (presumably year 11 of Amenemhat III): LUFT, *Archiv von Illahun*: *Briefe* 1, s.v. P 10023B.

26 R. PARKINSON/S. QUIRKE, *Papyrus* (*Egyptian Bookshelf*), London 1995, 38-39. As a fine example for a letter written in horizontal lines with reply in red in the margin, see P UC 32124: COLLIER/QUIRKE, *Lahun Letters*, 58-61, CD file UC32124-f.

27 This observation was confirmed by autopsy; I am greatly indebted to Stephen Quirke (UCL) for allowing me to consult the original.

28 E.g. P Berlin 10023B: see footnote 25 above.

29 COLLIER/QUIRKE, *Lahun Letters*, 120-123, CD files UC32205-f, UC32205-b. The arrival of a high-ranking person at Sekhem-Senusret is otherwise a recurring topic in the el-Lahun correspondence, see furthermore e.g. P BM 10864, a letter addressed by a superior to the seal-bearer Neni announcing his arrival at Sekhem-Senusret-true-of-voice; B. GRDSELOFF, A New Middle Kingdom Letter from El-Lāhūn, *Journal of Egyptian Archaeology* 35 (1949), 59-62; WENTE, *Letters from Ancient Egypt*, 78-79.

Little attention has been paid so far to the rubricized columns on the reverse of P UC 32204. It has been argued that no palaeographical evidence may be cited to establish how this text is related to the inscriptions on the recto, yet it follows from the full character of the second scribe's reply that the three columns were most probably written by the first scribe again, in response to the second scribe's arrogant answer. This interpretation makes perfect sense for the conversation as a whole: a situation, in which further interaction is severely interfered by the mutually unsupportive behaviour of the antagonists, might be resolved through a face-to-face meeting: "Come that I may see you!".[30] This usually happens when, like in this case, the parties are engaged in an interaction not as private persons but as representatives of institutions, so the decision of maintaining or breaking off relations falls outside their personal competence.

Although set phrases in the message of the first scribe may suggest subordination, to outline a constellation in which the words of an impudent official receive an angry response from his superior would be highly deceiving[31]: terms of respect, like the self-referent *b3k-jm* as well as the formal address *nb ˁ.w.s.* should rather be seen here as a means of sarcasm destined to challenge the values building up the other party's "face"[32], and to maximize the distance between the offender and the offended. Moreover, irony and arrogance are particularly avoided in letters of complaint addressed to a person of higher rank.[33] In this respect, Ramesside correspondence is much more indicative, showing that addressing the other with rude terms is peculiar to complaints to one's equal or subordinate, but not acceptable in letters to superiors.[34]

The study of individual documents characterised by deviation from norms and conventions, such as this small papyrus from the collection of the University College London representing three turns of correspondence between conflicting literates, could be extremely rewarding for ongoing research on interpersonal relations in ancient Egypt. In his review article, D. Warburton surmised that reading this manuscript "we may be closer to the Egyptians than in many other cases"[35], and indeed, P UC 32204 offers the modern reader a rare chance to look behind the repertoire of epistolary terms and idioms and to wonder if some universal patterns of human behaviour are found there.

Papyrus UC 32204 was also cited in studies focusing on the cult topography of the Fayum, since the manuscript mentions "the manager of the temple of Heqet, Pepi", which is up to now the single explicit reference to a Middle Kingdom sanctuary of the frog-goddess.[36] The significance of the source would be paramount: despite the widespread use of her figure on amulets and grave goods as a popular protective deity connected with the concept of birth and resurrection, the cult of Heqet during the

---

30 In a passage of a poorly-preserved letter, the personal mediation of the addressee is called upon to resolve a conflict between the letter-writer and a third party, P UC 32106A ii (2): *jr ẖnn.n=f k3=j ẖnn=j jr jw.t=k dj.tw h3 r t3*, "If he has been impudent, then I will be impudent, too. But if were you to come, this would lead to an easing off". Translation follows COLLIER/QUIRKE, *Lahun Letters*, 16-17.

31 So in PARKINSON, *Voices from Ancient Egypt*, 93, note 4.

32 For the concept of "face", one's public self-image, as borrowed from the field of pragmatics, see SWEENEY, *Correspondence and Dialogue*, 232.

33 Illustrated by the strategy of the letter-writer in P Berlin 10025: U. LUFT, Illahunstudien II: Ein Verteidigungsbrief aus Illahun, *Oikumene* 4 (1983), 121-179.

34 Cf. SWEENEY, *Correspondence and Dialogue*, 237-241 with examples.

35 D.A. WARBURTON, Review of M. Collier/S. Quirke, The UCL Lahun Papyri: Letters, *Discussions in Egyptology* 58 (2004), 111.

36 Recto (4)-(5). The reading of the deity's name is certain, see fn. 15 above. The reference is discussed in S. QUIRKE, Gods in the Temple of the King: Anubis at Lahun, in: S. QUIRKE (ed.), *The Temple in Ancient Egypt. New Discoveries and Recent Research*, London 1991, 26-27; M. ZECCHI, *Geografia Religiosa del Fayyum dalle origini al IV secolo a.C.* (*Archeologia e storia della civiltà egiziana e del vicino oriente antico, Materiali e studi* 7), Imola 2001, 104-105.

Middle Kingdom is rather poorly documented.[37] She is mostly known from offering formulae and consecration texts on early Middle Kingdom stelae of Abydene origin, where Heqet, along with Khnum, played a prominent role in the transformation of the dead.[38] Epithets of the deceased in early Middle Kingdom tombs at Beni Hasan give evidence that Heqet acquired the status of local deity at Hor-wer (later Antinoe) and received cult there as the spouse of Khnum[39] – presumably in the temple of the latter, as textual sources keep silent about a separate sanctuary dedicated to the frog-goddess.

There are good indications that the edifice referred to as the temple of Heqet in P UC 32204 may have been situated somewhere in the Fayum, at a site under heavy exploitation during the late Middle Kingdom:

- the papyrus was found at the settlement site "Kahun";
- formal characteristics of the letter suggest that the correspondents were officials in close relationship with each other;
- both correspondents were associated in one way or another with the royal mortuary foundation of Senusret II at el-Lahun[40];
- both parties were well acquainted with Pepi, manager of the Heqet-temple.

Given the adherence of the goddess to the watery element, the mouth of the swampy Fayum could have been an ideal place for her cult to evolve[41], yet the surviving hieratic sources, which, admittedly, can be employed to substitute the missing architectural, pictorial and hieroglyphic record only with serious limitations, do not corroborate this hypothesis. Hieratic manuscripts from el-Lahun yield but negative evidence for the goddess Heqet, though temple files as well as letters, accounts, even legal documents from the town-site do convey ample attestations of various deities of the Memphis-Fayum zone and beyond[42], allowing one to study the royal foundation of Senusret II within the network of interconnected sacral installations.[43] From the evincible correlation between prominent cult places like the temple of Hathor Mistress of Atfih, Sobek Lord of Rasehuy, and frequent theopohorous names like

---

37 For general characteristics of the goddess, see L. KÁKOSY, s.v. *Heqet*, in: W. HELCK/W. WESTENDORF (eds.), *Lexikon der Ägyptologie* II, Wiesbaden 1977, 1123-1124; H. KEES, *Der Götterglaube im alten Ägypten*, Berlin 1956, 61-63. Examples for amulets and offering vessels decorated with the figure of Heqet, see E. HORNUNG/E. STAEHELIN, *Skarabäen und andere Siegelamulette aus Basler Sammlungen*, Mainz 1976, 112; W.C. HAYES, *The Scepter of Egypt. A Background for the Study of Egyptian Antiquities in the Metropolitan Museum of Art* I: *From the Earliest Times to the End of the Middle Kingdom*, New York 1953, 227-228 with fig. 143, 236-237, 249 with fig. 159.

38 This is a wide corpus; for sake of convenience, see the stelae assembled and commented in J. SPIEGEL, *Die Götter von Abydos. Studien zum ägyptischen Synkretismus* (*Göttinger Orientforschungen IV.Reihe Ägypten* 1), Wiesbaden 1973, 82.

39 For a brief overview, see F. GOMAÀ, *Die Besiedlung Ägyptens während des Mittleren Reiches* I*: Oberägypten und das Fayyūm* (Tübinger Atlas des Vorderen Orients Reihe B 66/1), Wiesbaden 1986, 313. For the epithets, see P. E. NEWBERRY, *Beni Hasan* II (*Archaeological Survey of Egypt* 3), London 1894, pl. 4, tomb of Baqet: *mrjj Ḥq.t Ḥr-wr*, pl. 13, tomb of Khety: *ḥsjj n Ḥq.t Ḥr-wr*.

40 It is evident that the first scribe was writing from Sekhem-Senusret-true-of-voice. The perverted blessing formula in the reply implies that the place, where the second scribe was coming, should be a locality where Sobek, Lord of Ra-sehuy was venerated. This cult place of the crocodile god is yet to be located, but its constant occurrence in the el-Lahun temple files is certainly not accidental. For the temple of Sobek, Lord of Ra-sehuy: H. BEINLICH, *Das Buch vom Fayum. Zum religiösen Eigenverständnis einer ägyptischen Landschaft* (*Ägyptologische Abhandlungen* 51) Wiesbaden 1991, 308-311, and especially in relation to the el-Lahun foundation, see my forthcoming paper *Temple(s) and town at el-Lahun* (see footnote 7 above).

41 M. BÁRTA has convincingly demonstrated the close association of Heqet with the three lakes of the Saqqara-Abusir region during the Old Kingdom (The Title "Priest of Heket" in the Egyptian Old Kingdom, *Journal of Near Eastern Studies* 58/2 (1999), 112-115).

42 The geographical scope of correspondence is much wider than the Memphis-Fayum zone which can be inferred from the mention of Amun and Month of Thebes (P UC 32212: COLLIER/QUIRKE, *Lahun Letters*, 138-141), Atum Lord of Heliopolis (P UC 32198: IBID., 92-95), and Khentykhety of Kemwer (P UC 32202: IBID., 110-113) – to cite a few – in the blessing formulae of letters delivered at el-Lahun.

43 For a thorough and systematic review of papyrological evidence for deities attested at el-Lahun, see QUIRKE, *Gods in the Temple of the King*, 25-32.

Sattepihu[44] (beside Sathathor) or Nebrasehuy[45] (beside various forms with Sobek-) in the yet unprocessed prosopographical corpus, I would conclude that the total absence of names compounded with or built on Heqet might also be taken indicative of the non-existence of her cult within the region.[46]

The perplexing reference to the temple may thus be related to and interpreted in the light of a somewhat similar hieratic group in two other manuscripts. P UC 32199 is a letter of Neni addressed to the steward Iy-ib, in which the letter-writer first urges the steward to pay attention to the household of Wah, and then continues[47]:

k3 jr.tw ḫft jrj r wn k3 n 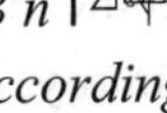 *ḥr ḥs.t=k*
Then let it be done accordingly so that the ka of the ruler can favour you.

The context is clear enough, since "being in the favour of the king or his ka" is a well-known and recurrent wish in the inscriptional record[48], and the group  is a common orthography of the word "ruler" both in contemporary manuscripts and in regular titles of the late Middle Kingdom.[49] Less clear is the reference of the other, partly damaged group in the *Great Festival Papyrus* in London (P UC 32191): *the festival of*  that takes place in the second month of shemu. Apparently the same festival is mentioned on a loose fragment: *ḥb*  that Griffith translated tentatively as "the festival of the reigning king".[50] In both cases *ḥq3*, i.e. the "reigning king" denotes most probably Amenemhat III.[51] More to the point is that in late Middle Kingdom titles, *ḥq3* seems to alternate with its feminine equivalent *ḥq3.t*; the difference being only orthographic: *ꜥnḫ n ṯ.t ḥq3.t*[52], *šmsw n ḥq3.t*[53],

---

44 E.g. P Berlin 10012A: BORCHARDT, *Zeitschrift für Ägyptische Sprache und Altertumskunde* 37 (1899), 99; P UC 32197: COLLIER/QUIRKE, *Lahun Letters*, 88-91.

45 E.g. P Berlin 10047: LUFT, *Urkunden zur Chronologie*, 91-96, pl. 28-29; P Berlin 10081C: IBID., 105-107, pl. 32-33.

46 Overall evidence for theophorous names honouring Heqet is scanty (all female): H. RANKE, *Die altägyptischen Personennamen* I, Glückstadt-Hamburg 1935, 255-256.

47 Recto (13)-(14). COLLIER/QUIRKE, *Lahun Letters*, 96-97. The letter dates to the end of the reign of Amenemhat III or to the earliest years of Amenemhat IV.

48 E.g. *wnn=ṯn ḥr ḥsw.t n.t jtjj=ṯn*, stela BM 101: *Hieroglyphic Texts from Egyptian Stelae, &c., in the British Museum* II, London 1912, pl. 1-2; K. SETHE, *Ägyptische Lesestücke zum Gebrauch im akademischen Unterricht. Texte des Mittleren Reiches*, Hildesheim 3rd ed. 1959, 89, line 17; *ḥs tw jtjj ḥs tw k3=f*, stela Louvre C 11: W.K. SIMPSON, *The Terrace of the Great God at Abydos. The Offering Chapels of Dynasties 12 and 13* (*Publications of the Pennsylvania-Yale Expedition to Egypt* 5), New Haven-Philadelphia 1974, ANOC 58.2, pl. 80; SETHE, *Lesestücke*, 76, line 19-20.

49 E.g. Sinuhe B 17 ; 86 and 113  (A.H. GARDINER, *Literarische Texte des Mittleren Reiches* II: *Die Erzählung des Sinuhe und die Hirtengeschichte* (*Hieratische Papyrus aus den Königlichen Museen zu Berlin* V), Leipzig 1909). From the titles listed under no. 13, 608, 1526, see as examples *3tw n ṯ.t ḥq(3)* – A. MARIETTE, *Catalogue générale des monuments d'Abydos découverts pendant les fouilles de cette ville*, Paris 1880, 364 no. 1018; *ꜥnḫ n ḫnw ḥq(3)* – GENERALVERWALTUNG (ed.), *Aegyptische Inschriften aus den Königlichen Museen zu Berlin* I. *Inschriften von der ältesten Zeit bis zur Hyksoszeit*, Berlin 1913, Nr. 1203; *šmsw n ḥq(3)* – J. GARSTANG, *El-Arabah. A Cemetery of the Middle Kingdom; Survey of the Old Kingdom Temenos; Graffiti from the Temple of Sety* (*Egyptian Research Account* 6), London 1901, pl. IV-V; SETHE, *Lesestücke*, 83, line 4.

50 GRIFFITH, *Petrie Papyri*, 61. For the festival and the later feast of Heqat in the inscription of the tomb of Petosiris at Hermopolis, see U. LUFT, *Die chronologische Fixierung des ägyptischen Mittleren Reiches nach dem Tempelarchiv von Illahun*, Wien 1992, 170-171.

51 P UC 32199 may be dated on the indirect evidence of its relationship with other datable documents in Lot I and II concerned with affairs of the family of Wah: P UC 32058, 32123, 32131, 32167 and 32292. See furthermore footnote 47 above. The *Festival Papyrus* dates to year 35.

52 MARIETTE, *Monuments d'Abydos*, 310 no. 891. For the title, see W.A. WARD, *Index of Egyptian Administrative and Religious Titles of the Middle Kingdom*, Beirut 1982, no. 611.

53 Sources listed in WARD, *Index of Titles*, Nr. 1527, to which add G. GOYON, *Nouvelles inscriptions rupestres du Wadi Hammamat*, Paris 1957, no. 85.

and even conversely *b3k.t n.t ḥq3*[54] beside *b3k.t n.t ḥq3.t*[55]. An early example of the interference of these forms can be attested in the Coffin Texts, where on two coffins *ḥq3* stands incorrectly in place of the goddess *Ḥq.t.*[56] Analogously, the orthographical difference between  (P UC 32204) and 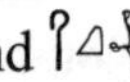 (P UC 32199 and P UC 32191) may also be attributed to a scribal error of this kind, which permits the restoration of the title in P UC 32204 as "the manager of the temple of the reigning king, Pepi".

A similar translation was already proposed by R. Parkinson in his excellent anthology, noting that by "ruler", the deceased Senusret II should be meant.[57] Indeed, a temple manager Pepi is known from a stela found in a tomb at the neighbouring site Harageh, a burial ground of a wealthy community at the time when cults at el-Lahun were flourishing[58], yet it does not necessarily follow that the temple mentioned in the letter is the mortuary temple of Senusret II, owing to the connotation of *ḥq3* in non-literary texts as "the one exerting his power", i.e., when applied to the royalty "the reigning king".[59] Whose temple should one then think of? Based on the evidence of dated texts in Lot VI, the papyrus might have been most likely written during the very last years of Amenemhat III or the earliest years of his successor, Amenemhat IV.[60] Given the paucity of monuments attributable to the short reign of Amenemhat IV[61] as opposed to his father's extensive building activity within the Fayum-Memphite region, the most probable candidate would be a temple built under Amenemhat III accommodating the cult of the reigning king. Suffice it to say that six of the account papyri from Lot VI are concerned with the labour-power employed at heavy constructions; P UC 32182 referring pronouncedly to "work in Ankh-Amenemhat-ankh-djet-er-neheh" in year 43, that is, at the Hawara foundation of Amenemhat III[62], where building activity was started around year 15 and work on the "Labyrinth" lasted well over the death of the king.[63] Thus it cannot at least be excluded that, reflecting a profound change in the ideology of kingship during the late Middle Kingdom, i.e. the merging of the royal cult with the cult of a deity[64], the complex religious architecture at Hawara within the domain of Sobek of Shedyet could have been the place, where a "temple of the reigning king" is to be looked for, yet any attempt at specification would remain essentially speculative.

---

54 Sources listed in WARD, *Index of Titles*, no. 778.

55 W.M.F. PETRIE, *Diospolis Parva. The Cemeteries of Abadiyeh and Hu 1898-9* (*Egypt Exploration Fund* 20), London 1901, 53, pl. XXVII; R.D. ANDERSON, *Musical Instruments* (*Catalogue of Egyptian Antiquities in the British Museum* III), London 1976, no. 12, fig. 24.

56 A. de Buck, *The Ancient Egyptian Coffin Texts* V (*Oriental Institute Publications* 73), Chicago 1954, 138; *mḏ3bt=s m ḥq3* (G1T, A1C) / *ḥq.t* (M46C, M2NY) *m r3-š=s*.

57 PARKINSON, *Voices from Ancient Egypt*, 93 with footnote 5.

58 B. GUNN, in: ENGELBACH, *Harageh*, 26-27, pl. XXIV,2; LXXI. The owner of the stela, Nebpu is strongly related to the royal cult at el-Lahun through the sequence of his titles in the offering formula; see QUIRKE, *Gods in the Temple of the King*, 33-34. Pepi, who seems to have been a close relative of Nebpu, can be seen on the right of the third register.

59 For the difficulties in proper rendering, cf. E. BLUMENTHAL, *Untersuchungen zum ägyptischen Königtum des Mittleren Reiches* I: *Die Phraseologie*, Berlin 1970, 25-26.

60 See the discussion and for details footnote 15 above.

61 For a review of his monuments, see I. MATZKER, *Die letzten Könige der 12. Dynastie*, Frankfurt-Bern-New York 1986, 173-174; GRAJETZKI, *Middle Kingdom of Ancient Egypt*, 61.

62 P UC 32057, P UC 32181, P UC 32174, P UC 32182, P UC 32178 and P UC 32168 may be related to building activities; see footnote 15 above.

63 D. ARNOLD, *Der Pyramidenbezirk des Königs Amenemhet III. in Dahschur* I: *Die Pyramide* (*Archäologische Veröffentlichungen* 53), Mainz 1987, 94.

64 See the elucidative remarks, in QUIRKE, *Gods in the Temple of the King*, 42 and 46.

Khenemet Nefer Hedjet Weret in the Great Temple of Tell Basta (Bubastis)

Eva Lange

In the remains of the Bastet temple in Bubastis there is preserved a fragment of a false door, made of red granite (N/5.36). It was found and documented in 1996 by the Egyptian-German Tell Basta-Project in the area of the Sed festival court of Osorkon II, lying between the remains of the relief decorated blocks of the building (*Planquadrat* N/5, see Fig. 1 and compare photo on the back of the cover). At the find spot there were no signs of any original architectural contexts.

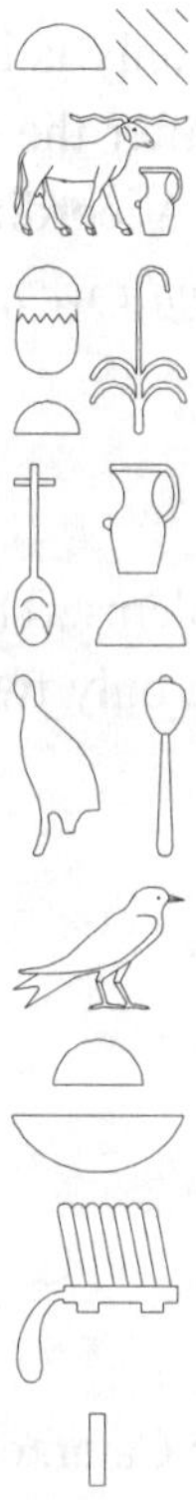

The fragment belongs to the left jamb of a false door. It is 0,77 m high and 0,67 m wide. It consists of the outer door jamb including the weathered torus moulding, the inner door jamb and a part of the niche of the door. The surface of the granite is highly polished; the modeling of the surface is very fine and worked with many details.

The inner door jamb shows the lower part of a carefully executed inscription of right-facing hieroglyphs. It contains the name and titles of the queen:

[…] [*ḥm.*]*t ẖnm*(*w*) *ḥm.t nsw.t ẖnm.t nfr ḥḏ.t wr.t nb*(*.t*) *jm*3*ḫ*(*jj.t*)

"[…] [Prieste]ss of Khnum, King's wife, she who is joined to the Beauty of the White Crown – the older –, mistress of provisions".

According to this inscription the false door belongs to a queen *ẖnm.t nfr ḥḏ.t wr.t*, a name which is first attested in the Twelfth Dynasty, i.e. the reign of Senusret II.[1]

1 Against L.K. Sabbahy, Comments on the Titel *ẖnm.t nfr ḥḏ.t*, *Studien zur Altägyptischen Kultur* 23 (1996), 22, who argued that *Ỉt*3*-wr.t* whose canopic chests are inscribed *s*3*.t nsw.t ẖnm.t nfr ḥḏ.t tn,* should be dated back to the reign of Amenemhat II. Against older opinions, the assembled pottery in her burial chamber shows that her burial took place no earlier than the reign of Amenemhat III: cf. D. Arnold, The Fragmented Head of a Queen Wearing the Vulture Headdress, in: E. Czerny/I. Hein/H. Hunger/D. Melman/A. Schwab (eds.), *Timelines. Studies in honour of Manfred Bietak* I (*Orientalia Lovaniensia Analecta* 149), Leuven-Paris-Dudley MA 2006, 47, note 3.

Altogether there are attested four Twelfth Dynasty queens and one king's daughter, all of them called *ḫnm.t nfr ḥḏ.t*:

ḥm.t nsw.t ḫnm.t nfr ḥḏ.t wr.t	→	queen of Senusret II[2]
ḥm.t nsw.t ḫnm.t nfr ḥḏ.t ḫrd	→	queen of Senusret III
ḥm.t nsw.t ḫnm.t nfr ḥḏ.t	→	queen of Senusret III
ḥm.t nsw.t ḫnm.t nfr ḥḏ.t ꜥꜣ.t	→	queen of Amenemhat III
Ỉtꜣ-wr.t sꜣ.t nsw.t ḫnm.t nfr ḥḏ.t tn	→	daughter of Amenemhat III[3]

From this overview, it becomes clear that these queens most often have an epithet relating to the age of the person with this name/title. It distinguishes them: *wr.t* means in this case "the older" and *ḫrd* "the younger". It seems possible to conclude that *ḫnm.t nfr ḥḏ.t wr.t* and *ḫnm.t nfr ḥḏ.t ḫrd* lived at about the same time and that at this time *ḫnm.t nfr ḥḏ.t* was a personal name which only is later used as a title.[4] This is supported by the observation that the expression always appears after the title *ḥm.t nsw.t*. This is the place normally reserved for the personal name of a queen. According to its inscription it is highly likely that this fragment of a door jamb belongs to *ḫnm.t nfr ḥḏ.t wr.t,* the wife of Senusret II, a queen attested by a high number of monuments.

Only the reading of the title here restored as *[Priest]ess of Khnum* creates problems. The title is only partly preserved at the upper edge of the inscription as [...].*t ḫnm(w)*. There are only two known examples of queenly titles which refer to Khnum, and they are much later. One is

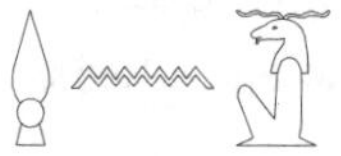

ḫkr.t n ḫnm(w)
"Ornament of Khnum"[5]

and the other

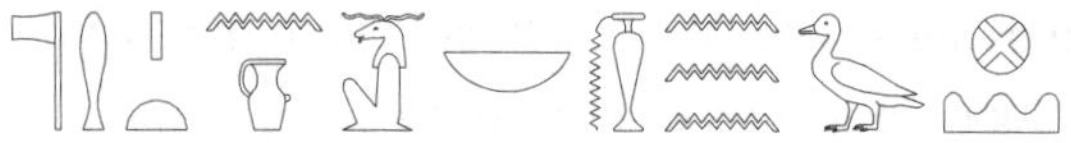

ḥm(.t)-nṯr n ḫnm(w) nb qbḥw
"Priestess of Khnum, Lord of the Cataract".[6]

The first title is known for two Ptolemaic queens, Berenike II und Cleopatra I, and the second title for Nesikhons, the daughter of Smendes II and wife of Pinodjem II.

2 Recently excavated evidence at the Dahshur pyramid of Senusret III seems to indicate the existence of another queen with the name *ḥm.t nsw.t ḫnm.t nfr ḥḏ.t wr.t*. Cf. W. GRAJETZKI, *Ancient Egyptian Queens. A Hieroglyphic Dictionary*, London 2005, 32.

3 See footnote 1.

4 S. ROTH, *Die Königsmütter des Alten Ägypten von der Frühzeit bis zum Ende der 12. Dynastie* (*Ägypten und Altes Testament* 46), 2001, 229, note 1294. For a discussion of *ḫnm.t nfr ḥḏ.t* as a ranking title and/or personal name see GRAJETZKI, *Ancient Egyptian Queens*, 34; SABBAHY, *Studien zur Altägyptischen Kultur* 23 (1996), 22-23.

5 Cf. L. TROY, *Patterns of Queenship in Ancient Egyptian Myth and History* (*Acta Universitas Upsaliensis. BOREAS. Uppsala Studies in Ancient Mediterranean and Near Eastern Civilizations* 14), Uppsala 1986, 186.

6 Cf. TROY, *Patterns of Queenship*, 189.

As mentioned above, there is no evidence at the find spot for the architectural context of the false door. Instead it can be assumed that the false door as fragment or still complete was brought to the Great Temple of Bubastis. It was re-used in the architecture of the great Sed festival court of Osorkon II. The original setting of this piece was most likely the (cenotaph ?-) pyramid of *ẖnm.t nfr ḥḏ.t wr.t* in Dahshur or her possible pyramid in Lahun.[7] However, it should be mentioned that only about 100 m north of the Great Temple of Bastet in Bubastis, there is a palace complex and a relating cemetery dating to the Twelfth Dynasty or even to the time of Amenemhat III. In the cemetery there were certainly no royal burials, but the palace was most likely not only used as residence of high officials, but also as a temporary place for the king. This is supported by a door lintel decorated with a relief showing the Sed festival of Amenemhat III, found at the north-east corner of the palace.[8] Therefore, it cannot be entirely excluded that the false door of *ẖnm.t nfr ḥḏ.t wr.t* belonged to a memory chapel constructed for this queen in Bubastis.

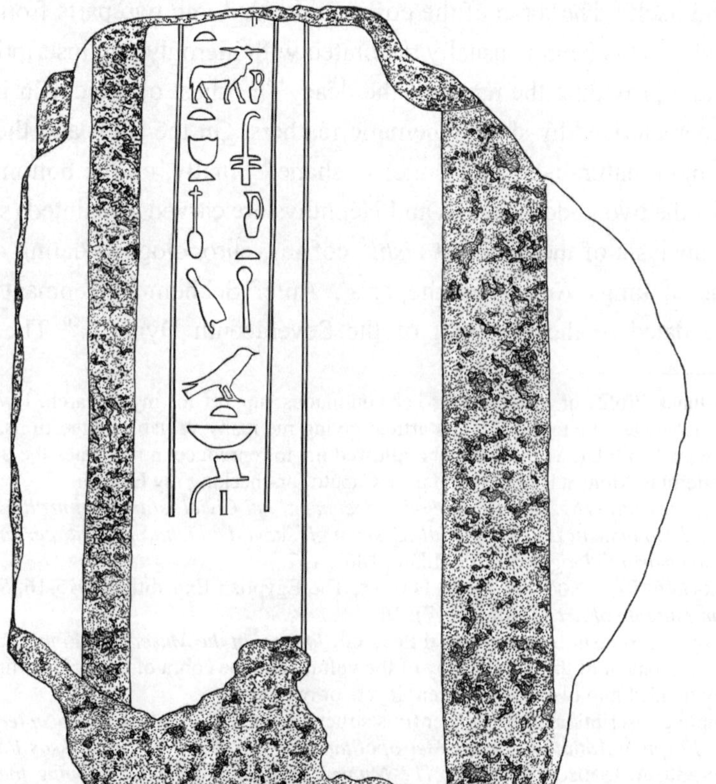

Fig. 1: False door of queen Khenemet Nefer Hedjet Weret (drawing by P. Whelan)

7 Cf. D. ARNOLD, *The Pyramid Complex of Senwosret III at Dahshur. Architectural Studies.* (*Publications of the Metropolitan Museum of Art Egyptian Expedition* 26), Yale 2002, 82.

8 S. FARID, Preliminary Report on the Excavations of the Antiquities Department at Tell Basta (Season 1961), *Annales du service des antiquités de l'Égypte* 58 (1964), 94.

Some Remarks on the Development of *rishi* Coffins*

Gianluca Miniaci

During the Second Intermediate Period there evolved a new kind of coffin characterized by feather patterns and an anthropoid form. The first scholar, who named this type of coffins as *rishi,* was Luigi Vassalli who coined it from the Arabic word for feathers.[1] The *rishi* coffins show a unitary structure based on a decorative repetitive pattern. The *nemes* headdress characterizes the upper part of the coffin. The face is usually poorly modelled and "wedge-shaped".[2] On the chest, there is a painted *wesekh* collar, under which there are drop-shaped beads. Over the collar, there is a vulture with its wings outstretched and a cobra, next to the body of the bird, standing with its hood extended and its tail curling around itself.[3] The torso of the coffin is divided into two parts from a vertical band with a border on either side. This band is usually decorated with hieroglyphic inscriptions, containing the *ḥtp dj nswt* formula and providing the name of the dead. The chest of the coffin is decorated with a first layer, which is characterized by short schematic feathers. On the sides and the legs of the coffin, the feathers become more naturalistic and longer in shape.[4] Finally, on the bottom of the coffin, beneath the feet, figures of the two goddesses Isis and Nephthys are carved or painted (see Pl. 7d).[5]

Through the analysis of the different *rishi*[6] coffins, chronological dating criteria can be reached. The *rishi* coffins of kings Antef Nubkheperra[7], Antef Sekhemra Wepmaat[8] and Antef Sekhemra Heruhirmaat[9] are dated to the first part of the Seventeenth Dynasty.[10] The *rishi* coffins of kings

---

* I would like to thank Professor M. Betrò for her continuous support for my research. I would like to thank Wolfram Grajetzki who encouraged me to publish this article giving me many valuable suggestions, and Stephen Quirke for his advice. I am indebted with Dr. M.J. Raven who allowed me to reproduce in the plates the picture of Montunakht coffin. Finally, I am grateful to Monica Hanna and Marina Caputo for checking my English.

1 *L'egittologo Luigi Vassalli (1812-1887). Disegni e documenti nei Civici Istituti Culturali Milanesi*, Milano 1994, 11-27 and L. VASSALLI, *I Monumenti istorici egizi. Il Museo e gli scavi d'antichità eseguiti per ordine di S.A. il Vicerè Ismail Pascia, notizia sommaria di Luigi Vassalli*, Milano 1867, 137.

2 See A.M. LYTHGOE/A. LANSING/N. DE GARIS DAVIES, The Egyptian Expedition 1915-16, *Supplement to the Bulletin of the Metropolitan Museum of Art* 12 (May 1917), 16.

3 See P. LACOVARA, An Ancient Egyptian Royal Pectoral, *Journal of the Museum of Fine Arts Boston* 2 (1990), 25-27, for a study on the development of the iconography of the vulture and the cobra of the *rishi* coffins.

4 They are usually divided into two other different layers or registers.

5 For a more complete description of the *rishi* coffins structure, see W.C. HAYES, *The Scepter of Egypt. A Background for the Study of the Egyptian Antiquities in the Metropolitan Museum of Art* II. *The Hyksos Period and the New Kingdom*, New York 1959, 30, A. DODSON/S. IKRAM, *The Mummy in Ancient Egypt. Equipping the Dead for Eternity*, London 1998, 204 or J.H. TAYLOR, *Death and the Afterlife in Ancient Egypt*, London 2001, 224.

6 In this article, the word *rishi* refers to the typology of coffins that belongs to a primary stage. A next stage shows a complete changed version of the *rishi* motif, more stylized, as illustrated by the coffins of king Ahmose or Queen Ahmes Nefertari, where "the body appears entirely sheathed in plumage, back and front", see J.H. TAYLOR, *Egyptian Coffins* (*Shire Egyptology* 11), Aylesbury 1989, 28.

7 Coffin of the king Antef Nubkheperra- British Museum EA 6652, see H.E. WINLOCK, The Tombs of the Kings of the Seventeenth Dynasty at Thebes, *Journal of Egyptian Archaeology* 10 (1924), 226-231, pl. XIV.

8 Coffin of the king Antef Wepmaat- Louvre Museum E 3091, see WINLOCK, *Journal of Egyptian Archaeology* 10 (1924), 234-236, pl. XIV.

9 Coffin of the king Antef Heruhirmaat- Louvre Museum E 3020, see WINLOCK, *Journal of Egyptian Archaeology* 10 (1924), 267, pl. XXI.

10 For the internal chronology of Seventeenth Dynasty, see A. DODSON, On the Internal Chronology of Seventeenth Dynasty, *Göttinger Miszellen* 120 (1991), 33-38; C. BENNETT, The first Three Sekhemre Kings of the Seventeenth Dynasty, *Göttinger Miszellen* 143 (1994), 21-28; K. RYHOLT, *The Political Situation in Egypt during the Second Intermediate Period c. 1800-1550 B.C.* (*Carsten Niebuhr Institute of Near Eastern Studies* 20), Copenhagen 1997, 168-171 and 266-281; J. VON BECKERATH, Theban Seventeenth Dynasty, in: E. TEETER/J.A. LARSON (eds.), *Gold of Praise. Studies on Ancient Egypt in Honor of Edward F. Wente* (*Studies in Oriental Civilizations* 58), Chicago 1999, 21-25;

Seqenenra Tao[11], Kamose[12] and the Queen Ahhotep[13] are precisely dated to the end of the Seventeenth Dynasty. In addition, there are four more dated *rishi* coffins: two of them are dated to the Seventeenth Dynasty; another one is the coffin of Hornakht[14] which was found with a staff that belongs to "king's son"[15] Tjuiu who lived under the reign of Seqenenra Tao; the last one is the coffin of Satdjehuty[16] daughter of Tetisheri, the grandmother of Ahmose.

All this collected evidence supports the idea that *rishi* coffins have originated and were spread out only during the Seventeenth Dynasty. However, all the previous examples act for a sort of standard form for *rishi* typology. On the other hand, there are other kinds of coffins, which show in their decorations an evolutionary phase. These coffins could be considered a transitional phase in the development of the anthropoid *rishi* coffin that can be placed either before or after the Seventeenth Dynasty, as they do not follow the standard model characterizing that period.

For example, the coffin of Montunakht[17] without the characteristic representation of the vulture and the cobra on the chest seems to be one of the first models of *rishi* coffin typology. The pattern of the feathers in the first layer is completely replaced by an abstract series of circles.[18] The feathers on the sides of the coffin are not yet divided into the usual registers, but rather into a single unit. The *nemes* is hardly outlined and it has a feathered decoration similar to the *rishi* mask decoration style. Finally, the lower part of the coffin is composed of a chess pattern, which could be an extension of some Middle Kingdom geometrical schemes as shown by the coffering decoration on the coffins of Nakhtankh and Khnumnakht (Pl. 7a-b).[19]

The coffin found by Petrie[20] during 1908, which was excavated north of Dra Abu el-Naga in an area called el-Khor[21], can be ascribed to a transitional phase. In fact, the first register of feathers is

---

C. Bennett, A Genealogical Chronology of the Seventeenth Dynasty, *Journal of the American Research Center in Egypt* 39 (2002), 123-155.

11 Coffin of the king Seqenenra- Egyptian Museum CG 61001, see G. Daressy, *Catalogue général des Antiquités égyptiennes du Musée du Caire N°s 61001-61044, Cercueils des cachettes royales*, Le Caire 1909, 1-2, pl. I-II.

12 Coffin of king Kamose- Egyptian Museum Cairo JE 4944, see G. Daressy, Le cercueil du roi Kames, *Annales du service des antiquités de l'Égypte* 9 (1908), 61-3, pl. 9 or Winlock, *Journal of Egyptian Archaeology* 10 (1924), 259-265, pl. XXI.

13 Coffin of the queen Ahhotep- Egyptian Museum Cairo CG 28501, see Winlock, *Journal of Egyptian Archaeology* 10 (1924), 250-255, pl. XVI), but also A.M. Roth, The Ahhotep Coffins. The Archaeology of an Egyptological Reconstruction, in: Teeter/Larson (eds.), *Gold of Praise*, Chicago 1999, 361-377.

14 Coffin of Hornakht- Vassalli excavations, see A. Mariette, *Monuments divers recueillis en Égypte et en Nubie par Auguste Mariette-Bey. Ouvrage publié sous les auspices de S.A. Ismail Pacha Khédive d'Égypte/Texte par G. Maspero*, Paris 1872/1889, 16, pl. 51. Vassalli misread the name written on the coffin and he named "Aqhor". Actually, the correct reading of his name is Hornakht as proposed by Stephen Quirke.

15 For this title during the Second Intermediate Period, see B. Schmitz, *Untersuchungen zum Titel s3-njswt "Königssohn"*, Bonn 1976, 217-262.

16 Coffin of Satdjehuti- Staatliches Museum Ägyptischer Kunst München ÄS 7163, see A. Grimm/S. Schoske, *Im Zeichen des Mondes. Ägypten zu Beginn des Neuen Reiches* (*Schriften aus der ägyptischen Sammlung* 7), München 1999, 92, cat. no. 1.

17 Coffin of Montunakht- Rijksmuseum van Oudheden Leiden AMM 25 [formerly S. 47, no. 9], see A.A. Boeser, *Beschreibung der aegyptischen Sammlung des niederländischen Reichsmuseums der Altertümer in Leiden, Die Denkmäler der Zeit zwischen dem Alten und Mittleren Reich und des Mittleren Reichs* II, Haag 1910, 3-4, pl. VIII, also M.J. Raven, *De dodencultus van het Oude Egypte*, Amsterdam 1992, 28-29.

18 Lacovara, *Journal of the Museum of Fine Arts Boston* 2 (1990), 25.

19 These coffins, which are dated to the Middle Kingdom, were found in the external court of the tomb no. 2 possible of Khnumaa at Rifeh, see W.M.F. Petrie, *Gizeh and Rifeh* (*British School of Archaeology in Egypt* 13), London 1907, 12, no. 26, pl. X B.

20 Coffin of an anonymous Queen- National Museums Scotland A.1909.527.1, see W.M.F Petrie., *Qurneh* (*British School of Archaeology in Egypt* 16) London 1909, 6-10, pl. XXII-XXIV, but also K. Eremin/E. Goring/B. Manley/C. Cartwright, A 17th Dynasty Egyptian Queen in Edinburgh?, *KMT* 11/3 (2000), 32-40.

21 I am indebted to Dr. Bill Manley for this information; for the location of the finding place, see Petrie, *Qurneh*, 6, pl. IV, point marked with B letter.

simply outlined, a way of decorating different from the classic feathered pattern (Pl. 7c). Otherwise, it is difficult to determine the dating of this coffin as a piece of the end of the Seventeenth Dynasty. The lid is made of tamarisk while the case is made of sycamore fig with acacia and sidder dowels in the case, all local material for Egypt.[22] As pointed out by Vivian Davies, it is assumed that the use of local wood can correspond to a poor economic period, when Thebes was not connected to the northern trading routes.[23] Following the end of the Second Intermediate Period, at least for royals, cedar wood returned back to fashion as attested in Seqenenra Tao and Ahhotep coffins.[24] This observation could date the Edinburgh coffin to the period of the initial phase of the Seventeenth Dynasty, or earlier, during which foreign resources of wood were still not available.

Similarly, in the coffin of king Antef Sekhemra Heruhirmaat, probably one of the first kings of the Seventeenth Dynasty[25], the vulture representation on the chest is missing. Apart from this distinctive feature the whole pattern is exactly similar to the prototype of *rishi* coffin. This evidence goes with the assumption that a progressive emergence of features of *rishi* coffins dates back to a period prior to the Seventeenth Dynasty, which could be attributed towards the end of the Thirteenth Dynasty.

Other coffins show that the *rishi* typology extends beyond the Seventeenth Dynasty and it is attested until the first part of the Eighteenth Dynasty. A coffin found in the eastern cemetery of Deir el-Medina by Bruyère[26] could be considered a successive phase for the evolution of *rishi* coffins, because it does not present the canonic feathered decoration. On the lid, alongside the ordinary vertical band there are two more vertical bands with a "basket-weave" pattern.[27] However, the feathered decoration is confined to the lateral and inferior parts of the lid of the coffin. This coffin is well dated because inside the tomb there were two jar stoppers with the name of king Thutmose III stamped (Pl. 7e).[28] Another coffin, which is similar in decoration, with the same "basket-weave" bands joint on the torso, has been found in Saqqara in a New Kingdom cemetery.[29] Therefore, it is possible to conclude that this model is a developed form of the *rishi* prototype coffin, during the first part of the Eighteenth Dynasty.

Another successive or alternative evolution of the standard *rishi* model is represented by a type of coffin that shows horizontal bands[30] joined to the vertical one directly on the feathered decoration. For example, the lid of the Rennefer coffin, found by Hayes in Western Thebes[31], shows the bands of a new style decoration combined with the painted feathers arranged in the same way of the prototype of *rishi* coffins. The piece is well dated, because of Rennefer's jewel box containing seven scarabs, and

---

22 EREMIN/GORING/MANLEY/CARTWRIGHT, *KMT* 11/3 (2000), 37.

23 W.V. DAVIES, Ancient Egyptian Timber Imports. An Analysis of Wooden Coffins in the British Museum, in: W.V. DAVIES/L. SCHOFIELD (eds.), *Egypt, the Aegean and the Levant. Interconnections in the Second Millennium BC*, London 1995, 148-149.

24 WINLOCK, *Journal of Egyptian Archaeology* 10 (1924), 251, note 5.

25 C. VANDERSLEYEN, Les trois Antef de la 17e dynastie, *Discussions in Egyptology* 59 (2004), 72.

26 Anonymous coffin- Bruyère excavations no. 1389, see B. BRUYERE, *Les fouilles de Deir el Médineh (1934-1935). Deuxième partie: la Nécropole de l'est* (*Fouilles de l'Institut français d'Archéologie orientale* 15), Le Caire 1937, 197-201, fig. a 25.

27 For the use of this pattern during the Second Intermediate Period, see N. REEVES, A Newly-Discovered Royal Diadem of the Second Intermediate Period, *Minerva* 7/2 (1996), 47-48.

28 It is important to stress that the tomb was not found intact, see BRUYERE, *Les fouilles de Deir el Médineh: la Nécropole de l'est*, 201.

29 Anonymous coffin- Saqqara NE 1, see C.B. FIRTH/B. GUNN, *Teti Pyramid Cemeteries* I (*Excavations at Saqqara*), Le Caire 1926, 69-70, pl. 42.

30 The model with horizontal bands is typical of "white" coffins of the first part of Eighteenth Dynasty.

31 Coffin of Rennefer- Metropolitan Museum of Art excavations of 1934-35 years, W.C. HAYES, The Tomb of Nefer-Khewet and His Family, *Section II of the Bulletin of the Metropolitan Museum of Art* 30 (November 1935), 21-22.

among them one bearing the titulary and name of king Thutmose I.[32] The coffin of Taiuwy[33], dated to the beginning of New Kingdom, adds a similar pattern to the *rishi* decoration.

These examples, for which there is a precise dating based on archaeological evidence, show a change in the standard typology corresponding to a change of the dating. Therefore, it is highly possible that the *rishi* type coffins that do not show yet a complete *rishi* pattern can be dated prior to the Seventeenth Dynasty.

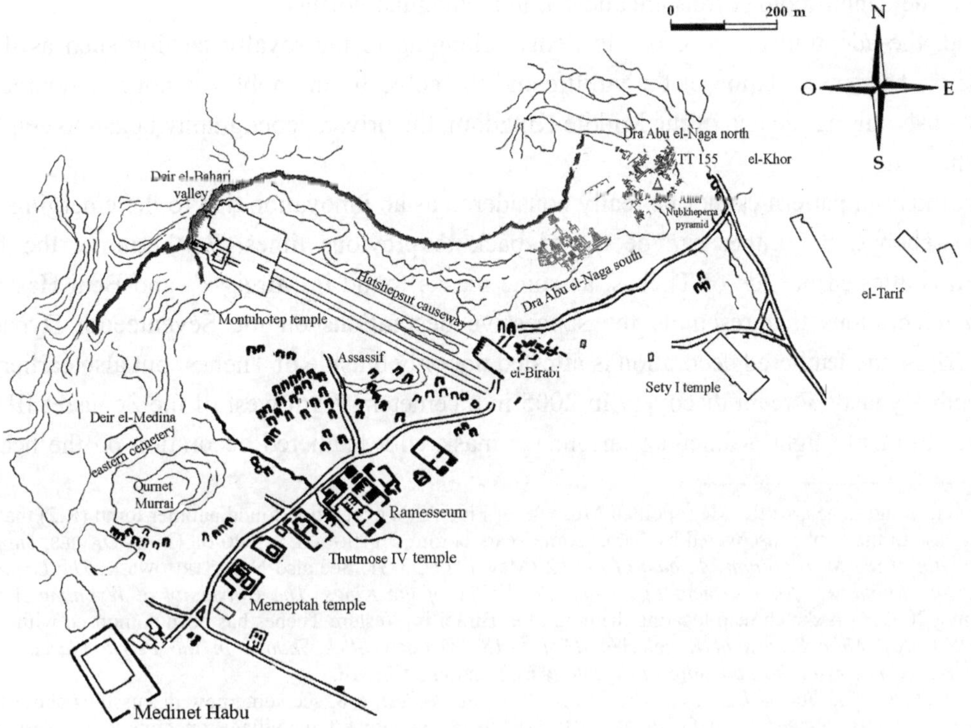

Fig. 1: Map of Western Thebes with find spots of *rishi* coffins

Through studying the provenance of the *rishi* coffins, it is remarkable that the main part of these coffins comes from the Theban Necropolis (Fig. 1): Dra Abu el-Naga north where there were the digs of Athanasi and Triantaphillos[34], Vassalli[35] and Petrie[36]; Dra Abu el-Naga south in an area called el-Birabi where Carter and Lord Carnarvon found two huge *saff* tombs with late Middle Kingdom/Early New Kingdom burials[37]; Deir el-Medina Eastern Cemetery where Bruyère found late Seventeenth/

32 HAYES, *Section II of the Bulletin of the Metropolitan Museum of Art* 30 (November 1935), 28.

33 Coffin of Taiuwy- British Museum 54350, see I.E.S. EDWARDS, *A Handbook to the Egyptian Mummies and Coffins Exhibited in the British Museum*, London 1938, 33 and C.N. REEVES/J.H. TAYLOR, *Howard Carter before Tutankhamun*, London 1992, 100 with fig.

34 M. DEWACHTER, Nouvelles informations relatives à l'exploitation de la nécropole de Drah Aboul Neggah, *Revue d'Égyptologie* 36 (1985), 49-59; ID., Un Grec de Louqsor collaborateur de Champollion et Lepsius : Ouardi Triantaphyllos, *Cahier de la Villa «Kérylos»* 5 (1995), 124; G. MINIACI, La tomba del re Antef Sekhem-Ra Wpmaat a Dra Abu el-Naga, *Egitto e Vicino Oriente* 27 (2004), 61-72.

35 Vassalli, who discovered the coffins of queen Ahhotep and king Kamose, found, in the nearby of TT 155, a cemetery of the late Seventeenth Dynasty, cf. F. TIRADRITTI, "*Luigi Vassalli*", communication held in the Mummification Museum of Luxor 20 November 2006.

36 PETRIE, *Qurneh,* 12, no. 26, pl. X B.

37 These tombs are no. 37 (MMA 5), according to Carter's numbering system, published in detail in EARL OF CARNARVON/H. CARTER, *Five Years' Explorations at Thebes: A Record of Work Done 1907-1911*, London 1912, 64-88, and no. 47, according to the latter's system, unfortunately unpublished, but rather mentioned in Gardiner's notes, A.H. GARDINER, The Tomb of a Much-Travelled Theban Official, *Journal of Egyptian Archaeology* 4 (1917), 28-38.

Eighteenth Dynasty burials.[38] Based on this archaeological evidence, the anthropoid *rishi* coffins probably originated in Thebes. Nevertheless, it is noticeable that all the distinctive features of *rishi* coffins can be already seen in an embryonic phase during the late Middle Kingdom and in the material culture of Middle and Lower Egypt.[39]

First, the anthropoid form of the Theban *rishi* coffin does not represent a new design, but rather comes from the previous tradition, developed in the centre and the north of Egypt during the Middle Kingdom, when anthropoid coffins are attested in rectangular coffins.[40]

Second, the adoption of some of the items belonging to the royalty fashion such as the *nemes* headdress or the representation of the vulture and the cobra by the nobles is not a new practice.[41] In fact, previously during the end of the Middle Kingdom, the private iconography began to employ royal items in the coffins.[42]

Third, the *rishi* pattern cannot be really considered as an innovation tied to the emerging of a new culture of Thebes, but rather can be traced back to previous times. Furthermore, the feathered decoration is attested outside of Thebes, as some masks found in Mirgissa[43] and Beni Hasan[44] show feathered decorations that resemble the successive decorations on the Seventeenth Dynasty *rishi* coffins.[45] Thus, the feathered decoration is attested not only outside of Thebes, but also earlier than the Seventeenth Dynasty. Recent discovery in 2005 in a cemetery 2 km west of the Senusret III pyramid at Dahshur brings to light a funerary cartonnage mask with feathered decoration on the headdress.[46]

Moreover, in the same area the Metropolitan Museum of Fine Art's expedition found another tomb (R.2) that showed a similar case to the tombs discovered by Carter some years before, LYTHGOE/LANSING/DE GARIS DAVIES, *Supplement of the Bulletin of the Metropolitan Museum of Art* 12 (May 1917), 3-31. See also N.C. STRUDWICK, *The Legacy of Lord Carnarvon. Miniatures from Ancient Egypt and the Valley of the Kings. The University of Wyoming Art Museum*, Wyoming 2001, 6. A sketch map locating the area of el-Birabi in Western Thebes has been composed with adaptations by P. WHELAN, *Mere Scraps of Rough Wood? 17th–18th Dynasty Stick Shabtis in the Petrie Museum and other Collections* (*Golden House Publications Egyptology* 6), London 2007, viii.

38 B. BRUYÈRE, *Les fouilles de Deir el Médineh: la Nécropole de l'est*, 6-8, see some new discussions about the eastern Necropolis of Deir el-Medina in G. PIERRAT-BONNEFOIS, Cimetière est du village ou cimetière à l'est de Deir el Medineh?, in: G. ANDREU (ed.), *Deir el-Médineh et la Vallée des Rois. La vie en Égypte au temps des pharaons du Nouvel Empire. Actes du colloque organisé par le musée du Louvre les 3 et 4 mai 2002*, Paris 2003, 51-66.

39 For more details and suggestions see G. MINIACI, L'origine dei sarcofagi rishi, *Aegyptus* 86 (2006), in press.

40 See, for example, the anthropoid coffin of Sepi (Cairo CG 28084), P. LACAU, *Catalogue général des antiquités égyptiennes du Musée du Caire Nos 28001-28086, Sarcophages antérieurs au Nouvel Empire*, Le Caire 1904, 199-200, pl. XX ; the anthropoid coffins of Nakhtankh and Khnumnakht, PETRIE, *Gizeh and Rifeh*, 12, no. 26; the anthropoid coffin of Userhet, found in the tomb no. 132 at Beni Hasan, J. GARSTANG, *Burial Customs of Ancient Egypt as Illustrated by Tombs of the Middle Kingdom. A Report of Excavations Made in the Necropolis of Beni Hassan during 1902-3-4*, London 1907, 173-174, fig. 181; the anthropoid coffin of Neferuptah, found in Hawara N. FARAG/Z. ISKANDER, *The Discovery of Neferwptah*, Le Caire 1971, 58-63; or the anthropoid coffin of Senebtisi, found at Lisht, A.C. MACE/H.E. WINLOCK, *The Tomb of Senebtisi at Lisht* (*Publications of the Metropolitan Museum of Fine Arts Egyptian Expedition* 1), New York 1916, 36-56.

41 G. JÉQUIER, *Les frises d'objets des sarcophages du Moyen Empire* (*Mémoires publiées par les membres de l'Institut français d'archéologie orientale* 47), Le Caire 1921, 13.

42 See, for example, the funerary mask of Khnumhotep from Meir, which adds on the headdress a golden uraeus, W.C. HAYES, *Scepter of Egypt* I, 310, fig. 201, or the representation of *nemes*, cobras and vultures between friezes of objects of Bersheh rectangular coffins, see H. WILLEMS, *Chests of Life. A Study of the Typology and Conceptual Development of Middle Kingdom Standard Class Coffins* (*Mededelingen en Verhandelingen van het Vooraziatisch-egyptisch Genootschap* "*Ex oriente lux*" 25), Leiden 1988, 220, group D.

43 Perhaps the best-conserved example is in the Louvre Museum (E 25702), see G. ANDREU/M. RUTSCHOWSCAYA/ C. ZIEGLER, *L'Égypte ancienne au Louvre*, Paris 1997, 100-101, no. 40. See also A. VILA, *Les masques funéraires*, in: J. VERCOUTTER, *Mirgissa* III. *Les Nécropoles*, Paris 1976, 151-263, pl. 1-4.

44 J. GARSTANG, *Burial Customs of Ancient Egypt*, 177, fig. 183.

45 A. DODSON, A Funerary Mask in Durham and Mummy Adornment in the Late Second Intermediate Period and Early Eighteenth Dynasty, *Journal of Egyptian Archaeology* 84 (1998), 93-99, pls. 14-15.

46 The mask belongs to a person called Senu, see S. YOSHIMURA, *Excavating in Egypt for 40 years, Waseda University Expedition 1966-2006*, Tokyo 2006, 194-197, 228, no. 249.

That mask can be dated back at least to the Thirteenth Dynasty, if not earlier, because it has been found in a rectangular coffin dated by style into the Twelfth Dynasty.[47] Therefore, the *rishi* design was known and already used in Lower Egypt during the Middle Kingdom, while in the south, in this period, there is no trace of such decorations.[48] Another significant case is a burial of a girl belonging to the tomb no. 1299 of Sedment cemetery, in which were found wing feathers of a hawk against the side of the head and neck under bandages.[49] This example could be considered as the archetype of the *rishi* decoration of coffins, once again found outside of Thebes.

Finally, the representation of the goddesses Isis and Nephthys under the feet of the *rishi* coffins is an element inherted from the rectangular coffins. Down to the time of Senusret III the rectangular coffins begin to represent the two goddesses on their short sides, at first without regularity, than constantly.[50]

To conclude[51], the appearance of *rishi* coffins during the Seventeenth Dynasty does not mean a sudden break with the previous traditions, but rather it expresses an evolution that probably begins at the end of the Middle Kingdom/Thirteenth Dynasty. It seems erroneous to consider the origin of the anthropoid *rishi* coffins as an external (either foreign or local – i.e. the Theban tradition) cultural tradition overlapping to a pre-existing one. However, it is possible that the power vacuum, which existed after the end of the Middle Kingdom, and the following rise of the Seventeenth Dynasty in Thebes, could have caused the emerging of new cultural and artistic stimuli. Nevertheless, most of these inputs went back to an ancient tradition that probably developed in Thebes over a long time at a lower level.

---

47 I would like to thank Wolfram Grajetzki and Masashiro Baba for the useful information and the bibliographic references.

48 The most ancient example coming from Thebes should be Cairo CG 28109 belonging to Nubhiredi that according to Dodson is datable to the very end of the Thirteenth Dynasty, see DODSON, *Journal of Egyptian Archaeology* 84 (1998), 95.

49 W.M.F. PETRIE/G. BRUNTON, *Sedment* I (*British School of Archaeology in Egypt* 34), London 1924, 18.

50 WILLEMS, *Chests of Life*, 163. See as examples for the Middle Kingdom, the coffin of Djehutihotep Cairo JE 37566 from Bersheh (A.B. KAMAL, Fouilles à Deir el-Barchè, *Annales du service des antiquités de l'Égypte* 3 (1902), 277-280); the coffin of Khnumnakht from Asiut (HAYES, *Scepter of Egypt* I, 318-319, fig. 207); as examples for the Thirteenth Dynasty, the coffin of Nekhta from Abydos (J. GARSTANG, *El-Arábah: A Cemetery of the Middle Kingdom*; *Survey of the Old Kingdom Temenos*; *Graffiti from the Temple of Sety* (*British School of Archaeology in Egypt* 6), London 1901, 6-7, pl. VI-VII, -E 252-); the coffins of Senebeni and Khensw (Cairo CG 28028, CG 28029) from Gurna (O. BERLEV, A Contemporary of King Sewah-en-Re, *Journal of Egyptian Archaeology* 60 (1974), 106-113 and P. LACAU, *Sarcophages antérieurs au Nouvel Empire*, 75-78, pl. XV); the coffin of Ikhet MMA 32.3.430 from Western Thebes (HAYES, *Scepter of Egypt* I, 348, fig. 228); the coffin of Senebhenaef Oxford Ashmolean Museum E 1953 from Abydos (W. GRAJETZKI, Another Early Source for the Book of the Dead. The Second Intermediate Period Burial D 25 at Abydos, *Studien zur altägyptischen Kultur* 34 (2006), 205-216, pl. 5-8).

51 Other published *rishi* coffins used in the present study are: Anonymous coffin- British Museum 52950 (DAVIES, *Ancient Egyptian Timber Imports*, pl. 32,2); Anonymous coffin- British Museum 52951 (TAYLOR/STRUDWICK, *Mummies. Death and Afterlife in Ancient Egypt*, 50-1); Coffin of Reri- Metropolitan Museum of Art 12.181.299 (HAYES, *Scepter of Egypt* II, 31, fig. 13); Anonymous coffin- Metropolitan Museum of Art 14.10.1 (HAYES, *Scepter of Egypt* II, 31, fig. 14, also A. HEYWOOD, The use of huntite as a white pigment in ancient Egypt, in: W.V. DAVIES (ed.), *Colour and Painting in Ancient Egypt*, 5-9, pl. II); Anonymous coffin- Metropolitan Museum of Art (LYTHGOE/LANSING/DE GARIS DAVIES, *Supplement to the Bulletin of the Metropolitan Museum of Art* 12 (May 1917), 13, fig. 10); Anonymous coffin- Boston 1987.490 a,b (D'AURIA/LACOVARA/ROEHRIG, *Mummies & Magic*, 131, no. 64); Anonymous coffin- Carter and Carnarvon excavations (EARL OF CARNARVON/CARTER, *Five Years' Explorations at Thebes*, 62, pl. LIII.3); Anonymous coffin- Staatliches Museum Ägyptischer Kunst München ÄS 1332 (GRIMM/SCHOSKE, *Im Zeichen des Mondes*, 95, cat. no. 11).

'Book of the Dead Chapter 178': A Late Middle Kingdom Compilation or Excerpts?

Stephen Quirke

1. 'Mortuary Liturgies' on Early Twelfth Dynasty Coffins

1.1. Liturgies in Coffin Texts 1-74

As Jan Assmann revealed, the outer coffin of Amenemhat (Egyptian Museum, Cairo CG 28092 = de Buck B10C), early Twelfth Dynasty mayor of Khemenu, buried at Deir el-Bersheh, carries fundamental significance for our knowledge of Middle Egyptian liturgies.[1] Like some one hundred other early Middle Kingdom coffins, the larger part of the interior faces are inscribed in cursive writings, of the position, type and date defining more or less the Egyptological corpus of Coffin Texts.[2] However, uniquely among these sources, its interior side-wall inscriptions are restricted to three main liturgical sequences, separated by a link-text unparalleled and so presumably composed for this context (CT 62 in De Buck). The recurrence of the linking-composition greatly eases the task of grasping the longer separated passages as liturgical sequences, and in one central passage Assmann could identify ancient names for the three sequences themselves:

ḫbs-tꜣ	"hacking of the earth" (in de Buck CT 1-29);
ḫnmw	"lamentations" (CT 44-61), and
ii-ṯhb-wr	"the great *ṯhb*-priest comes" (CT 63-74).

1.2. Liturgies used later as "Glorifications" of Osiris

Assmann applied this same powerfully source-grounded approach to Middle Kingdom and later sequences of passages that are individually first found inscribed in the pyramid chambers of late Old Kingdom kings and queens, known in Egyptology as the corpus of Pyramid Texts.[3] Two selections of Pyramid Texts occur in a sequence found for the first time, not on Old Kingdom monuments, but on the lid of the same outer coffin of Amenemhat and the lid of his middle coffin (Egyptian Museum, Cairo CG 28091 = de Buck B9C). The start of the same pair of selections also occurs on another early Twelfth Dynasty coffin, that of the lector Khenu from Saqqara (Egyptian Museum Cairo J 39052 = de Buck Sq4C). Over a thousand years later, the two PT sequences were inscribed on doorways of the greatest Twenty-sixth Dynasty Theban Tomb-chapels. Finally, entitled *sꜣḫw* "Glorifications" or "Transfigurations" of Osiris, the sequences appear on Ptolemaic Period temple papyri that survived because they were taken out of liturgical use and buried with individuals for their afterlife.[4] Assmann has assigned numbers to the *sꜣḫw* in order of their frequency in Ptolemaic manuscripts (*sꜣḫw* I

---

1 See now J. ASSMANN/M. BOMMAS, *Altägyptische Totenliturgien* 1 (*Supplemente zu den Schriften der Heidelberger Akademie der Wissenschaften Philosophisch-Historische Klasse* 14), Heidelberg 2002, 39-52.

2 Synoptic edition A. DE BUCK, *Egyptian Coffin Texts* I-VII (*Oriental Institute Publications* 34, 49, 64, 67, 73, 81, 87), Chicago 1935-1961; "Coffin Text" abbreviated henceforth CT in this article.

3 Synoptic edition K. SETHE, *Die altaegyptischen Pyramidentexte* I-IV, Leipzig 1908-1922: henceforth here PT; the introduction to the Middle Kingdom and later sequences is J. ASSMANN, Egyptian Mortuary Liturgies, in: S. ISRAELIT-GROLL (ed.), *Studies in Egyptology presented to Miriam Lichtheim* I, Jerusalem 1990, 1-45.

4 ASSMANN, *Egyptian Mortuary Liturgies*, 'Glorifications' II and III.

occurring on seven papyri, *s3ḫw* II on four, *s3ḫw* III on just one). On the manuscripts, they are distinguished by long titles:

> "Beginning of the Great *s3ḫw* to be recited at the 6-day, 15-day and month festivals, and at every festival of Osiris, by the chief lector of this temple" (*s3ḫw* II).
>
> "*s3ḫw* to be performed in the temple of Osiris by the chief lector of this temple, to be recited in *h3-snd* at every funerary festival" (*s3ḫw* III).

On the Middle Kingdom coffin lids inscribed for the mayor Amenemhat, the passages that became the central part of *s3ḫw* III (sections 7-9) precede the PT sequence of *s3ḫw* II, whereas on the Khenu coffin they occur with only an initial passage of *s3ḫw* II, PT 373, and on the coffin bottom rather than lid: the Assmann concordance of these sources is given below (Fig. 1).[5]

PT/CT	Sq4C	B9C	B10C 1	B10C 2	*s3ḫw* III	*s3ḫw* II
PT 593	X	X	X	X	7a	
PT 356-7	X	X	X	X	7b-c	
PT 364	X	X	X	X	7d	
PT 677	X	X	X	X	8	
PT 365	X	X	X	X	9a	
PT 373	X	X	X	X		2
PT 721	X	X	X	X	9b	3
PT 422		X	X	X		4
PT 374+CT 517		X	X	X		5
PT 424		X		X		6
PT 366-9		X		X		7-10
PT 423		X		X		11
PT 370-2		X		X		12-14
PT 332+ CT518		X		X		15
PT 468		X		X		16
PT 412		X		X		17
CT519		X		X		18
PT 690		X		X		19
PT 674		X		X		20
PT 462				X		21
PT 675-6				X		22-23
CT 837						24
CT 838-9						25

Fig. 1: PT and CT on the coffins of Khenu and Amenemhat and in *s3ḫw* II, III

5 ASSMANN, *Egyptian Mortuary Liturgies*, 36, fig. 6.

Pursuing the observations by Assmann, the same central passage of *s3ḫw* III (his sections 7-9) is included in the unique scroll-like series of funerary literature painted on the walls of the underground burial chamber of another man named Amenemhat, an accountant of grain in the Amun domain during the mid-Eighteenth Dynasty (Theban Tomb 82, see Fig. 2).[6] The PT sequence occurs on the south wall, after another ancient liturgical sequence, PT 220 to 224. The presence of PT 593-356-357-364-677-365-373 in that order already on the Middle Kingdom coffins of Khenu and Amenemhat without the other parts of *s3ḫw* III suggests that the sequence formed an important separate element, only later incorporated into the middle of the longer sequence *s3ḫw* III. However, it is also possible that the earlier sources represent extracts from an already existing longer liturgical sequence.

WEST WALL	NORTH WALL	EAST WALL	SOUTH WALL
BD 125	BD 17,18	BD 188-108-117-96+97-50-119-63B-8-93-95-94-66-119-102-38-132-45-38-29-	PT liturgy A (= PT 220 to 224) **PT liturgy B (= PT 593-356-357-364-677-365-373)** BD 80-133-134-65

Fig. 2: Burial chamber of Amenemhat, Theban Tomb 82

1.3. A Related Liturgy – 'Book of the Dead Chapter 178'

Four or five centuries later, in the mid- to late Twenty-first Dynasty, elements from these same passages are found in a remarkable composition written out on three closely-related funerary papyri, of Gautseshen, Pennesuttawy, and Ankheseniset.[7] Naville numbered the composition 'Book of the Dead chapter 178'.[8] This 'chapter', though, gives generally shorter excerpts, and they follow a different order to that of *s3ḫw* III. The other elements in BD 178 mostly comprise other PT that are also found, individually or grouped, on a range of different Middle Kingdom monument types: the Delta burial-chambers of the mayor Neha at Qatta, and Khesuwer at Kom al-Hisn; CT 788 from Twelfth and Thirteenth Dynasty coffins and stelae, also found on the pyramidia of kings Amenemhat III and Khendjer; and a group of formulae known from late Middle and Second Intermediate Period coffins found at Thebes and Abydos (numbered by de Buck as CT 777-785, but noted by Wolfram Grajetzki with additional sources as external to the main corpus of CT in the sense of the bulk of writings on early Middle Kingdom coffins).[9] A shorter version without the *s3ḫw* III elements is found on one earlier funerary papyrus, closer in time to the tomb of Amenemhat, the mid-Eighteenth

---

6 N. DE GARIS DAVIES, *The Tomb of Amenemhet (no. 82)* (*Theban Tomb Series* 1), London 1915.

7 As listed in I. MUNRO, *Spruchvorkommen auf Totenbuch-Textzeugen der Dritten Zwischenzeit* (*Studien zum Altägyptischen Totenbuch* 5), Wiesbaden 2001, 91.

8 E. NAVILLE, *Das aegyptische Todtenbuch der XVIII. bis XX. Dynastie*, Berlin 1886, and see the list of related antecedents, T.G. ALLEN, *The Book of the Dead, or Going Forth by Day. Ideas of the Ancient Egyptians Concerning the Hereafter as Expressed in Their Own Terms* (*Studies in Oriental Civilization* 37), Chicago 1974, 239: 'Book of the Dead' henceforth cited as BD.

9 W. GRAJETZKI, Bemerkungen zu einigen Spruchtypen auf Särgen des späten Mittleren Reiches, *Göttinger Miszellen* 166 (1998), 29-37.

Dynasty Book of the Dead papyrus of Nebseny, and there it has a title “formula for raising the body”.[10] Rita Lucarelli has compared the two versions of BD 178 in several details, interpreting them as a “hymn of transfiguration” in the two periods.[11]

In this contribution I seek to explore the various sources for separate elements of this “formula”, to consider their relation to larger units in which they elsewhere seem embedded, and to raise the question of the date at which the elements might have been brought together as a sequence.

2. Chronological Distribution of Elements of the “Formula for Raising the Body”

2.1 Nebseny Version, Mid- to Late Eighteenth Dynasty

T.G. Allen divided the full “formula” BD 178 into twenty-three sections, guided by the interpellation of the phrase “words spoken” in the Eighteenth and Twenty-first Dynasty papyri, and, secondarily, by the different history of segments (see appendix below for translation). He assigned to the twenty-three sections thus obtained the letters a-x (omitting j). Fifteen of these occur in the earlier version, on the mid- to late Eighteenth Dynasty papyrus of Nebseny:

a	compare PT 65b
b-h	PT Utterances 204-212 (sections 118-133)
i	CT 785 part 2
	CT 783 part 2
l	
n	
o part 1	PT Utterance 368 part (section 638) (= Utterance 588, section 1607)
s	PT Utterance 251 start (section 269) (start in CT 788 section b)
t	PT Utterance 249 end (section 266)

2.1.1 Section (a): Offering-list Recitation

The ‘formula’ begins with the address to the deceased:

“Take to yourself the eye of Horus,
Of your requirement,
The requirement of offerings”.

Though not precisely paralleled, the initial phrase is familiar as the refrain in the recitations accompanying tabulated lists of offerings, from the earliest example on the north wall of the burial chamber in the pyramid of Unas (PT 23-171).[12] In these recitations, by “sacramental interpretation” each presentation of an offering marks the restoration of the “eye of Horus”, in other words full bodily integrity and health. The “requirement of offerings” is the phrase used as caption to tabulated offering-

---

10 British Museum EA 9900: used as the main manuscript in NAVILLE, *Das aegyptische Todtenbuch*, republished by G. LAPP, *The Papyrus of Nebseny* (*Catalogue of the Books of the Dead in the British Museum* 3), London 2004.

11 R. LUCARELLI, Some Remarks about Ch.178 of the Book of the Dead, in: R. PIRELLI (ed.), *Egyptological Studies for Claudio Barocas* (*Istituto Universitario Orientale Dipartimento di Studi e Ricerche su Africa e Paesi Arabi Serie Egittologia* 1), Napoli 1999, 27-54.

12 J. OSING, Zur Disposition der Pyramidentexte des Unas, *Mitteilungen des Deutschen Archäologischen Instituts Kairo* 42 (1986), 131-144.

lists.[13] This sentence could act, then, as a summary notation for recitating the full tabulated list of offerings. Part of the Unas offering liturgy follows in BD 178, supporting this general interpretation.

2.1.2 Section (b-h): Liturgy for Presentation of Food-offerings

Sections b-h = PT 204-212, is first found on the east wall gable over the entrance in the burial chamber in the pyramid of Unas. The sequence is one of the offering-liturgies most widely-attested throughout the second and first millennia.[14] In the Middle Kingdom it occurs on the early to mid-Twelfth Dynasty burial-chamber of the mayor Neha at al-Qatta in the western Delta (East wall, lines 32-60).[15] The bulk, sections b-f, also occurs on the late Middle Kingdom stela of the greatest of tens of Upper Egypt Nehy (Egyptian Museum, Cairo CG 20520, d, lines 15-36).[16] There, it follows the earliest known occurrence of BD 148, a formula for offerings prominent in New Kingdom sources.[17] As Lucarelli observes, the combination BD 148 + BD 178 also occurs then on the rear wall of the north chapel in the mid-Eighteenth Dynasty offering-complex over the tomb of Puyemra, Theban Tomb 39.[18] There, BD 148 fills the lateral area, below an offering-frieze of depictions of kilts, sceptres, cloth, falcon-terminal broad-collars, and ointment-vessels, while elements of BD 110 and BD 178 are inscribed on the central feature of the wall, a red granite false-door stela (see below paragraph 3).

2.1.3 Section (i, k): Hour Vigil Night-offerings and Preparations to Move Outside

Sections i and k occur within a distinctive inscriptional programme on a group of late Thirteenth to early Seventeenth Dynasty coffins in Upper Egypt, in compositions numbered by de Buck CT 777-785 although not in fact found among the main CT corpus defined as writings in blocks of cursive columns on coffin exteriors and interiors.[19] In this group, CT 785 is on the exterior lid, CT 783 on the exterior front, on the two sources cited by de Buck, the coffins of Senebni and Khons (Egyptian Museum, Cairo CG 28028-9 = de Buck T6C, T10C).[20]

CT 785 (BD 178i) ends on the motif of bread-offerings in their hour of the night-offerings. The night hour reference may evoke the Hour Vigil for the embalming of Osiris, known in greatest detail from inscriptions in the Ptolemaic Period temple of Horus at Edfu.[21] The most direct evidence for Middle Kingdom use, if not composition, of the Hour Vigil is perhaps a passage inscribed on calcite

---

13 W. BARTA, *Aufbau und Bedeutung der altägyptischen Opferformel* (*Ägyptologische Forschungen* 24), Glückstadt 1968.

14 T.G. ALLEN, *Occurrences of Pyramid Texts, with Cross Indexes of These and Other Egyptian Mortuary Texts* (*Studies in Oriental Civilizations* 27), Chicago 1950.

15 L.H. LESKO, *Index of the Spells on Egyptian Middle Kingdom Coffins and Related Documents*, Berkeley 1979, 76 (Q1Q).

16 H. LANGE/H. SCHÄFER, *Catalogue général des antiquités égyptiennes du Musée du Caire Nos 20001-20780, Grab- und Denksteine des Mittleren Reiches* II, Berlin 1908, 116-120 (118-120 for lines 15-36 with BD 178b-f).

17 LUCARELLI, *Remarks on Ch.178*, 39.

18 N. DE GARIS DAVIES, *The Tomb of Puyemre at Thebes* (*Publications of the Metropolitan Museum of Art Egyptian Expedition* 2-3), New York 1922-1923, pl. XLVIII.

19 GRAJETZKI, *Göttinger Miszellen* 166 (1998), 29-37 (see footnote 7).

20 'CT 777-784' are arranged similarly on the lost coffin of a king's wife Mentuhotep dated to the Second Intermediate Period (late Thirteenth to early Seventeenth Dynasty); the missing 'CT 785' might have been on the lid, not recorded, see C. GEISEN, *Die Totentexte des verschollenen Sarges der Königin Mentuhotep aus der 13. Dynastie. Ein Textzeuge aus der Übergangszeit von den Sargtexten zum Totenbuch* (*Studien zum altägyptischen Totenbuch* 8), Wiesbaden 2004, 28-30.

21 H. JUNKER, *Die Stundenwachen in den Osirismysterien nach den Inschriften von Dendera, Edfu und Philae* (*Denkschriften der Kaiserlichen Akademie der Wissenschaften Philosophisch-Historische Klasse* 54), Wien 1910.

libation vessels found in late Twelfth Dynasty royal burials.[22] The Edfu inscription identifies these words as accompanying the second libation in the second night hour of the Osiris Hour Vigil. The Book of the Dead papyri of Gautseshen and Pennesuttawy, two of the four sources for BD 178, contain a copy of this libation passage.[23]

In CT 783, Horus destroys enemies, notably a "thief", at the entrance of the threshold. Conceivably, this is the moment when an embalmer intruded, to make the necessary, but sacrilegious cut into the body, enabling removal of dangerously soft matter. A move to the entrance might be related to this removal of the internal organs. However, the following sections l-n involve justification, suggesting instead that the body was being moved outside for a ritual judgement of the deceased. If the two motifs are to be combined, cutting the body (presumably near the start of the seventy days of embalming) might have been followed by an initial judgement ritual. This would not tally with other evidence for a judgement ritual on the dawn of the day of burial, unless a judgement rite occurred more than once in the long cycle of rites from death to burial.

2.1.4 Section (l, n): Middle Egyptian Liturgical Declarations of Justification

Allen noted no earlier parallels for sections l and n. They refer to the balance and the night of silencing lament, evoking the judgement of the deceased. Section l sets the scene in Hutwer, perhaps the place of a bull-sacrifice in association with judgement during the burial rites.[24]

2.1.5 Section (o, part 1): 'Nut Formula', Liturgical Declarations at Packing Body in Natron

Section o part 1 is the 'Nut formula' PT 638, found on mid-Twelfth Dynasty and later coffin-lids, including those of the early Thirteenth Dynasty king Auibra Hor and the king's daughter Nubhetepti-khered buried at Dahshur (Egyptian Museum, Cairo CG 28106, 28104 = de Buck Da4C, Da2C). According to its phrasing, the sky-goddess Nut is to spread herself over the deceased as *štt-pt*, perhaps "lake-lady of the sky" and protects the deceased as "the Great Sieve". Harco Willems has drawn attention to, and given a full explanation for, the prominence of the sieve in Middle Kingdom and later depictions and inscriptions.[25] The phrase might, then, specifically denote the salt lake sources for natron, Wadi Natrun and/or the Upper Egyptian sources near Elkab. If so, this widely-attested passage PT 638 would provide a "sacramental interpretation" for the sieving of natron over the body, presumably the crucial stage in the physical treatment to preserve the body of the deceased. Like the possible reference to the embalming-cut, the sieving seems to place this part of BD 178 as a liturgy relatively early in the process of embalming. However, the same passage recurs in the 'Glorifications'

---

22 From Lahun, vessel of Sathathoriunet, W.M.F. PETRIE/G. BRUNTON/M.A. MURRAY, *Lahun* II (*British School of Archaeology in Egypt* 33), London 1923; from Hawara, vessel fragments of king Amenemhat III and king's daughter Neferuptah, W.M.F. PETRIE, *Kahun, Gurob, and Hawara*, London 1890, pl. V.

23 E. NAVILLE, *Papyrus funéraires de la XXIe dynastie* II, *Le Papyrus hiératique de Katsehsni au Musée du Caire*, Paris 1914, pl. I-LXV; MUNRO, *Spruchvorkommen*, 91.

24 F. GOMAÀ, *Die Besiedlung Ägyptens während des Mittleren Reiches* II: *Unterägypten und die angrenzenden Gebiete* (*Beihefte zum Tübinger Atlas des Vorderen Orients Reihe B* 66.2), Wiesbaden 1987, 325-326, sources including an inscription of king Khaneferra Sobekhotep from Abydos, Louvre C10, evoking the judgement vindicating Osiris and Horus, see W. HELCK, *Historisch-biographische Inschriften der Zweiten Zwischenzeit* (*Kleine Ägyptische Texte* 6.1), 2nd edition Wiesbaden 1983, 5, line 7, and depictions of burial rites in the Twelfth Dynasty chapels of Intefiqer for his wife Senet at Thebes, and Djehutyhotep at Deir el-Bersheh, for which see J. SETTGAST, *Untersuchungen zu altägyptischen Bestattungsdarstellungen* (*Abhandlungen des Deutschen Archäologischen Instituts Kairo Ägyptologische Reihe* 3), Glückstadt 1963, 27.

25 H. WILLEMS, The Embalmer Embalmed. Remarks on the Meaning of the Decoration of Some Middle Kingdom Coffins, in: J. VAN DIJK (ed.), *Essays on Ancient Egypt in Honour of Herman te Velde* (*Egyptological Memoirs* 1), Leiden 1997, 343-372.

that seem to mark the last twenty-four hours before burial. The passage may, then, recall and merge in the person of Nut two different physical presences over the body of the deceased – first the sieve and the natron sifted through it onto the body, early in embalming, and later the coffin-lid lowered into place after embalming has been completed.

2.1.6 Section (s): Address to the Masters of Hours

Section s is an appeal for free passage to the "masters of hours", PT 269, in the second part of CT 788, found on the early Thirteenth Dynasty coffin of the lady of the house Satsobek, buried at Dahshur (Egyptian Museum, Cairo CG 28105 = de Buck Da3C). The designation "master of hours" again evokes the Hour Vigil, perhaps serving as the appeal on each hour at the arrival of the new set of watchers.

2.1.7 Section (t): 'Nefertem Formula'

Section t is the 'Nefertem formula' PT 266, recurrent among late Thirteenth to early Seventeenth Dynasty coffins in Upper Egypt, the best preserved and only fully published being that of the king's ornament Nubherredi (Egyptian Museum, Cairo CG 28030 = de Buck T7C). As Grajetzki notes, the formula is attested on coffin fragments from Second Intermediate Period cemeteries at Hu, as well as at Thebes.[26] In the mid-Eighteenth Dynasty, it also occurs in the inscriptions of the chapel of Puyemra, Theban Tomb-chapel 39 (see below paragraph 3). As the culmination of the liturgy in the Nebseny version, this passage evidently carried particular weight. Nefertem seems an incarnation of the divine essence of scented oils, which would be of especial importance in the final stages of embalming and anointing; a closing rite of anointing would account for the relevant prominence of the formula among the inscriptions on the Upper Egyptian Second Intermediate Period coffins.[27]

Section t also occurs in a PT sequence found in two unusual Book of the Dead papyri (Neferwebenef, mid-Eighteenth Dynasty, and Muthetepti, Twenty-first Dynasty), and numbered by Naville BD 174, section c end.

2.1.8 Nebseny Version Summary

In the Nebseny version, the sequence of actions seems to move from food-offerings (a-h), to preparations for moving outside (i-k), declarations of the deceased as true of voice (l, n), preservation of the body in natron (o), a request for access (s), and a revivifying final application of unguent = Nefertem (t). The whole sequence in this shorter version on the papyrus of Nebseny bears the title "formula for raising the body", indicating perhaps the dawn of the funerary procession, as the body was raised for the last time into the coffin and moved out of the embalming-place.

---

26 W. GRAJETZKI, The Second Intermediate Period Model Coffin of Teti in the British Museum (EA 35016), *British Museum Studies in Ancient Egypt and Sudan* 5 (2006), 4.

27 For Nefertem and scented oil, see H. SCHLÖGL, s.v. *Nefertem*, in: W. HELCK/W. WESTENDORF (eds.), *Lexikon der Ägyptologie* IV, Wiesbaden 1982, 378-380.

2.2 Twenty-first Dynasty Version

The longer version of the Twenty-first Dynasty adds these nine further elements, mainly from the Pyramid Texts found in *s3ḫw* II start and *s3ḫw* III sections 7-9:

m	
o part 2	PT Utterance 422 part (sections 752-754a start) (*s3ḫw* II.4)
p	PT Utterance 677 start (sections 2018-2021a) (in *s3ḫw* III.8)
q	CT 788 section a
r	PT Utterance 356 part (sections 575-576a) (*s3ḫw* III.7b)
u	PT Utterance 252 start (section 272) (M57C lines 74-81; T13C lines 2)
v	PT Utterance 364 part (sections 609-610b) (*s3ḫw* III.7d)
w	PT Utterance 677 end (section 2028) (in *s3ḫw* III.8)
x	PT Utterance 677 part (section 2023) (in *s3ḫw* III.8)

2.2.1 Section (m): Justification Declarations

Section m, not previously known, is inserted between the two sections in the Nebseny version not known from sources before the New Kingdom (Allen sections l, n), and expands on the theme of justification.

2.2.2 Section (q): Opening the Sight to See the Lord of the Horizon

Section q comes from the 'pyramidion formula' CT 788, a composition inscribed on the east face of the pyramidia of Amenemhat III and Khendjer.[28] The end of 'CT 788' occurs already in the Nebseny version section s, also found in the Twenty-first Dynasty manuscripts. At this stage, the deceased, mummified and coffined, is perhaps exposed for the first time since death to the sunlight.

2.2.3 Section (u): Address to the "Gods of the Underworld", Deceased as the "Great God"

The start of PT 252 is written at the head of the mid- to late Twelfth Dynasty coffin of Sobekherheb from Meir (M57C) and on the lid of the coffin of Hemenhotep (T13C), in the Second Intermediate Period Upper Egyptian group to which the coffin of Nubherredi also belongs. It is also inscribed on the mid-Eighteenth Dynasty red granite false-door stela of Puyemra from Theban Tomb-chapel 39, and ends Book of the Dead chapter 112 (see below paragraph 3). From these sources, it may be identified as an address marking a moment of outstanding significance within the rites from embalming to burial, perhaps to the deceased in the cemetery ("gods of the underworld") who would be passed in procession after the completion of embalming. By the process of mummification, the deceased has become a "great god", the status of Ra and Osiris.

28 For locations on sources in chronological order, see P. VERNUS, Deux inscriptions de la XIIe dynastie provenant de Saqqara, *Revue d'Égyptologie* 28 (1976), 124; on the "opening of the face", see too H. WILLEMS, *Chests of Life. A Study of the typology and Conceptual Development of Middle Kingdom Standard Class Coffins* (*Mededelingen en Verhandelingen van het Vooraziatisch-egyptisch Genootschap "Ex Oriente Lux"* 25), Leiden 1988, 168-9, and A. LOHWASSER, *Die Formel "Öffnen des Gesichts"* (*Veröffentlichungen der Institute für Afrikanistik und Ägyptologie der Universität Wien* 58 = *Beiträge zur Ägyptologie* 11), Wien (1991).

2.2.4 Sections from *s3ḫw*

The remaining six sections, individually discussed below 2.2.5-2.2.10, are all from the Pyramid Text sequence first found on the early Twelfth Dynasty coffins of Amenemhat and Khenu, and finally on the Ptolemaic Period papyri, entitled *s3ḫw* "glorifications" of Osiris (*s3ḫw* II start, and *s3ḫw* III, central part).

2.2.5 Section (o, part 2): Departure of the Deceased Transfigured and Crowned

PT 422 opens with this acclamation, which becomes an element in the Glorifications of Osiris (*s3ḫw* II section 4), PT sequences found on the middle and outer coffins of mayor Amenemhat. A slightly shorter excerpt is inscribed around the outer right band of the red granite stela of Puyemra, mid-Eighteenth Dynasty (Theban Tomb-chapel 39, see below paragraph 3), and the middle part is inscribed after CT 1, 20-21 from the funeral liturgy *ḫbs-t3* in the tomb-chamber of Khesuwer at Kom al-Hisn.[29]

The wording implies an acclamation of the mummified body as it moves finally out of the embalming-chamber, after the seventy days of treatment.

2.2.6 Section (p): Raising and Crowning of the Deceased after Being Prostrate

PT 677 begins with a recurrent phrase in the funerary literature, announcing that the "great god is fallen on his side" followed by the declaration that he stands, and is crowned. Further passages from PT 677 occur at the end of BD 178 separately as sections w and x (cf. below 2.2.9-10). In the Glorifications of Osiris on Middle Kingdom coffins and the Late Period to Ptolemaic Period sources, PT 677 is not divided in this way, forming instead an integral part of a sequence PT 677+365+373 (respectively *s3ḫw* III, sections 8-9a, *s3ḫw* II, section 2).[30] This section is also found on the lid from the coffin of Khutkhentkhety, wife of Ipiankhu (Egyptian Museum, Berlin 18105).[31]

2.2.7 Section (r): Arrival of Horus to Protect the Deceased, Now "Fixed"

PT 356 recounts the presence of Horus, arrived to drive off the enemies of the deceased, who is now said to be "fixed", presumably, then, after completion of the treatment and perhaps wrapping of the body. The phrase "to drive off enemies" may imply that Horus arrives to lead the deceased on a journey during which protection is required, here most likely the final journey from embalming-place to burial-place, or a stage of that journey. A slightly longer excerpt of PT 356 occurs in the Glorifications of Osiris (*s3ḫw* III, section 7b) also found in the mid-Eighteenth Dynasty Theban Tomb of Amenemhat TT 82 (burial chamber, lines 37-41).

2.2.8 Section (v): Arrival of Horus to Open the Eye, the Gods to Bind the Face

In PT 364 Horus arrives to equip the deceased with his eye, and to open his eye, after which the gods tie on the "face". Presumably these actions denote a ritual of opening the eyes and mouth, preceding the definitive fastening of the mummy-mask in place over the head of the deceased. It is not clear whether this presents from a different speaker or role the same action as in section t, where Horus arrives and the mask is fastened, or whether this is a second rite of arrival and fastening. Again, the

[29] LESKO, *Index of Spells*, 57 (KH1KH).

[30] In that sequence on middle and outer coffins of Amenemhat B9C-B10C and coffin of Khenu Sq4C; also in the mid-Eighteenth Dynasty Theban Tomb of Amenemhat TT 82, burial chamber, lines 67-75.

[31] ALLEN, *Occurrences of Pyramid Texts*, 98.

Glorifications of Osiris give a longer excerpt, also found in the Theban Tomb of Amenemhat TT 82 (burial chamber, lines 47-66; *s3ḫw* III, section 7d). Further excerpted or expanded versions of PT 364 occur in the Deir al-Bahri tomb-chamber of Senenmut.[32]

2.2.9 Section (w): Ra Purifies the Deceased Standing with Nut, They Lead Him to the Burial-place

The final words of PT 677 inform the deceased that the sun-god purifies him as he stands with Nut, so under the open sky, and/or in his coffin, and that they then "lead him on the ways of the horizon" to make his good monuments there with his ka-spirit forever. This part of PT 677 is inscribed on the red granite stela of Puyemra (see below, section 3), and occurs in a Middle Kingdom sequence preceding, rather than following, PT 364, as preserved in the Deir al-Bahri tomb of Senenmut from the mid-Eighteenth Dynasty.[33] For other parts of PT 677 (see above 2.2.6 on section p), with its occurrence in "Glorifications" *s3ḫw* III.

2.2.10 Section (x): The Deceased Issues Commands to the "Secret of Places"

This final section of the long version of BD 178 found in the Twenty-first Dynasty papyri presents the deceased as law-giver for the "secret of places", perhaps a reference to those buried in the cemetery. The deceased becomes, like Ra and Osiris, the foremost of the westerners. This seems also to be the part of PT 677 with which the central part of "Glorifications" *s3ḫw* III finishes in the version on the wall of the burial-chamber of Amenemhat in Theban Tomb TT 82.[34]

2.2.11 Twenty-first Dynasty Version Summary

The first half of the liturgy follows the model seen in Nebseny, with offering liturgy (a-h), preparations to move outside (i, k) and a here extended declaration that the deceased is true of voice (l-n). After justification, as in the Nebseny version, a passage evokes the treatment of the body where natron is passed through a sieve over the deceased (o part 1). The next section (o part 2) contains the acclamation of the deceased preparing for his final journey; accompanying this is the statement on the raising and arraying of the deceased after the period of lying prostrate (p), and, continuing the theme of emergence, the formula to open the sight to the sun-god (q). Horus now arrives to lead the procession in which the deceased needs to be protected against enemies (r). Returning to the Nebseny version, there is the appeal to the masters of hours for access, perhaps, in this context after r, spoken by the Horus role (s), and the anointing associated with opening the eyes and fastening the mask over the head (t). The longer version concludes with four passages added to the Nebseny version: the "gods of the underworld" (those already buried in the cemetery?) are told of the divine, specifically Ra/Osirian status of the deceased (u); Horus arrives (again?) to open the eyes, as the gods fasten the mask over the head (v, cf. t); Ra shines on the deceased standing with Nut, and the two deities lead him to his funerary monument – this then is the burial procession (w); the deceased is declared to be the lawgiver of the "secret of places" (again, those already buried in the cemetery?) (x).

---

32 ALLEN, *Occurrences of Pyramid Texts*, 78: PT sections 609-610b on South wall, line 48 = ceiling inscription B, ASSMANN/BOMMAS, *Totenliturgien* I, 517-8, inscription A comprising PT 424-366-367 from the *s3ḫw* II sequence; PT sections 609-613a on North wall, lines 33-35 cf. Assmann's spells 14 and 20 of 'Glorifications CT 4', ASSMANN/BOMMAS, *Totenliturgien* I, 500 and 508-513.

33 ASSMANN/BOMMAS, *Totenliturgien* I, 499-500, 'Glorifications CT 4' section 13.

34 ALLEN, *Occurrences of Pyramid Texts*, 98, PT sections 2018-2023a in lines 67-75.

3. The Red Granite Stela of Puyemra: Link to a Processional Liturgy of Sacred Places

To this point it is not clear whether this is a Middle or a New Kingdom liturgical sequence: that is, whether (1) the array of different earlier sources represent excerpts from an already existing unitary Middle Kingdom liturgy BD 178, though only alluded to earlier, in elements attested separately on different sets of coffins and other monuments, or (2) BD 178 is a New Kingdom compilation of excerpts of previously separate compositions and liturgies. This question can be developed with reference to another New Kingdom source, the red granite false-door stela of Puyemra. This monument introduces a further source-group, far commoner in the extant written record of both the Middle and the New Kingdoms: the 'formulae for knowing the ba-souls of sacred places'.

Theban Tomb 39 is the offering-complex over the burial-place of Puyemra, god's father and second god's servant of Amun in the mid-Eighteenth Dynasty. The rear wall of its north chapel was clad in inscribed limestone blocks, only partly preserved, but with elements of BD 148, one of the main New Kingdom formulae for offerings, under a frieze of offerings. The frieze includes, on left, a capped hes-vase, two axes on a box, cloth, and a falcon-terminal collar with counterpoise, and, on the right, two *ḫrp*-sceptres, two *šndyt*-kilts, and another falcon-terminal collar.[35] The centre-piece of the wall was the great red granite false-door stela with image of Puyemra and his wife before a ka-sign and table of offerings, over double vertical column of inscription identifying him as *imȝḫy*, and then elements of BD 110 and 178 arranged in three framing bands of inscription (Fig. 3).

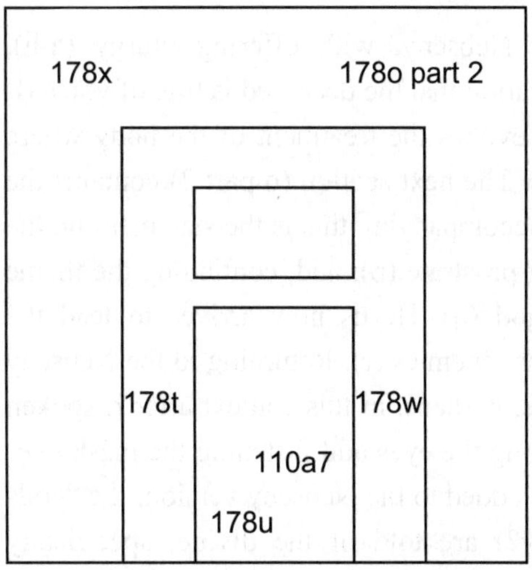

BD 178o part 2: **departure** transfigured and crowned

BD 178w: Ra purifies deceased standing with Nut, they lead him to burial place

BD 178t: Nefertem = final anointing?

BD 110a7: **arrival** clad with headcloth

BD 178u: **arrived** as great god (address to gods of underworld)

BD 178x: issues commands (address to those "secret of places")

Fig. 3: False-door stela of Puyemra, showing distribution of parts of BD 110 and BD 178

The right inner band of inscription presents an excerpt from the culmination of the guide to the Marsh of Offerings, BD 110, in which the deceased declares to the Hesat-cow, embodying milk, that he has arrived, equipped with the head of the blue-eyed Horus.[36]

35 DAVIES, *Tomb of Puyemre*, pl. XLVIII, LI.

36 ALLEN, *Egyptian Book of the Dead*, 89, BD 110 a7 section 2.

"O Hesat, I have come with you.
Lapis-lazuli encircles,
I have followed the winds of the Nine Gods.
It is the great god who gives me my head,
Who binds my head for me,
The blue-eyed Horus."

This passage evokes the blue and gold striped nemes-headcloth familiar from anthropoid coffins and mummy masks starting from the mid-Twelfth Dynasty.[37] Here the passage appears incorporated into a setting otherwise dominated by passages found in the second half of BD 178. One of these passages, BD 178u in the same band to the left, terminates another of the CT/BD formulae for knowing sacred places, BD 112.[38] There, it stands separate from the main body of the formula with its aetiology of the abomination of the black boar by the followers of Horus. In general the formulae for knowing sacred places CT 154-160/BD 107-116 form a distinctive group in their narration of mythological episode, and are often found as a spatially bound unit on both Middle Kingdom CT coffins, and New Kingdom and later BD papyri. The phrase ending BD 112, and found also as BD 178u, reads:

"Raise your faces, O gods who are in the underworld, for I am come to you.
You shall see him, now that he is become the great god."

The address to underworld gods would suit a procession through the cemetery area, and the reference to "become the great god" indicates the transformation of the deceased in acquiring the status of the two deities known at this period as "great god", Osiris and Ra.[39] Therefore the passage can be read as the wording of a declamation at a station along the route of the procession from embalming-chamber to burial-place. The formulae for knowing ba-souls of named places might involve in part, then, a "sacramental interpretation" of landscapes passed by the funeral procession on its way from embalming-chamber to burial-place. This view has been argued for another set of sources by Willems, after Altenmüller: "After mummification, the procession left the place of embalmment (*sḥ-nṯr*), passing by three halting places symbolizing holy cities in the Delta: Sais, Buto and Hut-ser"[40], moving by small boat on water to Sais, and on ox-drawn sled to Buto overland. Willems also interprets depictions and inscriptions concerning a funerary journey to Abydos as a nocturnal rite, leaving the security of the embalming place for a dawn ritual judging and justifying the deceased.[41] Not all these rites need have involved movement by boat along stretches of river or canal: if the Egyptians conceived of the coffin as a boat, and libations as its sailings, funerary rites of "sailings" might be cast as rites within the embalming-chamber.[42] However, it seems plausible that the messy business of treating the body, involving quantities of water constantly renewed in the washing of the body, took place in a separate space, ideally close to a water-source, and that some literal journey was involved in

---

37 Tomb of Two Brothers: W.M.F. PETRIE, *Gizeh and Rifeh* (*British School of Archaeology in Egypt* 13), London 1907, pl. XB; general Sep: Egyptian Museum, Cairo CG 28084.

38 ALLEN, *Egyptian Book of the Dead*, 91, BD 112b.

39 O.D. BERLEV, Two Kings - Two Suns. On the Worldview of the Ancient Egyptians, in: S. QUIRKE (ed.), *Discovering Egypt from the Neva. The Egyptological Legacy of O.D. Berlev*, Berlin 2003, 19-35.

40 WILLEMS, *Chests of Life*, 145-146.

41 H. WILLEMS, *The Coffin of Heqata* (*Cairo JdE 36418*). *A Case Study of Egyptian Funerary Culture of the Early Middle Kingdom* (*Orientalia Lovaniensia Analecta* 70), Leuven 1996, 132-133.

42 WILLEMS, *Chests of Life*, 157; ID., *Heqata*, 176-7.

moving from that space to the burial-place. Only more careful archaeological excavation of cemetery sites can resolve the question.

The 'formulae for knowing the ba-souls of places' refer to other spaces, with the one overlap of Pe (Buto) but even that counterpoised here not to other Delta cities but rather to its Upper Egyptian opposite Nekhen. The ba-souls of Pe and Nekhen are regularly depicted as trios kneeling and striking their chests, a gesture designated *hnw* in Egyptian.[43] The 'formulae for knowing' these participants in ritual could have been deployed either within the embalming-chamber, or on the final and risky procession from there to the tomb; only the inclusion of the "Raise your faces" address implies a journey passing by the blessed dead resting in the cemetery. In the Middle Kingdom version, the formulae titles refer to the following beings of places:

CT 154	know ba-souls of Iunu, entering Iunu
CT 155	know ba-souls of New Moon, entering House of Osiris of Djedu
CT 156	know ba-souls of Khemenu, be among followers of Osiris of Djedu
CT 157	know ba-souls of Pe
CT 158	know ba-souls of Nekhen
CT 159	know ba-souls of the Easterners
CT 160	know ba-souls of the Westerners

In the New Kingdom, some reinterpretation can be seen in the changes in selection (CT 155 dropped, CT 156, 159, 160 reworked as multiple chapters) and titles (marked bold here):

CT 154	BD 115	Iunu
CT 155	-	
CT 156	BD 114, 116	Khemenu
CT 157	BD 112	Pe
CT 158	BD 113	Nekhen
CT 159	BD 107 (later BD 109)	**Westerners** BD 107, Easterners BD 109
CT 160	BD 108, BD 111	Westerners BD 108, **Pe** BD 111 in Dynasty 19

Only one other of these formulae includes such an address appended to aetiologies, following the account of the conflict of Seth and the serpent on the mountain of Bakhu, the eastern horizon terrain, in BD 111:

> "Raise yourself from your right side, alive, renewed, youthful, like Ra every day.
> You shall never die".[44]

Such declarations might be expected to accompany mummification, at moments when the embalmers had to raise it during the treatment of the body, rather than a journey. However, they might also be appropriate at later moments when the body was raised, for example, to be placed into the coffin, or

43 WILLEMS, *Heqata*, 56 as the gesture of officiants in the offering-ritual; ASSMANN/BOMMAS, *Totenliturgien* I, 14 as gesture accompanying *sꜣḫw* "glorifications".

44 ALLEN, *Egyptian Book of the Dead*, 91, BD 111b, from the mid-Eighteenth Dynasty burial chamber of Amenemhat, Theban Tomb-chapel 82.

when the coffin itself was raised at any stage of its last journey, or at the very end of the journey when the coffin was moved off its bier, down the tomb-shaft, and into its final resting-place.

These two exhortations to arise are found on Middle Kingdom coffins, but not within the series CT 154-160 (that is, in CT 157 = BD 112, CT 160 = BD 111). Accordingly they might be interpreted as New Kingdom additions to the series, extraneous to the Middle Kingdom sequence. Nevertheless, they could provide a contemporary liturgical dimension, as that seems appropriate to the series of 'formulae for knowing sacred places' if understood as an "accompanying composition" for a liturgy of embalming and procession. As outlined in the list below, despite variation, the preferred location for CT 154-160 on Middle Kingdom coffins seems to be the head and foot ends, so below precisely the offering-frieze areas where Willems has noted the concentration of images of purification materials – sieve, ankh-shaped cloths, and sacred oils.[45]

Locations of CT 154-160 on Middle Kingdom coffins:

1. Top: B2Bo (Djehutynakht inner), B17C (Neferi)
2. **Front, head-end**: B4Bo (Djehutynakht inner), also perhaps but only CT 154 to 157 S3C (Itib)
3. **Foot to back, foot-end**: B1C (Sep outer), B1Y
4. Front to back: CT 154, 160 only B3C (Sathedjhotep); CT 154 to 157 only S9C (Tjuau)
5. **Head to foot**: B9C (Amenemhat middle), B1L (Gua inner)
6. **Head to foot to front**: B2P (Sep inner)
7. **Head to front**: and second time on back B4L (Sen outer)
8. **Head**: S2P (Nakhti inner); CT 154 to 158 only S1C (Mesehty inner) perhaps completed CT 157 to 160 on S2C top (Mesehty outer)

Pursuing equivalences proposed by Willems, and taking as guide the liturgical addenda to BD 112 = CT 157 and BD 111 = CT 160, the formulae CT 154-160 might be aligned with the following moments or themes, in a speculative manner intended only to illustrate the kinds of possibilities for future interpretation and research:

CT 154	enter Iunu	to open court after embalming
CT 155	enter House of Osiris of Djedu	place on vehicle for journey?
CT 156	know ba-souls of Khemenu	accompaniment of lector=Thoth?
CT 157	know ba-souls of Pe	address blessed dead (BD 112b)
CT 158	know ba-souls of Nekhen	pendant address (to south side?)
CT 159	know ba-souls of the Easterners	burial dawn rites?
CT 160	know ba-souls of the Westerners	raising coffin (BD 111b)

On the themes of 'knowing souls of sacred places' and embalming, it may also be worth considering the association of purification vignettes with BD 110 and BD 178 in the papyri of Nebseny and Gautseshen. For Gautseshen, the two formulae and vignette of purification mark the end of the whole papyrus. For Nebseny BD 178 is placed at the centre of the manuscript, after BD 110 with its purification vignette, and BD 177, a PT liturgical sequence entitled on this source "formula for raising the transfigured spirit".[46]

[45] WILLEMS, *The Embalmer Embalmed*, 343-372 (see footnote 25).
[46] LAPP, *Papyrus of Nebseny*, pl. 49-57.

4. Liturgical Sequences as Excerpts of Varying Separability

From the discussion of BD 178 and related series of compositions, the inscribed funerary monuments throughout second and first millennia appear to capture varying moments and sequences of moments in a single vaster cycle of action, the seventy days from first death to revivifying burial. Each inscribed surface mediates our encounter with that long and intensely verbalised process; even the liturgical papyri do not provide either a comprehensive or even necessarily a direct guide to the drama. To call this drama the embalming ritual, would fail to recognise its scope and multifocal essence; instead, paradoxically, it may better be grasped by articulating it as a web of active communicative sequences with overlapping intent. Embalming as the physical treatment of the deceased is one part of the drama: the body has to be packed in natron, which is sieved to remove any impurities and perhaps to obtain the particular density most suited to preservation of the body. The embalming moment appears to be evoked by the Nut formula, in BD 178, section o part 1. It is preceded by the entire, already composite, task, ritualised, of bringing the body of the deceased from place of death into embalming chamber. Here may belong the rite of justification, as well as after the embalming: the deceased must deserve the rites of mummification. This may be why the justification passages of BD 178 precede the sieving of natron (sections l-n). To be sustained, though, the deceased already first needs food and drink: accordingly, BD 178 begins with a food-offering liturgy, before even the deceased has been declared true of voice (sections a-h). Before judgement, the night-offerings are followed by the protection of the deceased by Horus against a "thief", possibly the person cutting the body for removal of soft organs, for preservation of the body but disturbing its wholeness (sections i-k). After justification (l-n), it seems, the final journey begins: by its end, the deceased rules the world of their afterlife as lawgiver to the gods whose places are hidden, the buried dead (section x).

Several of the sequences seem stable across sources, and Assmann has shown how, in the context of the middle coffin of mayor Amenemhat, three even received their own name as anciently/ "emically" separable units. Yet, it remains the case that names for sequences of funerary rituals are an exception. The paratextual habit of nominalising each "compositional unit/sequence" seems not to have obsessed the ancient world as it does our print-trained minds; that should already place us on guard against reifying repeated ancient deployments of words as inscription. As always in Egyptology, our corpora are necessary tools of research, establishing stable objects of reference without which further understanding would be near impossible, and yet the very existence of the object of reference should not blind us to the essentially modern motivation – to provide objects of study. In other words, instead of liturgies, the monuments communicate to us liturgical sequences variably excerpted more or less often in varying contexts. Out of these more or less flexible written sequences, as distributed by date over different types of inscribed funerary monuments, we can reconstruct more of an original broader sequence. Equally important, we can understand more of their deployments, and more of the limits to our ability ever to reconstruct a full sequence of the hundreds of thousands of words uttered by any one cast in the ancient Egyptian drama from death to rebirth.

APPENDIX: TRANSLATIONS

Version in the Papyrus of Nebseny, copyist in the Ptah temple at Memphis, late Eighteenth Dynasty, about 1375 BC, British Museum EA 9900

[Title]
Formula for raising up the body,
Opening the eyes, strengthening the ears,
Establishing the head set in its protection.
Words spoken by
The writer, copyist of the Ptah temple, Nebseny, lord of reverence,
Who says:

[Allen section a]
Take to yourself the eye of Horus,
Of your requirement,
The requirement of offerings (= the offering-list).

[Allen section b]
Words spoken:
The hoer rejoices,
The heart is lifted, to purify the chest,
When they consume the gleaming eye of Horus,
That is in Iunu.

O this the writer, copyist of the Ptah temple, Nebseny,
They remove what is in the body of Osiris,
Made by the thirsting of the mouth of
The writer, Nebseny, lord of reverence before his god.
He shall not hunger, he shall not thirst,
The writer of the Ptah temple, Nebseny,
The desert-god has rescued him,
Removing his hunger,
Filled, filled, of hearts.

Version in the Papyrus of Pennesuttawy, late Twenty-first Dynasty, about 975 BC, British Museum EA 10064

[Title]

Words spoken by
The Osiris, pure-priest, head boat captain of the Amun domain, Pennesuttawy, true of voice:

[Allen section a]
Take to yourself the eye of Horus,
Of your requirement,
The requirement of offerings (= the offering-list).

[Allen section b]
Words spoken:
The hoer rejoices,
The heart is lifted, to purify the chest,
When they consume the gleaming eye of Horus,
That is in Iunu.

O this Osiris Pennesuttawy, true of voice, small of voice,
They remove what is in the body of Osiris,
Made by the thirsting of the mouth of
Osiris Pennesuttawy, true of voice.
He shall not hunger, he shall not thirst,
This Osiris Pennesuttawy, true of voice,
The desert-god has rescued him,
Removing his hunger,
Filled, filled, of hearts.

Version in the Papyrus of Nebseny

[Allen section c]
Those in charge of pouring of bread,
That is, the keepers of the flood-rise,
Command for
The writer, copyist of the Ptah temple, Nebseny,
As commanded by Ra himself.

Ra has commanded him to
Those who are in charge of the victuals of this year.
They grasp and give him barley and emmer,
His bread is indeed for the Great Bull-god.

May you give to
The writer, Nebseny,
The (role of) keeper of the five loaves in the temple,
Three loaves being in the sky, before Ra,
Two leaves being at the land, before the Nine Gods.
See then (?) Nun, he sees, he sees, O Ra.
It is good for
The writer, copyist of the Ptah temple, Nebseny,
On this good day.

The writer, Nebseny,
Is lord of reverence,
By command of Shu and Isis.
The writer, Nebseny,
Has joined with reverence,
Beautiful before his god.
May they give bread and beer to
The writer, Nebseny,
May they do for him all good and pure things
On this good day.

[Allen section d]
Offerings for his guide,
Offerings are transported,
For the one who is in the eye.
Offerings for the boat,
All who shall enter to see the god.
May you have power over water,
May you tread amid the offering-table,
After an offering-loaf and four basins of water,
Under the command of Osiris for
The writer, Nebseny.

[Allen section e]
Shu has commanded his things for
The writer, Nebseny.
That is your bread and your beer.

Version in the Papyrus of Pennesuttawy

[Allen section c]
Those in charge of pouring of bread,
the keepers of the flood-rise,
He commands for
This Osiris Pennesuttawy, true of voice,
Your bread, cupbearer of Ra,
As Ra has commanded himself for him.
Ra has commanded him to
Those who are in charge of the victuals of this year.
They grasp and give, they clench and give him
barley and emmer, bread and beer.
He is the Great Bull-god.
May you strike Seth,
This Osiris Pennesuttawy, true of voice,
The keeper of the four loaves in the temple,
Three loaves to the sky, before Ra,
Three loaves to the land, before the Nine Gods.
See then (?) Nun, he sees, good keeper,
The Osiris Pennesuttawy, true of voice,
Today more than yesterday.
He has copulated with male liquid (?),
He has breathed Shu in place (?),
Osiris Pennesuttawy, true of voice,
Has joined the titulary (?),
He has copulated with the beautiful woman,
Terror (?) of the Two goddesses Right,
As she hovers to the count (?).
Good is the terror of
This Osiris Pennesuttawy, true of voice.
She gives bread to
This Osiris Pennesuttawy, true of voice,
May all good and pure things be done for him
On this day.
[Allen section d]
Offerings for his guide,
Offerings are transported,
For those who are in the eye.
Offerings for the boat.
The one who is in the eye of the god enters
To the control of water, and flame of fire.
Tread with the offering of a loaf and four basins of water.
The Osiris Pennesuttawy, true of voice,
flourishes.

[Allen section e]
Shu shall not take his things and vice versa,
Repeat your deliveries,
open your bread and your beer.

Version in the Papyrus of Nebseny

[Allen section f]
The opener awakes,
Thoth is tall,
The sleeper awakes,
The one who is in Kenset (?) stirs.
You are given offerings
In the presence of Thoth.
The Great God is gone out as the Nile-flood god.
Wepwawet is gone out from the tamarisk city.
Pure is the mouth of
The writer, copyist of the Ptah temple, Nebseny,
The Nine Gods cense the mouth of
The writer, Nebseny.
Pure is his mouth, truly (?),
And this tongue that is in his mouth.
Excrement is the abomination of
This the writer, Nebseny,
He avoids urine,
like the avoidance of it by the town Two Companions.
Thoth proceeds to the sky.
May you all take with you
The writer, Nebseny,
May he eat of what you eat,
May he drink of what you drink,
May he sit where you sit, where you have power,
May he sail where you sail.
The pavilion of
The writer, Nebseny,
Is woven in the town Rushes.
The flood-rise of
The writer, Nebseny,
Is in the Marsh of Offerings.
His offering-piles are among the gods.
The waters of
The writer, Nebseny,
Are as the wine of Ra.
He circles the sky, he roams like Thoth.

Version in the Papyrus of Pennesuttawy

[Allen section f]
Message of Osiris,
Thoth is tall,
The sleeper awakes,
The one who is in Kenset (?) stirs
In the presence of Thoth.
The Great God is gone out as the Nile-flood god.
[Wepwawet is gone out from the tamarisk city.]
Pure is the mouth of
The Osiris Pennesuttawy, true of voice,
The Nine Gods cense the mouth of
This Osiris Pennesuttawy, true of voice,
His mouth, and this tongue that is in his mouth.
Excrement is the abomination of
The Osiris Pennesuttawy, true of voice,
He shall not drink urine,
like the avoidance of it by the town Two Companions.
Proceed to the sky, travel with Thoth.
May you all take with you
The Osiris Pennesuttawy, true of voice,
May he eat of what you eat,
May he drink of what you drink,
May he sit where you sit,
May he have power as they have power,
May he sail where you sail.
The pavilion of
The Osiris Pennesuttawy, true of voice,
Is in the Marsh of Reeds.
The flood-rise of
The Osiris Pennesuttawy, true of voice,
Is in the Marsh of Offerings.
His offering-piles are among you, O gods.
The waters of
This Osiris Pennesuttawy, true of voice,
Are as the wine of Ra.
He circles the sky, he roams like Thoth.

Version in the Papyrus of Nebseny

[Allen section g]
Hunger is the abomination of
The writer, Nebseny,
He does not eat it.
Thirst is his abomination.

The writer, Nebseny,
Is the one to whom bread has been given
By the lord of eternity.
His command is carried out.
The writer, Nebseny,
Was conceived in the night,
He was born at dawn.
He belongs to the following,
before the god of the Morning Star.

He has brought to you the bread that he found.

[Allen section h]
The eye of Horus waters over a bush of ...
The Foremost of the Westerners [comes to him].
He has brought provisions and offerings
To Horus foremost of the Houses.
What he lives on,
The writer, copyist of the Ptah temple, Nebseny, lord of reverence,
Lives on;
What he drinks of,
The writer, copyist of the Ptah temple, Nebseny,
Drinks of;
A haunch together with a loaf are his offerings.
True of voice is
The writer, Nebseny,
Favoured by Anubis who is upon his mountain.

[Allen section i]
Words spoken:
O writer Nebseny,
Your form is that in which you existed on earth,
Alive, youthful every day.
May your face be opened
To see the lord of the horizon,
That he may give bread to
The writer, Nebseny,
In his hour, at his time of night.

[Allen section k]
Horus has greeted you,
He has destroyed the jaws of your enemies,
Seizing the thief at the entrance of the stronghold.

Version in the Papyrus of Pennesuttawy

[Allen section g]
Hunger is the abomination of
This Osiris Pennesuttawy, true of voice,
He shall not eat it.
Thirst is his abomination,
He shall not drink it.
This Osiris Pennesuttawy, true of voice,
Shall be the one to whom bread is given forever.
His two nurses are She who is powerful in her action
And She whom he praises (?).
This Osiris Pennesuttawy, true of voice,
Shall be one conceived as Osiris in the night,
This Osiris Pennesuttawy, true of voice,
Shall be born at daybreak.
He belongs to the following,
The god preceding the morning-star god.
This Osiris Pennesuttawy, true of voice,
Is conceived in the Primeval Waters,
And is born in the Primeval Waters.
He comes, binding the bread for you,
And he shall not be found.

[Allen section h]
The eye of Horus waters over a bush of the *denu*-plant,
Keeper of its mouth for the Foremost (?) of the Westerners.
He has brought provisions
To Horus foremost of the Houses.
What he lives on,
This Osiris Pennesuttawy, true of voice,
Lives on,
and what he drinks of;

A haunch together with a loaf are his offerings.
True of voice is
Osiris, pure-priest, head boat captain of the Amun domain, Pennesuttawy, true of voice,
Favoured by Anubis who is upon his mountain.

[Allen section i]
Words spoken:
This Osiris Pennesuttawy, true of voice, born to Tameni
This your form is that in which you existed on earth,
Alive, youthful (?) every day.
May your face be opened
To see the lord of the horizon,
That he may give bread to the one who has no bread
At the hour of their time of night.

[Allen section k]
Horus has greeted you,
He has destroyed the jaws of your enemies,
Seizing the thief at the entrance of the stronghold.

Version in the Papyrus of Nebseny

[Allen section l]
Words spoken:
O writer Nebseny,
You have no enemies in Hutwer,
The balance is level on your moment,
That is its breadth for Osiris,
Who is lord of victuals of the west.
He goes in at his desire,
To see the great god in his forms.
He is given life at his nose,
And justification against his enemies.

[Allen section n]
Words spoken:
O writer Nebseny,
Lies are your abomination.
The lords of offerings have pacified you,
On that night of silencing lament.
You are given sweet life
From the mouth of the Nine Gods.
Thoth is content over it,
You are justified against your enemies.

[Allen section o, part 1]

Writer, Nebseny,
Nut has spread herself over you,
In her name of lake-lady of the sky.
She causes you to be in the following of the great god.
You have no enemies.

She rescues you from all evil things,
In her name of the Great Sieve.
You are the eldest among her children,
O writer, Nebseny.

Version in the Papyrus of Pennesuttawy

[Allen section l]
Words spoken:
O this Osiris Pennesuttawy, true of voice,
There is no slaughter of you in Hutwer,
The balance is free from a fault of yours,
That is its breadth for Osiris,
Who is lord of victuals of the west.
It means that he can go in and out in the temples,
To see the great god in his forms.
He is given life at his nose,
And justification against his enemies.

[Allen section m]
Words spoken:
Osiris Pennesuttawy, son of Inpehefnakht, true of voice,
You are a transfigured spirit who is in the god's land,
Embraced in the broad court
of the Judge of the Two Companion-gods, who acted against you,
The one bearing your wound is against their head,
(*space left blank = part missing in source from which this was copied*),
Sky and earth are opened (?),
You have sweetened the eye that was raging,
As you were over the heads of those who acted against you.
I have saved you in the broad court.
Horus has made your ka-spirit,
As you are over this noble god, living forever.

[Allen section n]
Words spoken:
O this Osiris Pennesuttawy, true of voice,
Slaughter is your abomination.
You shall not perish, there shall be no blood.
The lords of offerings have pacified you,
On that night of silencing lament.
Your offering is sweet life
(*space left blank = part missing in source from which this was copied*),
… from the mouth of the Nine Gods.
Thoth is content with you,
You are justified against your enemies.

[Allen section o, part 1]
Words spoken:
O this Osiris head boat captain of the Amun domain,
Pennesuttawy, true of voice,
Your mother Nut spreads herself over you,
In her name of spread of the sky.
She causes you to be a god,
You have no enemies,
In your name of god.
She unites you away from all things,
In her name of the Great Sieve.
You are the one among their children,
O this Osiris Pennesuttawy, true of voice,

Version in the Papyrus of Pennesuttawy

[Allen section o, part 2]
You have gone, you have been transfigured,
You have become powerful in the places of the god.
Your ba-soul has acted for you within her,
With your power behind you,
And your Great Crown yours upon you,
As foretold for you, in front of you,
With your face in your presence,
And your mourners in front of you,
With the followers of the gods following you,
O this Osiris Pennesuttawy, true of voice.

[Allen section p]
Words spoken:
O this Osiris head boat captain of the Amun domain,
Pennesuttawy, true of voice,
The great god falls on his side,
The god stands, he is powerful with him.
His Great Crown on his head is as the Great Crown of Ra,
When he goes out from the horizon,
You are greeted by Horus in the horizon.

O this Osiris head boat captain of the Amun domain,
Pennesuttawy, true of voice,
Take to yourself this his dignity,
Made for you by the Nine Gods,
You shall be on the throne of Osiris,
In the seat of the Foremost of Westerners.

[Allen section q]
Words spoken:
The face is opened of
This Osiris head boat captain of the Amun domain,
Pennesuttawy, true of voice,
That he may see as he sails across the sky.
May he ascend,
This Osiris Pennesuttawy, true of voice,
To the great god.
It is a never-perishing star, lord of eternity,
Osiris head boat captain of the Amun domain,
Pennesuttawy, true of voice.

[Allen section r]
Words spoken:
O this Osiris, pure-priest, head boat captain of the Amun domain,
Horus comes to you to save you,
He has caused Thoth to make Seth retreat from you,
He has brought them to you, the two nests,
He has forced back for you the heart of your enemy.
You are this fixed god.

Version in the Papyrus of Nebseny

[Allen section s]
Words spoken:
O master(s) of the hours,
Those who are first of Ra,
Make a way for
The writer, Nebseny, lord of reverence,
That he may pass by within the circuit
of Osiris, lord of the life of the two lands,
Living for eternity.

[Allen section t]
Words spoken:
The writer, copyist of the Ptah temple,
Nebseny, lord of reverence, fair one,
Is in the following of Nefertem,
The lotus at the nose of Ra,
He ..[…]
Pure and godly, in the presence of the gods,
To see Ra for eternity.

Version in the Papyrus of Pennesuttawy

[Allen section s]
Words spoken:
O master of the hours,
He who is first of Ra,
Make a way for
Osiris Pennesuttawy, true of voice,
That he may pass by within the circuit
of Osiris, lord of life, living for eternity.

[Allen section t]
Words spoken:
Osiris, pure-priest, head boat captain of the Amun domain, Pennesuttawy, true of voice,
Arises as Atum,
The lotus at the nose of Ra,
As he goes out from the horizon
The gods are pure
To see him every day.

[Allen section u]
Words spoken:
Raise your faces, you who are in the underworld.
There has come
Osiris Pennesuttawy, true of voice, born of Tameni,
You see him as he becomes a god.
Initiate
Osiris Pennesuttawy, true of voice,
He shall not perish, he shall not be destroyed, forever.

[Allen section v]
Words spoken:
O Osiris, pure-priest, head boat captain of the Amun domain, Pennesuttawy, true of voice,
Horus has come to count you among the gods.
Horus loves you, he has provided you with his eye,
Horus has joined you with his eye, then,
Horus opens your eye for you,
So that you may see by it,
And the gods bind your face,
Osiris Pennesuttawy, true of voice.

[Allen section w]
Words spoken:
O Osiris, pure-priest, head boat captain of the Amun domain, Pennesuttawy, true of voice,
Pure one, [Ra finds you standing] with your mother Nut,
They lead to the way of the horizon,
Where you have made your resting-place,
It is good with your ka-spirit forever.

Version in the Papyrus of Pennesuttawy

[Allen section x]
Words spoken:
O Osiris, pure-priest, head boat captain of the Amun domain, Pennesuttawy, true of voice,
You issue commands to those whose places are secret,
Noble guide in all their transfigurations,
In their name of secret of place,
O this Osiris, pure-priest, head boat captain of the Amun domain, Pennesuttawy, true of voice.

ꜥḥ3wtyw of the Middle Kingdom

Danijela Stefanović

smn tw n.i di.i ptr.k ḏrt ꜥḥ3wty

Establish yourself for me, for I shall cause you to see the hand of a warrior[1]

The title *ꜥḥ3wty* belongs to the regular military titles of the Middle Kingdom.[2] R.O. Faulkner has suggested that the *ꜥḥ3wtyw* are professional, trained soldiers.[3] According to S. Quirke this title was lower in rank than that of the ordinary soldier (*ꜥnḫ*).[4] In the literature, *ꜥḥ3wty* is usually rendered as a term that defines "soldier" or "warrior".

The twenty-one known holders of the title *ꜥḥ3wty* are attested on monuments of the Middle Kingdom.[5] Within the titulary of the *ꜥḥ3wtyw* other administrative or rank titles are not recorded.[6] The members of their families, if and when they are mentioned with titles, belong to the lower stratum of society. The activities in which the *ꜥḥ3wtyw* are involved point to their military engagement. Their tasks, including communication between forts, monitoring and controlling local Nubians, are well attested in the Semna Despatches.[7] Despatch no. 2 reports about their monitoring action:[8]

> ... *iw* [*h3b*] *n b3k-*[*im*] ... (3) *ꜥḥ3wty 5 nty* ... *p3 ꜥ* ... *rdi.n sn b3k-im ḥr* ... (4) *h3b b3k-im* ... *iw.sn r smi.t* [*n*] ... (5) *b3k-im ḥr.s r n3 n* ... *m dd(t) mnw n mnw swḏ*[*3-ib pw ḥr.s*]
>
> ... [This] servant [wrote] ... five *ꜥḥ3wtyw* who (?) ... the track upon [which] this servant had placed them (?) ... (when?) this servant writes/wrote ... (when?) they come to report [to] ... this servant because of it, regarding (?) these ... (this) being something a fortress gives to (another) fortress [= official mail]. [It is a communica]tion [because of it] ...

1 W.F. Edgerton/J.A. Wilson, *Historical Records of Ramses III: The Texts in Medinet Habu Volumes I and II translated with explanatory notes* (*Studies in Ancient Oriental Civilizations* 12), Chicago 1936, 140, pl. 111, col. 30.

2 A. Erman/H. Grapow (eds.), *Wörterbuch der Ägyptischen Sprache* I, Berlin-Leipzig 2nd ed. 1957, 217; W. Ward, *Index of Egyptian Administrative and Religious Titles of the Middle Kingdom*, Beirut 1982, no. 618, 619-624; S. Quirke, The Regular Titles of the Late Middle Kingdom, *Revue d'Égyptologie* 37 (1986), 122; Id., *Titles and bureaux of Egypt 1850-1700 BC.* (*GHP Egyptology* 1), London 2004, 100.

3 R.O. Faulkner, Egyptian Military Organization, *Journal of Egyptian Archaeology* 39 (1954), 40. Cf. R.J. Leprohon, Les forces du maintein de l'ordre dans la Nubie au Moyen Empire, in: C. Berger/G. Clerc/N. Grimal (eds.), *Hommages à Jean Leclant* II (*Bibliothèque d'Études* 106/2), Le Caire 1994, 287; J. Bourriau, *Pharaohs and Mortals. Egyptian Art in the Middle Kingdom* (exhibition catalogue), Cambridge 1988, 55-56.

4 S. Quirke, *The Administration of Egypt in the Late Middle Kingdom*, New Malden 1990, 192.

5 As for the prosopography of the holders of this title, contained in the work of D. Stefanović, *The Holders of the Regular Military Titles in the Period of the Middle Kingdom: Dossiers* (*GHP Egyptology* 4), London 2006, Doss. 957-976, there can be added the *ꜥḥ3wty* Nekht (*nḫt*) attested on two fragments of a coffin from Beni Hasan tomb no. 135 (Fitzwilliam Museum Cambridge E.216.1903; cf. J. Garstang, *The Burial Customs of Ancient Egypt as Illustrated by Tombs of the Middle Kingdom Being a Report of Excavations Made in the Necropolis of Beni Hassan during 1902-3-4*, London 1906, 217, tomb register). I wish to thank Dr. W. Grajetzki for bringing the monument to my attention.

6 Except Khusobek (*ḫwj-sbk*); see below p. 127.

7 P.C. Smither, The Semnah Despatches, *Journal of Egyptian Archaeology* 31 (1945), no. 2, 3, 4.

8 Smither, *Journal of Egyptian Archaeology* 31 (1945), 7; C. Vogel, *Ägyptische Festungen und Garnisonen bis zum Ende des Mittleren Reiches* (*Hildesheimer Ägyptologische Beiträge* 46), Hildesheim 2004, 79.

The duties of the *ꜥḥ3wtyw* from Mirgissa, according to the Despatch no. 3 were similar:[9]

> (7) *kt šꜥt init n.f m inyt m-ꜥ mr šnṯ sbk-wr nti m iḳn* (8) *m dd(t) mnw n mnw* (9) *swḏ3-ib pw n sš.k ꜥnḫ wḏ3 snb r ntt p3 ꜥḥ3wty 2 mḏ3y 70 (?)* (10) *šm m-s3 p3-ꜥ m 3bd 4 prt sw 4 iwi r smit n.i m hrw pn (11) ḥr tr n mšrw ini.n.sn mḏ3y 3 ḥr (?)... ḥr ... 4 (?)* ... (12) *r ḏd gmi.n.n st ḥr rsyt p3 ꜥḏ ḥr ḫrw t3 ḫtit nt šmw* (13) *mitt st 3 ḫrw.fy st ꜥḥꜥ.n wšd.n.i n n3 n mḏ3yw r ḏd* (14) *ij.n.ṯn tn ꜥḥꜥn ḏd.n.sn ij.n.n ḥr ḫnmt ibh3y*
>
> Another letter which was brought to him, being one that was brought from *mr šnṯ*[10] Sobekwer (*Sbk-wr*), who is in Iken, (this) being something a fortress gives to (another) fortress. It is a communication to your scribe - may he live, prosper and be healthy - about the fact that those two *ꜥḥ3wtyw* and seventy (?) Medjay-people who went following the track in the fourth month of the Seed season, day 4, came to report to me on this day at the time of evening, having brought three Medjay-men ... four ... saying, "We found them on the south of the desert's edge, below the inscription of the Harvest season, (and) likewise three women (?)" – so they said. Then I addressed these Medjayu, saying: "Where have you come from ?" – Thereupon they said, "We have come from the well of Ibhay!".

Despatch no. 4, sent from Serra East, records:

> (7) *kt šꜥt init n.f m-ꜥ šmsw imny nt ḫsf mḏ3(y)w m dd(t) mnw n mnw* (8) *swḏ3-ib pw n nb.i ꜥnḫ wḏ3 snb r ntt ꜥḥ3wty n nḫn snw s3 ḥrw s3 rn-iḳr* (9) *ꜥḥ3wty n ṯbw rnsi s3 s-n-wsrt sp* (10) *iwi r smit n b3k-im rnpt sp 3 3bd 4 prt sw 2 ḥr tr n iꜥw* (11) *m wpwt ꜥnḫ n niwt ḫwi-sbk mnṯw-ḥtp ḫwi-sbk ...irti m* ... (12) *nti m idn ꜥnḫ n ṯt ḥḳ3 m iwꜥyt nt mh3 r ḏd iwꜥit pri (?)* (13) *r pḫrt ꜥḏ 3wt ... mnnw ḫsf mḏ3iw m rnpt sp 3 3bd 3 prt sw ꜥrḳi* (14) *iwi r smit n.i rḏd gmin.n ꜥ n siw 32 ꜥ3 3 ḫnd.n.sn*
>
> Another letter which was brought to him by the *šmsw* Ameny (*imny*), who is in (the fortress called) "Repelling the Medjay", (this) being something a fortress gives to (another) fortress. It is a communication to my Master, l.p.h., about the fact that the *ꜥḥ3wty* of Hierakonpolis Senu's (*snw*) son Heru's (*ḥrw*) son Reniker (*rn-iḳr*) and the *ꜥḥ3wty* of Qaw el-Kebir Renesi's (*rnsi*) son Senusret's (*s-n-wsrt*) son Sepi (*sp*) came to report to this servant in regnal year 3, fourth month of the Seed season, day 2, at the time of breakfast, on the business of the *ꜥnḫ n niwt* Khusobek's (*ḫwj-sbk*) son Mentuhotep's (*mnṯw-ḥtp*) son Khusobek (*ḫwj-sbk*) ... who represents (?) the *ꜥnḫ n ṯt ḥḳ3* in the garrison troop of Meha, saying: "The patrol that went forth to survey the desert's edge [which extends to] the fortress 'Repelling the Medjay' in regnal year 3, third month of the Seed season, last day, have come to report to me, saying 'We have found the track of 32 men and three asses, which they trod'".[11]

In the source mentioned above the title *ꜥḥ3wty* is followed by territorial designation[12], which means that these "soldiers" probably originated from Hierakonpolis and Qau el-Kebir and their units were

---

9 SMITHER, *Journal of Egyptian Archaeology* 31, (1945), 7-8; VOGEL, *Festungen und Garnisonen*, 80, 107.

10 For the title in question see QUIRKE, *Revue d'Égyptologie* 37 (1986), 122, note 45: WARD, *Index of Titles*, no. 390; QUIRKE, *Titles and Bureaux*, 106; R.J. LEPROHON, A New Look at an Old Object. Stela M.F.A. 13.3967/20.1222, *Journal of the Society for the Study of Egyptian Antiquities* 12/2 (1982), 75-76.

11 SMITHER, *Journal of Egyptian Archaeology* 31, 1945, 8; VOGEL, *Festungen und Garnisonen*, 81, 107. Cf. D. FRANKE, Ursprung und Bedeutung der Titelsequenz Sab Ra-Nechen, *Studien zur Altägyptischen Kultur* 11 (1984), 168.

12 WARD, *Index of Titles*, no. 621, 624.

organized in the frame of a specific territory. However, as C. Vogel points out, we do not know anything about the system for sending those people to the garrisons of Nubia.[13] The *ʿḥ3wtyw* are also recorded on the Nubian stela from el-Girgawi near Korosko (*RILN* 74) dated in the year 18 of Senusert I. The monument belongs to the "overseer of the double granary" Mentuhotep (*Mnṯw-ḥtp*). The inscription is not in a good condition, but it is clear that the text reports, as do stela Florence 2540 and the tomb inscriptions of Sarenput I (*S3-rnp.wt*) at Qubbet el-Hawa and of Amenemhat (*Ỉmn-m-ḥ3.t*) at Beni Hasan, the main campaign of Senusret I against Kush.[14]

The further Nubian examples are coming from Areika. The Areika settlement with its pottery, stamp and scarab sealings, and graffiti indicate that Egyptians occupied it during the first half of the Twelfth Dynasty. Among the Egyptians present at the site during the Middle Kingdom there were – according to the evidence – soldiers who appear to have had a role in controlling the C-group population. Their duties were perhaps similar to those attested in the Semna Despatches.

J.W. Wegner states that Areika was originally built as a military and administrative installation and that it may be understood as a manifestation of Middle Kingdom military and administrative control in the Amada region.[15] He points to the group of eight mud stamp-sealings, all produced from the same seal, with the striding upright figure wearing a feather on his head and holding a bound captive. Above the captive is a zoomorphic symbol.[16] Objects similar to the Areika sealings have also been found at other sites in Lower Nubia. The fortresses of Buhen and Kuban provide stamp-sealings which are direct parallels of those from Areika; the figure on the Buhen and Kuban examples holds a bow in hand.[17] The fact that they were associated with the Egyptian fortresses argues that they were used within activities of the military and administrative control of Lower Nubia during the Middle Kingdom. According to Wegner, the iconography of seals is iconography of an *ʿḥ3wty*.[18] It is known from the Semna Despatches, and already mentioned above, that *ʿḥ3wtyw* were present in the zone of Lower Nubia during the Middle Kingdom, as well as that such soldiers were concerned with controlling and monitoring the Nubians. In this case, the kneeling bound figure on the stamp-sealing is a Nubian. Hieroglyphic and animal symbols used on these seals, according to him, may be identified as emblems of *ʿḥ3wtyw* military companies, or the different regions with which various units were associated because they correspond to both nome symbols and attested military standards.[19] For Wegner these troops of *ʿḥ3wtyw* "came from different nomes during the conquest of Lower Nubia and

---

13 SMITHER, *Journal of Egyptian Archaeology* 31 (1945), SD no. 4, 8, pl. IV/1; VOGEL, *Festungen und Garnisonen*, 115.

14 Cf. C. OBSOMER, *Sésostris Ier. Étude chronologique et historique du règne* (*Collection Connaissance de l'Égypte ancienne* 5), Bruxelles 1995, doc. 120, 319-321; W.K. SIMPSON, Mentuhotep, Vizier of Sesostris I, Patron of Art and Architecture, *Mitteilungen des Deutschen Archäologischen Instituts Kairo* 47 (1991), 331-340; W. GRAJETZKI, *The Middle Kingdom of Ancient Egypt*, London 2006, 42; D. STEFANOVIĆ, *The Army of Pharaonic Egypt in the Period of the Middle Kingdom* (in Serbian; unpublished PhD thesis), Belgrade 2006, chap. I.4.

15 J.W. WEGNER, Regional Control in the MK Lower Nubia: The Function and History of the Site of Areika, *Journal of the American Research Center in Egypt* 32 (1995), 128.

16 WEGNER, *Journal of the American Research Center in Egypt* 32 (1995), 144-145, fig. 9; cf. D.M. RANDALL-MACIVER/ C.L. WOOLLEY, *Areika* (*University of Pennsylvania, Publications of the Egyptian Department of the University Museum, Eckley B. Coxe Junior Expedition to Nubia* 1), Oxford 1909, 9; T. SÄVE-SÖDERBERG, *Ägypten und Nubien. Ein Beitrag zur Geschichte altägyptischer Außenpolitik*, Lund 1941, 132.

17 H.S. SMITH, *The Fortress of Buhen. The Inscriptions* (*Egypt Exploration Society Excavation Memoir* 48), London 1976, pl. XLVIII and W.B. EMERY/L.P. KIRWAN, *The Excavations and Survey between Wadi es-Sebua and Adindan 1929-1931*, Cairo 1935, 55 fig. 36; cf. WEGNER, *Journal of the American Research Center in Egypt* 32 (1995), 146, fig. 10.

18 WEGNER, *Journal of the American Research Center in Egypt* 32 (1995), 147. Compare with WH no. 6. (A. FAKHRY, *The Egyptian Deserts. The Inscriptions of the Amethyst Quarries at Wadi el Hudi*, Cairo 1952, fig. 20).

19 WEGNER, *Journal of the American Research Center in Egypt* 32 (1995), 147; cf. R.O. FAULKNER, Egyptian Military Standards, *Journal of Egyptian Archaeology* 27 (1941), 12-19.

formed the foundation of the military force used in the conquest".[20] He therefore suggests that different units of *ʿḥ3wtyw* possessed military emblems closely associated with the nome symbols of the regions they came from although it is not just limited to nome symbol.[21] The same system is perhaps attested on the geographical additions to the title itself.

The role of *ʿḥ3wtyw* in Nubia seams to be clear. However, the holders of the title in question are also attested north of Elephantine. What do we know about their duties in their homeland? Were they used by government for more peaceful actions? The inscription Wadi el-Hudi no. 6 dates to year 16 of Senusret I and reports the bringing of amethyst.[22] The expedition was led by *mr mnf3t*, *šmsw* Rensi (*rnsi*). Among the expedition members we find *ḏ3mw nḫt mšʿ n nfrw* from Thebes, 200 *ʿḥ3wtyw* from *3bw* (Elephantine) and 100 *ʿḥ3wtyw* from *nbyt* (Ombos).[23] One *ʿḥ3wty n niwt* is attested on rock inscription Wadi el-Hudi no. 84.[24] The rock inscription Wadi Hammamat no. 61, also from the reign of Senusret I, gives a detailed list of all expedition members. The segment of a text, defined by D. Farout as a "military" one (it lists various categories of "soldiers" engaged in mission), is "captioned" with *ʿḥ3wty*.[25] We may suppose that the term *ʿḥ3wty* in this case, as well as for the example mentioned above, was used as common modifier for all expedition members under the arm. The aim of missions was not the military one, but it is more than possible that such enterprises had armed escort. Moreover, soldiers might serve as additional source of labour.

The further evidence for *ʿḥ3wtyw* comes from the tomb of Djehuty-Hetep (*Ḏḥwtj-ḥtp*) from Deir el-Bersheh. In the depiction of a colossal statue being hauled along a road by a large number of men divided in four rows we may see, among others, the *ḏ3mw nw ʿḥ3wtyw n wnw* ("*ḏ3mw* of the warriors/soldiers of the Hare nome"). According to Faulkner's conclusion *ḏ3mw nw ʿḥ3wtyw* refers to the "troops of the warriors".[26] In the beginning of the inscription above the group of the *ḏ3mw nw ʿḥ3wtyw* it says:[27]

> *ḏd mdw (in) nfrw n ḏ3mw ir n nb.f*
> Words spoken by the young men of *ḏ3mw*, those created by their lord.

Some differences can be seen through the clothing of the hauliers. In the two external rows ("*ḏ3mw* of the west of the Hare nome" and "*ḏ3mw* of the east of the Hare nome") the men are all dressed in a close-fitting linen loincloth and a few have shaven heads. The priests ("the phyla of the *wʿb*-priests of the Hare nome") have the same loincloth but are distinguished by the large proportion of shaven heads. The *ʿḥ3wtyw* have a greater variety of clothing, with loincloths open at the front which is hidden

---

20 WEGNER, *Journal of the American Research Center in Egypt* 32 (1995), 147.

21 WEGNER, *Journal of the American Research Center in Egypt* 32 (1995), 147.

22 A.I. SADEK, *The Amethyst Mining Inscriptions of Wadi el-Hudi* I, Warminster 1980, 16-19 (no. 6); FRANKE, *Studien zur Altägyptischen Kultur* 10 (1983), 168, n. 38; K-J. SEYFRIED, *Beiträge zu den Expeditionen des Mittleren Reiches in die Ost-Wüste* (*Hildesheimer Ägyptologische Beiträge* 15), Hildesheim 1981, 11-16; O. БЕРЛЕВ, Общественные отношения в Египте эпохи Среднего царства, Москва 1978, 168-170; ID., A Social Experiment in Nubia during the Years 9-17 of Sesostris I, in: M.A. POWELL (ed.), *Labor in the Ancient Near East*, New Haven 1987, 144-148; ID., Les prétendus "citadins" au Moyen Empire, *Revue d'Égyptologie* 23 (1971), 37-38; OBSOMER, *Sésostris Ier*, doc. 67.

23 WARD, *Index of Titles*, no. 619, 620.

24 SADEK, *Wadi el-Hudi* I, 72-73; STEFANOVIĆ, *Military Titles*, Doss. 976.

25 D. FAROUT, La carrière du *wḥmw* Ameny et l'organisation des expéditions au Ouadi Hammamat au Moyen Empire, *Bulletin de l'Institut français d'archéologie orientale* 94 (1994), 143-172.

26 FAULKNER, *Journal of Egyptian Archaeology* 39 (1954), 40; ID., *A Concise Dictionary of Middle Egyptian*, Oxford 1962, 319; cf. F.L. GRIFFITH/P.E. NEWBERRY, *El Bersheh* I (*Archaeological Survey of Egypt* 3), London 1895, 21, pl. XV.

27 GRIFFITH/NEWBERRY, *El Bersheh* I, 21, pl. XV.

by a white, brown or green piece of material, fastened to the belt. Others have a much shorter rounded loincloth. They are not shaved and some wear ostrich feathers in their hair.[28] The appearance of the *ḏ3mw nw ʿḥ3wtyw* engaged in the transport of the statue of the nomarch Djehuty-Hetep is almost identical with the depiction of soldiers in the war scenes from the Middle Kingdom tombs.[29] There is one more attestation from Bersheh. In the tomb no. 1 we find one *ʿḥ3wty (n) t3-mḥw*.[30] However, Akhanakht (*ʿḥ3-nḫt*), the nomarch of Bersheh during the First Intermediate Period, claims for himself: *ink ʿḥ3[wty]* – "I am the one who *ʿḥ3[wty]*".[31]

The *Cursus honorum* of Khusobek[32], the famous soldier of the Middle Kingdom, may speak in favour of the military character of the title in question. The stela Manchester 3306, the most important written source for campaigns into Levant under Senusret III, reports his military actions. According to Faulkner's translation Khusobek, at the beginning of his carrier, was appointed as *ʿḥ3wty m ḫt* – "warrior of the bodyguard".[33] Faulkner, as H.G. Fischer notes, suggested the reading of the title with a query, and the meaning may also be "rear guard".[34]

Beside Khusobek, seven more *ʿḥ3wtyw* are attested on stelae.[35] The Abydos stela CG 20746 is of special importance. The main person on this monument is *mr ʿḥ3wty* Senbu (*snbw*) and along with him there are two *ʿḥ3wtyw*: Seneb-em (*snb-m*) and Senen (*snn*). One family of *ʿḥ3wtyw* is attested in the Lahun area.[36] The census lists found there list the household of two *ʿḥ3wtyw*: father Heri (*ḥri*) and son Seneferu (*snfrw*). Sneferu, who held the title *ʿḥ3wty* when the final list was drawn up, mentioned his father who belonged to the *sn.nwt nt ḏ3mw*[37] – "second[38]/'reserve'[39] *ḏ3mw*" of *wʿrt mḥtt*.[40] According to D. Franke, the existence of men under arm in the area of Lahun is an indication that the soldiers were settled there with grants of land.[41] Most of the building projects of the rulers of Twelfth Dynasty

---

28 GRIFFITH/NEWBERRY, *El Bersheh* I, 19-21 (tomb no. 2), pl. XII-XVI.

29 Cf. A.R. SCHULMAN, The Battle Scenes of the Middle Kingdom, *Journal of the Society for the Study of Egyptian Antiquities* 12/4 (1982), 164-183.

30 F.L.GRIFFITH/P.E. NEWBERRY, *El Bersheh* II (*Archaeological Survey of Egypt* 4), London 1895, 19; WARD, *Index of Titles*, no. 623; STEFANOVIĆ, *Military Titles*, Doss. 975.

31 GRIFFITH/NEWBERRY, *El Bersheh* II, 33, pl. 13.

32 STEFANOVIĆ, *Military Titles*, Doss. 291, 324, 443, 659, 831, 875, 974.

33 FAULKNER, *Journal of Egyptian Archaeology* 39 (1954), 39; WARD, *Index of Titles*, no. 622; STEFANOVIĆ, *Military Titles*, Doss. 974; cf. J. BAINES, The Stela of Khusobek. Private and Royal Military Narrative and Values, in: J. OSING/G. DREYER, *Form und Mass. Beiträge zur Literatur, Sprache und Kunst des Alten Ägypten. Festschrift für Gerhard Fecht zum 65. Geburtstag am 6. Februar 1987* (*Ägypten und Altes Testament* 12), Wiesbaden 1987, 46, 49.

34 H.G. FISCHER, *Egyptian Titles of the Middle Kingdom. A Supplement to Wm. Ward's Index*, New York 1985, 59.

35 STEFANOVIĆ, *Military Titles*, Doss. 958 (Beni Hasan/Tomb 283; S.E. OREL, Two Unpublished Stelae from Beni Hasan, *Journal of Egyptian Archaeology* 81 (1995), 218-219); Doss. 960 (Abydos?; P.A.A. BOESER, *Beschreibung der aegyptischen Sammlung des niederländischen Reichsmuseums der Altertümer in Leiden. Die Denkmäler der Zeit zwischen dem Alten und Mittlerem Reich und des Mittleren Reiches. Erste Abteilung Stelen* II, Haag 1909, 51), Doss. 961 (Edfu; Cairo JdE 52456; B. Gunn, A Middle Kingdom Stela from Edfu, *Annales du service des antiquités de l'Égypte* 29 (1929), 5-14, О. Д. БЕРЛЕВ, Стоимость раба в Египте эпохи Среднего царства, *Вестник Древней Истории* 42/1 (1966), 28-39); Doss. 967 (Sheikh Farag/Tomb 217; Boston MFA 13.3844; R.J. LEPROHON, *Stelae* I. *The Early Dynastic Period to the Late Middle Kingdom* (*Corpus Antiquitatum Aegyptiacarum Museum of Fine Arts Boston Fasc.* 2), Mainz 1985, 2,86); Doss. 968 and 970 (Abydos; CCG 20746; H.O. LANGE/H. SCHÄFER, *Catalogue général des antiquités égyptiennes du Musée du Caire Nos 20001-20780, Grab- und Denksteine des Mittleren Reiches* II, Berlin 1908, 378-380); Doss. 971 (Abydos; CCG 20313; LANGE/SCHÄFER, *Catalogue général des antiquités égyptiennes du Musée du Caire Nos 20001-20780, Grab- und Denksteine des Mittleren Reiches* I, Berlin 1902, 325-326).

36 F.L. GRIFFITH, *The Petrie Papyrus. Hieratic Papyri from Kahun and Gurob* (*Principally of the Middle Kingdom*), London 1898, I.3, pl. IX, lines 1-16; cf. B.J. KEMP, *Ancient Egypt. Anatomy of a Civilization*, London 1989, 157.

37 GRIFFITH, *Petrie Papyrus*, I.3, pl. IX., line 2; cf. I.5, pl. IX. line 16.

38 OBSOMER, *Sesostris Ier*, 277.

39 W. HELCK, s.v. *Militär*, in: W. HELCK/W. WESTENDORF (eds.), *Lexikon der Ägyptologie* IV, Wiesbaden 1982, 130.

40 See D. STEFANOVIĆ, *wʿrt mḥtt* on the Stela Sinai 115, *Göttinger Miszellen* 190 (2002), 75-82.

41 FRANKE, *Studien zur Altägyptischen Kultur* 10 (1983), 168; cf. W. HELCK, s.v. *Militärkolonie*, in: *Lexikon der Ägyptologie* IV, 135.

in the area of Lahun and Hawara were connected with their funerary complexes. The active soldiers and veterans settled there were used by government, when the need arose, as expedition members, workers at the building projects, or in border patrols.[42]

In considering the role of *ʿḥ3wtyw* – assuming that we are speaking about a military "profession" – we have to ask ourselves two basic questions: how regular was their garrison duty? Where did they fit into the military organization of the Middle Kingdom?

C. Vogel points out that we may just guess about duration of the duties of men under arms, among others *ʿḥ3wtyw*, in Nubian forts. As we know that by the end of the Twelfth Dynasty the Nubian fortresses were manned not by rotating garrisons, but by permanent settler families,[43] Vogel suggests two models:

> Case A: "Der ägyptische Soldat versah nur befristet (vielleicht 1-2 Jahre) seinen Militärdienst in einer (nubischen) Festung und kehrte dann in seine Heimat zurück. Dann hätte er auch eine Familie besitzen können".
>
> Case B: "Der ägyptische Soldat versah seinen Dienst solange es seine körperliche Verfassung erlaubte, in der ihm zugewiesenen Festung. In diesem Fall ist nicht anzunehmen, daß er Familie besaß".[44]

It seems, however, that there is one more specific case attested on the late Middle Kingdom stela from Edfu, belonging to the *ʿḥ3wty* Ha-ankh (*ḥ3-ʿnḫ*).[45] According to Berlev's interpretation of the text, Ha-ankh arrived in Edfu after thirteen days he had spend in Kush separated from his family. He was "rewarded" for six years of his "duty" and he could buy (*jnị*)[46] the servant Wesha-sekhet *b3kt wšʿ-sḫt*[47] and three cubits of land.[48] It is very tempting to assume that he spent all six years of his "military carrier" in Nubia, and that he was rewarded after the last "task" mentioned on his monument. Furthermore, it is clear that Ha-ankh's family and estate were in his homeland. However, we do not know anything neither about his past or future task (military or civil one, if any), nor about similar career of any other *ʿḥ3wty*.

We do not know much about the place of the *ʿḥ3wty* within the military organization of the Middle Kingdom. Quirke points out that "soldier" (*ʿḥ3wty*) would be the lowest rank of official, "but even that was probably above the level of the main mass of fighters, to judge from the quality of sources attesting to them (from the early Middle Kingdom, the fine coffin set of the 'soldier' from Beni Hasan,

---

42 FRANKE notes that various categories of soldiers were settled in such areas. According to his opinion the common living place of men under arms and civilians may explain the frequent attestation of "soldiers" on the stelae belonging to the staff of civil administration (*Studien zur Altägyptischen Kultur* 10 (1983), 168).

43 S.T. SMITH, *Askut in Nubia. The Economics and Ideology of Egyptian Imperialism in the Second Millennium BC*, London 1995; ID., Sealing Practice at Askut and the Nubian Fortresses, in: M. BIETAK/E. CZERNY (eds.), *Scarabs of the Second Millennium BC from Egypt, Nubia, Crete and the Levant: Chronological and Historical Implications*, Wien 2004, 207; VOGEL, *Festungen und Garnisonen*, 116. Cf. SMITH, *Fortress of Buhen. Inscriptions*, 220-223.

44 VOGEL, *Festungen und Garnisonen*, 116.

45 GUNN, *Annales du service des antiquités de l'Égypte* 29 (1929), 5-14; БЕРЛЕВ, *Вестник Древней Истории* 42/1 (1966), 28-39; cf. T. SÄVE-SÖDERBERGH, A Buhen Stela from the Second Intermediate Period, *Journal of Egyptian Archaeology* 35 (1949), 57-58.

46 ERMAN/GRAPOW, *Wörterbuch der Ägyptischen Sprache* I 90.2-91.10

47 See Berlev's comment concerning her price (*Вестник Древней Истории* 42/1 (1966), 33-36). Unfortunately, this very important example is not recorded by T. HOFMANN, *Zur sozialen Bedeutung zweier Begriffe für 'Diener': b3k und ḥm untersucht an Quellen vom Alten Reich bis zur Ramessidenzeit* (*Aegyptiaca Helvetica* 18), Basel 2005.

48 Cf. H.G. FISCHER, Lend Records on the Stelae of the Twelfth Dynasty, *Revue d'Égyptologie* 13 (1961), 108.

in the Fitzwilliam and Liverpool City Museum)".[49] However, the titles *mr ꜥḥ3wtyw*[50] and *3ṯw n ꜥḥ3wtyw*[51] are also attested.

On the stela Cairo CG 20746, as it was mentioned above, beside *mr ꜥḥ3wtyw* Senbu there are two "ordinary" *ꜥḥ3wtyw*: Seneb-em and Senen. As there is no kinship indication, we may suppose that they belonged to the same "profession" and that *mr ꜥḥ3wtyw* Senbu perhaps was their superior. The inscription *RIK* 117 is not helpful. Qatiu (*k3tjw*), according to Habachi's reading, mentioned on an offering table from the Heqaib sanctuary, served as "administrator of the warrior, Heqaib"[52] and probably was attached to the sanctuary of the saint.

According to the records, the *ꜥḥ3wtyw* were organized groups of men under arms. They were recruited from the inhabitants of a nome or of towns and, in some cases, organized in *ḏ3mw*-groups. We may ask whether the formations of these groups were limited to certain social positions, or by age. What seems to be clear is that *ꜥḥ3wtyw* formed a combat group which could be also used by the Court, as many other such units, for the purposes of a less military character.

---

49 QUIRKE, *Titles and bureaux*, 97; see above footnote 5.

50 RIK 117 (F. HINTZE/W.F. REINEKE, *Felsinschriften aus dem sudanesischen Nubien* I (*Publikation der Nubien-Expedition 1961-1963* 1), Berlin 1989, no. 493) and CCG 20746 (LANGE/SCHÄFER, *Grab- und Denksteine des Mittleren Reiches* II, 378-380). VOGEL points to the RIK 117 (*Festungen und Garnisonen*, 108). See also D. JONES, *An Index of Ancient Egyptian Titles, Epithets and Phrases of the Old Kingdom* (*British Archaeological Reports International Series* 866), London 2000, 360.

51 Not recorded by WARD, *Index of Titles*. L. HABACHI, *Elephantine* IV: *The Sanctuary of Heqaib* (*Archäologische Veröffentlichungen* 33), Mainz 1985, no. 94; D. FRANKE, *Das Heiligtum des Heqaib auf Elephantine. Geschichte eines Provinzheiligtums im Mittleren Reich* (*Studien zur Archäologie und Geschichte Altägyptens* 9), 84-86.

52 HABACHI, *Elephantine* IV: *The Sanctuary of Heqaib*, 108, 161.

An Unfinished Late Middle Kingdom Stela From Abydos

Paul Whelan

This article presents a detailed examination of an interesting Middle Kingdom stela in the reserve collection of the Musées Royaux d'Art et d'Histoire, Brussels (Pl. 8).[1] Although in poor condition, having been broken in two and intentionally defaced in antiquity, the stela is nonetheless deserving attention. It belongs to a small group of unusual late Middle Kingdom stone monuments distinguished by having one or more niches incorporating single or multiple mummiform statuettes carved in half-round relief.[2] Few examples of this type have been studied in any detail and the majority are known only from brief catalogue entries, as is indeed the case with the Brussels stela. The lack of attention afforded the latter is no doubt due to its ruined condition as well as the absence of any genealogical or prosopographical data in its incomplete inscriptions. However, as this study will show, other criteria are apparent which, although less conclusive, suggest the stela is one of the earliest examples of this uncommon class of object. Furthermore, closer inspection of the various decorative elements reveals something about the use-life of the object and the commercial activities of an artisan or workshop producing cult objects at Abydos in the Middle Kingdom.

Description

The stela entered the museum collection in 1913 and bears the registration number E.4860. In 1923 Louis Speleers published an inaccurate sketch of the object which shows the layout of its inscriptions, but not the distinctively shaped base, fracture, or damaged mummiform figure.[3] These and other details, most of which are clearly visible in the photograph and line drawing of the stela, are hereby described (Pl. 8 and Fig. 1).

Brussels E.4860 is an arch-topped stela carved from a single limestone slab measuring 46.9 cm high, 26.5 cm wide, 8 cm deep. The decorated front surface is dominated by a central arch-topped niche, 31 cm high, 17 cm wide, 3.7 cm deep, which accommodates the damaged and intentionally defaced remains of a mummiform statuette carved in half-round relief. The edges of this niche have a pronounced batter, which slopes inwards towards the back, of between 0.5-0.6 cm around the sides and base (approx. 9°), and by 1.3 cm around the arch (approx. 19°). These edges, together with the back of the niche, have been carefully smoothed and bear no trace of additional decoration. Two bands of symmetrically reversed hieroglyphs carved in sunk relief and framed within lightly incised border lines begin at the centre of the arch and run down the sides of the niche. The signs are shallow cut with

1 I am indebted to Luc Limme in the Musées Royaux d'Art et d'Histoire, Brussels for his help during my research and for permission to publish the photograph of the object. I would like also to thank Pat Winker in the School of Archaeology, Classics and Egyptology, University of Liverpool for access to archive material relating to Garstang's excavations at Abydos, and to Wolfram Grajetzki for his comments on an early draft of this article.

2 To avoid over cluttering the article, I have included a catalogue of the objects belonging to this category at the end of the article, to which the capital letters A-O used throughout refer. A separate study exploring the purpose of these objects in the context of Abydos is in preparation by the present writer.

3 L. Speleers, *Recueil des Egyptiennes des Musées Royaux du Cinquantenaire à Bruxelles*, Brussels 1923, 33 no. 107, 129; B. Porter/R. Moss, *Topographical Bibliography of Ancient Egyptian Hieroglyphic Texts, Reliefs, and Paintings* V *Upper Egypt: Sites,* Oxford 1937, 99. Speleers's brief written entry for the figure is thus: "Dans cette cavité est sculptée une statuette du mort, enveloppé dans un manteau, et croisant les mains (abîmée)".

no internal detail and are coloured with green pigment; black draft lines are still visible around the edges of several signs. The inner incised border line terminates roughly at the same point as the inscriptions while the outer border line continues down for approximately 4 cm below where the formulae end. The carefully smoothed lower part of the stela immediately below the niche is undecorated except for traces of a rectangular frame drawn in black pigment,[4] the horizontal lines of which are spaced 3.5 cm apart which exactly matches the distance between the two incised border lines around the niche.

Two notches carved from either side of the stela's base together with a rebate running across its width creates a projection 19 cm wide, 2.5 cm high, 4.9 cm deep, which was probably intended to act as a tenon enabling the stela to be securely fixed into a separately fashioned offering table or pedestal. The tenon appears to be contemporary with the manufacture of the object, although there is no obvious wear, abrasion marks or discolouration of the stone to indicate that the stela had ever been inserted into a separate base – at least not for any length of time for weathering to have occurred, as appears to be the case with other examples.[5]

At some point, most probably in antiquity, the stela was broken in two and a fracture runs diagonally across the object, roughly a third of the way down the left edge to midway on the right edge. The break affects both vertical sections of inscription, but particularly the left column, which is missing a portion of stone resulting in the loss of about a quarter of the text. In modern times this area has been filled with plaster and the inscription restored; presumably the two halves of the stela were rejoined at the same time.

The ruined state of the mummiform statuette is apparently the result of a failed attempt to chisel out the image. Only battered parts of the figure's upper half remain and nothing of the lower portion has survived other than the merest suggestion of a gently tapered body form indicated by chisel marks in the stone. Despite such extensive damage it is still possible to offer a few observations as to the original appearance of the statuette. The rounded outer shape of a large tripartite wig as well as parts of its front lappets is clearly visible, on which a few small patches of blue pigment are still preserved. The top of both narrow shoulders and part of the upper chest and left arm remain intact, but only the outlines of the upper right arm and torso are preserved in the otherwise shattered stone. Although Speelers described the figure as having "croisant les mains," the damage to the chest area makes it impossible to determine whether the lower arms and/or hands were once modelled in relief or merely implied by the slight projection of the elbows captured in the outline of the statuette.[6] Similarly, due to the missing chin and central portion of the neck immediately below, it cannot be established whether the figure originally sported a short beard. However, traces of reddish skin colour preserved on the sides and base of the neck indicate that it was almost certainly a male figure.[7] Green pigment in the area immediately below the neckline is undoubtedly the remains of a decorative collar, the modest size

---

4 A sketch of the stela in the *journal d'entrée* indicates a vertical line on the left, although this is no longer visible.

5 The similarly notched base of Leiden stela 35 appears to show some discolouration in the area between the "tenon" and the decorated surface, possibly as a result of it having weathered differently while inserted into a separate base. P.A.A. BOESER, *Beschreibung der Aegyptischen Sammlung des Niederländischen Reichsmuseum der Altertümer in Leiden* II, Haag 1909, No. 35, pl. 25. Object F has a similar horizontal rebate without the side notches, presumably also to facilitate its secure installation into a separate base.

6 In all but one instance, the arms modelled on mummiform figures of eleven objects from this type-group are depicted crossed, right over left.

7 Where identification is possible on other examples in the type-group the main dedicator is always male. In every instance where female mummiform figures are depicted, they are secondary individuals.

of which is indicated by the fact that the green colour does not continue beyond the outer sides of the lappets[8] where traces of the original white coloured garment are preserved.

As a result of the extensive damage to the lower half of the figure it is not possible to determine whether the tight-fitting garment terminated above the ankles, thus exposing the feet, or enveloped the entire lower body. One would favour the latter type of garment, since this is found on all but two mummiform figures from this object group.[9]

The back of the stela has a rough chiselled surface with a slightly curved hull-like section; however, there are no traces of plaster to indicate that it was ever fixed to a wall or other structure.[10]

The Inscriptions

ḥtp dj nsw [a] *ꜣsjr nb ꜣbḏw* [b] *d[.f..........]* [c] *ḫt nb.t nfr(.t) wꜥb(.t) n kꜣ n(j)* [d] (left)
"An offering which the king has given and Osiris, lord of Abydos, so that [he] may give [...] everything good and pure for the ka of ..."

ḥtp dj nsw jnpw [e] *tp(j) ḏw.f jm(j) w(t)* [f] *nb tꜣ-ḏsr* [g] *d.f prt-ḫrw t ḥnḳt kꜣ ꜣpd ḫt nb.t nfr(.t) wꜥb(.t)* [h] *n kꜣ n(j)* [i] (right)
"An offering which the king has given and Anubis, who-is-upon-his-mountain, the one in the *wt*, lord of the sacred land, so that he may give a voice offering of bread, beer, ox and fowl and everything good and pure for the ka of ..."

Notes to Inscriptions

a) The use of a single sedge plant sign shared by both symmetrically reversed offering formula is uncommon: W. BARTA, *Aufbau und Bedeutung der altägyptischen Opferformel* (*Ägyptologische Forschungen* 24), Glückstadt 1968, 53 note 1. The possible chronological implication of this is discussed later. The single *t* sign following *ḥtp* is not indicated in the transliteration as it has been shown that its use in horizontal inscriptions simply follows the arrangement often found in vertical arrangements of the formula where it serves only as a phonetic complement of *ḥtp*: G. LAPP, *Die Opferformel des Alten Reiches unter Berücksichtigung einiger späterer Formen* (*Sonderschriften des Deutschen Archäologischen Instituts Kairo* 21), Mainz 1986, 4-5. However, the *nsw ḥtp t dj* arrangement rarely occurs in horizontal stelae inscriptions of the Middle Kingdom, although it is firmly attested in offering formulae of the Old Kingdom and First Intermediate Period. Barta, for example, lists only sources from these earlier periods; none from the Middle Kingdom: *Aufbau und Bedeutung der altägyptischen Opferformel*, 12-14 and 43. I know of only one other Middle Kingdom stela with the same arrangement, Cairo CG 20427, which interestingly also derives from North

---

8 Although broad collars which extend beyond the lappets are more commonly represented, narrow examples are to be found, e.g. W.C. HAYES, *The Scepter of Egypt. A Background for the Study of Egyptian Antiquities in the Metropolitan Museum of Art*, Part I: *From the Earliest Time to the End of the Middle Kingdom*, New York 1953, 328, fig. 216 (left statuette).

9 Only K has figures with garments terminating around the ankle area. In this respect, the statuettes are not strictly mummiform.

10 The unfinished back suggests that the stela was intended to be erected against or set into a wall. For an example of an *in situ* stela with a separate stone plinth erected against the wall of an Abydene memorial chapel see W.K. SIMPSON, *Inscribed Material from the Pennsylvania-Yale Excavations at Abydos* (*Publications of the Pennsylvania-Yale Expedition to Egypt* 6), New Haven-Philadelphia 1995, pl. 6 B and 7 A-B.

Abydos: H.O. LANGE/H. SCHÄFER, *Catalogue général des antiquités égyptiennes du Musée du Caire N°s 20001-20780, Grab- und Denksteine des Mittleren Reiches* II, Berlin 1908, 22-24. It is perhaps tempting to see this as evidence of a regional variation of the formula; however its occurrence on the Cairo stela might be explained simply as one of a number of orthographic blunders in the inscriptions. These include the wrong order of signs writing *ḫt* in the offering formula and similar errors in two of the personal names, and most significantly by the fact that the second line of the formula continues above the first!

b) This combination of Osirian epithets regularly occurs on Abydene stelae and is second only in frequency to the epithet string *ꜣsjr nb ḏdw nṯr ꜥꜣ nb ꜣbḏw*: BARTA, *Aufbau und Bedeutung der altägyptischen Opferformel*, 56. For the range and frequency of epithet combinations on Abydene stelae see: J. SPIEGEL, *Die Götter von Abydos* (*Göttinger Orientforschungen IV.Reihe Ägypten* 7), Wiesbaden 1975, 173-176.

c) The damaged portion may have borne a list of the same offerings as those preserved in the inscription on the right side, although the lower ends of four plural strokes which are visible above the *ḫt nb.t* group are not apparent on the opposite formula.

d) At this point one would expect the name (and titles) of the deceased to follow as well as one, or both, of the expected epithets *nb jmꜣḫ* and *mꜣꜥ ḫrw*. An explanation for their absence is presented later.

e) The way of writing the name Anubis with an ideogram of a recumbent canid on a shrine (Gardiner-Sign E16) without additional phonetic complements is attested from the Old Kingdom (A. ERMAN/H. GRAPOW (eds.), *Wörterbuch der ägyptischen Sprache* I, Berlin 2nd ed. 1957, 96). The symbolism of this sign has been discussed in some detail, most recently by H. WILLEMS, *The Coffin of Heqata* (*Cairo JdE 36418*). *A Case Study of Egyptian Culture of the Early Middle Kingdom* (*Orientalia Lovaniensia Analecta* 70), Leuven 1996, 144-146. Willems concludes that the object beneath the animal originally represented a container of equipment associated with rituals carried out in the Place of Embalming. In this respect its singular use here instead of, or combined with, the phonetic spelling of the god's name certainly seems more appropriate for a stela bearing a three-dimensional representation of an embalmed and mummified body before which one can imagine rituals were also performed. However, unlike the name of Osiris which occurs in most of the inscriptions on objects from this type group, Anubis is found on only two other examples G[11] and N.[12] Of these, only the latter bears the name written with the ideogram of a canid upon a shrine, while on the former the name is written phonetically.

f) The *w*(*t*) determinative (Gardiner-Sign Aa2) is rather small and indistinctly carved above the quail chick. Lacking a definitive explanation for the *w*(*t*) I have chosen to leave the word untranslated. A comprehensive discussion of its development and possible meaning is offered by U. KÖHLER, *Das Imiut. Untersuchungen zur Darstellung eines mit Anubis verbundenen religiösen Symbols* II (*Göttinger Orientforschungen IV.Reihe Ägypten* 4), Wiesbaden 1975, 444-452.

g) *tp*(*j*) *ḏw.f jm*(*j*) *w*(*t*) *nb tꜣ-ḏsr* is the most frequent Anubis epithet combination found on Middle Kingdom stelae from Abydos – examples are listed in SPIEGEL, *Götter von Abydos,* 42, 171. Spiegel suggests that the Osirian cult had a direct bearing upon the development of Anubis's epithets, and in particular that of *tp*(*j*) *ḏw.f*, which supplanted *ḫnty zḥ-nṯr* as the principal epithet (SPIEGEL, *Götter von*

11 The inscriptions on this object remain unpublished, and this observation is based on a hand copy of the text made by the writer.

12 G. LAPP, Die Stelenkapelle des *Kmz* aus der 13. Dynastie, *Mitteilungen des Deutschen Archäologischen Instituts Kairo* 50 (1994), 251-252 fig. 7 and 8.

Abydos, 42-49). In addition, there is reason to believe that *tp(j) ḏw.f* may have held greater significance in the late Twelfth and Thirteenth Dynasties as a result of developments at South Abydos during the reign of Senusret III. A recently discovered seal impression bearing the mountain (*ḏw*) hieroglyph surmounted by a recumbent canid upon a shrine has been interpreted as the toponym *ḏw-jnpw* (Mountain-of-Anubis) associated with the tomb complex of Senusret III and the nearby pyramid-like gebel formation at South Abydos, where it would seem that this natural topographical feature became identified as the symbolic domain of the god: J.W. WEGNER/M.A. ABU EL-YAZID, The Mountain-of-Anubis: Necropolis Seal of the Senusret III Tomb Enclosure at Abydos, in: E. CZERNY/I. HEIN/H. HUNGER/D. MELMAN/A. SCHWAB (eds.), *Timelines. Studies in Honour of Manfred Bietak* I (*Orientalia Lovaniensia Analecta* 149), Leuven 2006, 419-435.

h) For this grouping of offerings see: BARTA, *Opferformel*, 57, Bitte 2 h.

f) See note d) above.

Provenance

The stela's provenance is recorded in the *Journal d'Entrée* as having been found at Abydos by John Garstang, to which Speleers's catalogue adds that it came from his excavations in 1907. This date precludes the stela's association with a group of 95 objects in the Musées Royaux d'Art et d'Histoire also excavated by Garstang at Abydos, since these all come from his 1908-9 seasons and were given in recognition of funding received from Jean Capart on behalf of the museum.[13] One can suppose therefore that the stela came from one of two areas of North Abydos excavated by Garstang and his team in 1907 (Fig. 2).[14] The first of these was located in the main wadi approximately 400 metres south of the Osiris temple enclosure and probably just beyond the southern limits of the Nineteenth Century excavations of Auguste Mariette who brought to light a large quantity of Middle Kingdom artefacts.[15] The 1907 wadi excavations were supervised by Garstang's assistant E. Harold Jones who it seems kept no record of the work. Analysis of archival material relating to the 1907 season suggests that few, if any, Middle Kingdom artefacts were found by Jones. His main discovery of about three hundred stelae came from a large Ptolemaic-Roman Period cemetery which had developed in the wadi as well as a cemetery of mummified hawks.[16] Some time after Jones's work began Garstang commenced excavations in an area of the western bank of the wadi roughly 500 metres south west of the Osiris temple enclosure. Here, Garstang encountered numerous Middle Kingdom burials, some containing later interments, which belonged to a continuation of a sector of the cemetery he had encountered seven years earlier at which time it was given the designation "E".[17] Given the concentration of Middle Kingdom remains this would seem to be the more likely location where Brussels E.4860 was found. However, it should also be borne in mind that Jones's earlier excavation

13 For a list of objects see S.R. SNAPE, *Mortuary Assemblages from Abydos* (unpublished PhD thesis), Liverpool 1986, 595. Jean Capart joined the committee overseeing Garstang's excavations at Abydos in September 1907 (IBID., 57).

14 The approximate locations were established by Kemp in B. KEMP/R. MERRILEES, *Minoan Pottery in Second Millennium Egypt* (*Sonderschriften des Deutschen Archäologischen Instituts Kairo* 7), Mainz 1980, 106 fig. 6 and 287-289.

15 A. MARIETTE, *Catalogue générale des monuments d'Abydos*, Paris 1880, 103-230. For a discussion of the area worked by Mariette see B.J. KEMP, s.v. *Abydos*, in: W. HELCK/W. WESTENDORF (eds.), *Lexikon der Ägyptologie* I, Wiesbaden 1975, 28-41.

16 The limited archival evidence concerning the wadi excavations is discussed in SNAPE, *Mortuary Assemblages from Abydos*, 52-57; and in KEMP/MERRILEES, *Minoan Pottery in Second Millennium Egypt*, 105-107.

17 IBID., 108-109; J. GARSTANG, *El Arábah: A Cemetery of the Middle Kingdom; Survey of the Old Kingdom Temenos; Graffiti from the Temple of Sety* (*Egyptian Research Account* 6), London 1900, 1-27.

in the wadi encompassed an area adjacent to, or possibly even overlapping, part of Mariette's "nécropole du nord" from where stelae I and K derive.

Dating

It has long been established that small-scale monuments incorporating niched mummiform figures appear in the reign of either Senusret III or Amenemhat III.[18] This date is confirmed by two arch-topped stelae, J and K, which belong to the Abydene offering chapel group of the celebrated official Iykhernofret.[19] Less secure dates have been proposed for half of the remaining fourteen objects in this type group which nevertheless suggest that this distinctive sculptural style continues in use into the early Thirteenth Dynasty and possibly later still.[20] So far, other than Speleers's overly vague "moyen empire" no precise date has been proposed for the Brussels stela however, the following analysis attempts to show that it should be considered as one of the earliest examples.

Its distinctive low-arched form was used for private stelae from the Eleventh Dynasty and throughout the Middle Kingdom; however the shape became increasingly popular from the reign of Amenemhat II[21] and remained in vogue into the Thirteenth Dynasty.[22] Besides E.4860, another four round-topped stelae within the type-group – H, I, K and L[23] – display the same abrupt transition between the low arch and the vertical sides;[24] of these only the aforementioned K has been securely dated to the last great period of the Twelfth Dynasty, when the stela's low-arch parallels funerary architecture, most notably the precisely executed vaulted ceilings and arched doorways used extensively in the subterranean compartments of the Dahshur pyramid complexes of Senusret III[25] and Amenemhat III.[26] In this respect, the preciseness of stela E.4860's low arch should be noted especially as it compliments what appears to be a more reliable dating criterion. The symmetrically reversed *ḥtp dj nsw* formulae around its niche, which serves to emphasise this architectural comparison, is regularly found on stone doorframes as well as offering tables, although far less often on stelae.[27] Indeed, the relative infrequency of this arrangement on stelae has clear chronological implications in dating

18 H.G. EVERS, *Staat aus dem Stein* II, Munich 1929, 81.

19 Both stelae, together with a further nine examples, make up the Abydos North Offering Chapel (ANOC) No. 1 (W.K. SIMPSON, *The Terrace of the Great God at Abydos. The Offering Chapels of Dynasties 12 and 13* (*Publications of the Pennsylvania-Yale Expedition to Egypt* 5), New Haven-Philadelphia 1974, 17). For a detailed discussion of the relationships between individuals named on the various stelae belonging to this offering chapel group see R.J. LEPROHON, The Personnel of the Middle Kingdom Funerary Stelae, *Journal of the American Research Center in Egypt* 15 (1978), 33-38.

20 For the possible dating of monument O to the latter half of the Thirteenth Dynasty, see P. VERNUS, Une formule des shaouabtis sur un pseudo-naos de la XIIIe Dynastie, *Revue d'Égyptologie* 26 (1974), 101-114.

21 K. PFLÜGER, The Private Funerary Stelae of the Middle Kingdom and Their Importance for the Study of Ancient Egyptian History, *Journal of the American Oriental Society* 67 (1947), 128.

22 R. HÖLZL, Round-Topped Stelae from the Middle Kingdom to the Late Period. Some Remarks on the Decoration of the Lunettes, *Sesto Congresso Internazionale di Egittologia Atti* I, Turin 1992, 285-286.

23 Although stela L still retains two corner tabs of the original rectangular slab, the actual decorated surface has an arch top.

24 It is possible that some of the rectangular slab monuments were originally round-topped stelae, since none appear to be complete and their original shapes are uncertain.

25 D. ARNOLD, *The Pyramid Complex of Senwosret III at Dahshur. Architectural Studies* (*Publications of the Metropolitan Museum of Art Egyptian Expedition* 26), New York 2002, in particular pl. 11b, 12a, c and d.

26 D. ARNOLD, *Der Pyramidenbezirk des Königs Amenemhet III. in Dahschur* I. *Die Pyramide* (*Archäologische Veröffentlichungen* 53), Mainz 1987, pl. 10-12 and 14. For a general discussion of the vault roof style in the Middle Kingdom see D. ARNOLD, *Building in Egypt. Pharaonic Stone Masonry*, New York 1991, 195-199.

27 Symmetrical reversal was used for two identical texts, so that they appear mirrored, or with different texts, as with E.4860. A discussion of this arrangement without however detailed analysis of its use on stelae, can be found in H.G. FISCHER, *Egyptian Studies* III*: The Orientation of Hieroglyphs, Part* I. *Reversals*, New York 1977, 13-14.

Brussels E.4860. A study of nearly a thousand Middle Kingdom stelae has revealed relatively few with symmetrically reversed *ḥtp dj nsw* formulae (cf. Fig. 3).[28] The most common arrangement of the formulae employs two centrally positioned and mirrored sedge plants (Gardiner-Sign M23) at the beginning.[29] This style occurs on rectangular and round-topped stelae, most frequently in horizontal inscriptions, but also in ten curved texts, from the early Twelfth to Thirteenth Dynasty.[30] However, far fewer stelae (fifteen examples) were found with symmetrically reversed *ḥtp dj nsw* formulae sharing a single centrally positioned sedge plant sign. Of these, thirteen have the offering formulae composed in a horizontal line,[31] while only two examples, Brussels E.4860 and the previously mentioned and firmly dated K, bear curved inscriptions. Based on the apparent rarity of this arrangement and, albeit to a much lesser extent, on the carefully fashioned low-arch shape, I believe that Brussels E.4860 should be dated to the same period, i.e. the reign of either Senusret III or Amenemhat III.

General Commentary

Already mentioned above is the fact that both symmetrically reversed inscriptions are incomplete ending with the phrase *n k3 n(j)* which lacks not only the name and title(s) of the dedicator, but also one or both of the expected epithets *m3ʿ ḫrw* and *nb jm3ḫ*. These undoubtedly remained to be added, and indeed the outer of the two incised border lines extends beyond both inscriptions and into the lower section of the stela in anticipation of additional text, for which the artisan had also marked out a rectangular frame in black draught lines immediately below the niche. It is unlikely that the mummiform figure alone would have been inscribed with any concluding text. Such an arrangement would have resulted in a large gap between the central inscription and those around the niche thus interrupting the visual relationship between all three and contrary to the artisan's otherwise carefully considered layout of the stela. In fact, the importance placed on the close spatial arrangement of inscription around a niche is evident from arch-topped stela I from the type-group, which also derives from Abydos and also bears a central niche containing a single mummiform figure. On this object, one text runs down the right side of the niche and then continues in a perpendicular plane beneath, while the left text maintains its vertical descent terminating at the base of the stela. A central column of inscription runs down, and immediately below, the mummiform figure where it continues in the remaining small blank area beneath the niche to the left. As a result there is very little space between the three lines of text and despite the fact that they are asymmetrical the overall composition appears visually balanced. However, the clumsy workmanship and inelegantly carved hieroglyphs indicate that stela I was not made by the sculptor of Brussels E.4860, which in any case could not have borne the same uneven text arrangement; although a number of different layouts could have been accommodated

---

28 I believe the scope of the survey, while not exhaustive, is sufficiently broad to validate the conclusions made herein.

29 Stelae with symmetrically reversed formulae separated by a single incised vertical line or with vertical inscriptions are not included in the survey.

30 An early date is attested, for example, by Cleveland Museum of Art 21.1017 which is assigned to the reign of Senusret I, cf. L.M. BERMAN, The Stele of Shemai, Chief of Police, of the Early Twelfth Dynasty, in The Cleveland Museum of Art, in: P. DER MANUELIAN (ed.), *Studies in Honor of William Kelly Simpson* I, Boston 1996, 98. One can cite Cairo CG 20391 as a stela of a later date which, on the basis of genealogical evidence, has been assigned to the reign of Sobekhotep II of the Thirteenth Dynasty, cf. D. FRANKE, *Personendaten aus dem Mittleren Reich (20.-16. Jahrhundert v. Chr.). Dossiers 1-796* (*Ägyptologische Abhandlungen* 41), Wiesbaden 1984, Doss. 167.

31 Five of the stelae with horizontal inscriptions have been dated to the late Twelfth to early Thirteenth Dynasties.

by a simple process of lengthening the existing border lines and utilising the space beneath the niche and on the body of the mummiform figure.

In his study of Elephantine stelae, Detlef Franke suggested that the wishes of the client was an important factor influencing the final appearance of a stela, along with the artistic and technical abilities of an artisan and the prevailing religious and social conventions of the time.[32] One option available to the potential client was to purchase a "blank" already carved stela bearing the main body of text, which could be personalised simply by the addition of the purchaser's name and epithets. A stela chosen from stock was likely not only to be less costly, but also would require the shortest time to complete. This might have been an important consideration for pilgrims on a brief visit to Abydos, or perhaps the only option available at certain times when increased demand for cult objects may have strained the capabilities of local workshops. In consideration of this point, it should be noted that although the Brussels stela is clearly unfinished, the fact that the mummiform figure and the inscriptions are painted suggests that this was not an object simply awaiting the name of the purchaser, but rather a finished sculptor's trial piece or display model that was presented in its final decorated form except for a personalised dedication. Even so, the artisan who created it seems to have deliberately left the border lines incomplete in acknowledgement of the different ways in which the concluding inscription could have been arranged on copies of the stela.

Interestingly, arch-topped stela H also appears to be an example of an unfinished workshop product. This unprovenanced round-topped stela has a central niche incorporating a single mummiform statuette flanked by two slender female figures depicted in everyday attire. The skilful carving and carefully prepared surfaces of the stela are conspicuous only by the absence of an inscription and painted decoration. Since it is unlikely to have been supplied to the customer in this state one can suppose that it represents yet another unfinished project, on which the text remained to be added.[33] It is also hard to believe that stela H can be anything other than either a display model used to demonstrate one of the stylistic options available to a would-be client or a sculptor's guide, since it would seem unlikely that a workshop would have speculatively created for stock a composition of two female and one mummiform figure in the hope of attracting a suitable customer.[34] Conversely, a greater demand can be envisaged for stelae such as E.4860 which incorporate a single mummiform figure and could, therefore, have been a pre-prepared stock item.[35]

Any attempt at reconstructing the use-life of the Brussels stela is hindered by the lack of a recorded archaeological context, however a plausible explanation based on the following observations may be proposed that would account for the damage and/or attempted removal of the mummiform figure. At first glance one can be forgiven for concluding that the same artisan who fashioned the stela was also responsible for trying to chisel out the mummiform figure, perhaps due to a mishap during manufacture, at which point the stela broke. However, this scenario does not readily explain why the hieroglyphs and figure were painted, or why both formulae end incomplete at exactly the same point

---

32 D. FRANKE, *Das Heiligtum des Heqaib auf Elephantine. Geschichte eines Provinzheiligtums im Mittleren Reich* (*Studien zur Archäologie und Geschichte Altägyptens* 9), Heidelberg 1994, 109.

33 It is possible that it bore an inked inscription now worn away. Finely carved stelae with inked inscriptions are known, for example Cairo CG 20325 and CG 20720. However, it should be noted that all of the texts on objects in the type-group are carved in sunk relief.

34 This view contrasts that of Wildung who suggested that group-statues were likely to have been a stock product of a temple workshop, D. WILDUNG, *Sesostris und Amenemhet. Ägypten im Mittleren Reich,* Munich 1984, 101.

35 The commercial appeal of the two most popular Abydene deities included in the inscriptions of Brussels E.4860 may also be relevant in this respect.

yet have the same extended outer border line in anticipation of additional text. It would seem more logical for the artisan to have finished carving the inscription before applying any colour decoration. While it is true that examples of unfinished Middle Kingdom stelae with two-dimensional decoration in sunk relief indicate that both image and hieroglyphic text were carved at the same time[36], a different procedure was used for the creation of statues and likely also for other three-dimensional objects. From the Old Kingdom, if not before, as many as eight stages were employed in the manufacture of statues, and it was only after the main carving and the final surface preparation of the object had been completed that inscriptions and painted decoration were added.[37] The same procedure was almost certainly followed for Brussels E.4860, in which case it makes little sense for the artisan to have coloured the existing hieroglyphs when there were others still to be carved. In addition, whoever removed the lower half of the mummiform figure left a coarsely chiselled area which is *below* the smoothed surface of the niche's back. Surely, the skilled artisan who created the stela was unlikely to have made such a clumsy attempt at removing the statuette if it was his intention to reuse the object.

Given these considerations, I believe the most logical explanation for the stela's condition is as follows: the stela represents an example of a sculptor's trial piece or display model, left unfinished at the point where the personalised portion of inscription was all that remained to be added. For reasons unknown the stela was abandoned/lost/misappropriated and only some time later was an attempt made to reuse it by someone lacking any stone-working skills, who sought to modify it perhaps into a stela-naos, by clumsily chiselling out the mummiform figure. It was during this attempted reuse that the object broke and was thus abandoned.[38] The lack of any personal name on the object would have made it more attractive for reuse by another individual whose own statue, for example, placed within the vacant niche would have effectively served to personalise the stela without the need for re-cutting the existing inscription. In the absence of a firm provenance, it remains unclear when or where the attempted re-use occurred, but perhaps it was during a period of later activity in the Middle Kingdom cemetery "E" excavated by Garstang.

Since it is unlikely that anyone would transport an unfinished object any considerable distance, it seems reasonable to assume that Brussels E.4860 was manufactured locally.[39] Firm evidence for the existence of stelae workshops at or near to Abydos in the Middle Kingdom is known principally from textual sources[40], or understood from the numerous Abydene stelae of similar appearance.[41] Likewise, a number of analogous Middle Kingdom statuettes deriving from Abydos may be taken as evidence of the commercial mass production of stone objects by a local workshop.[42] Until recently there was little

---

36 J. Bourriau, *Pharaohs and Mortals. Egyptian Art in the Middle Kingdom* (exhibition catalogue), Cambridge 1988, 29-31.

37 Best attested by the well-known group of Fourth Dynasty royal statues, cf. G.A. Reisner, *Mycerinus. The Temples of the Third Pyramid at Giza*, Massachusetts 1931, 115-116 and pl. 62-63. For a discussion of statue production using evidence from different periods see J. Vandier, *Manuel d'Archéologie Égyptienne* III, *Les Grandes Époques, La Statuaire*, Paris 1958, 3-13. The final stages of statue production including the addition of inscriptions are most vividly depicted in a scene in the New Kingdom tomb of Rekhmire, for which see N. de G. Davies, *The Tomb of Rekh-mi-Rēʻ at Thebes* II (*Publication of the Metropolitan Museum of Art Egyptian Expedition* 11), New York 1943, pl. LX.

38 Although the stela's original context is not known it would seem unlikely, given its damaged and un-personalised state, that it served as a memorial.

39 Seven of the fifteen stelae with the same unusual arrangement of the *ḥtp dj nsw* formulae were excavated at North Abydos, while the remaining unprovenanced examples are also considered to have come from the site, either by association with an Abydene offering chapel or by internal evidence.

40 R.O. Faulkner, The Stela of the Master-Sculptor Shen, *Journal of Egyptian Archaeology* 38 (1952), 3-5; O. Berlev, Review of W.K. Simpson, The Terrace of the Great God at Abydos, *Bibliotheca Orientalis* 33 (1976), 326.

41 Simpson, *Terrace of the Great God*, 13-16.

42 Vandier, *Manuel d'Archéologie* III, 270-272.

to suggest the presence of workshops at North Abydos even though this was the area where most of the temple and funerary activity was located. However, evidence for specialised craft production has been found within the south western corner of the Osiris enclosure, which included a number of circular faience kilns dated by the excavators to the First Intermediate Period and possibly into the Middle Kingdom.[43] Although no evidence of stone working was found, the discoveries nevertheless reveal the existence of specialised craft workshops operating in relatively close proximity to the main temple and cultic area of North Abydos, and at a time when such production centres are considered to have been attached only to private establishments.[44] Stela E.4860's probable place of discovery in the northern cemetery suggests that a stone workshop was likely to have been located not too far away and may have been attached to the Osiris temple complex.

Furthermore, the likelihood that Brussels E.4860 represents an example of a workshop's pre-prepared display or trial piece implies a degree of popularity for this distinctive class of stela that is otherwise unapparent from the small number of examples known.

43 M.D. ADAMS, The Abydos Settlement Project, in: C.J. EYRE (ed.), *Proceedings of the Seventh International Congress of Egyptologists, Cambridge, 3-9 September 1995* (*Orientalia Lovaniensia Analecta* 82), Leuven 1998, 25-28. See also P.T. NICHOLSON/E. PELTENBURG, Egyptian Faience, in: P.T. NICHOLSON/I. SHAW (eds.), *Ancient Egyptian Materials and Technology*, Cambridge 2000, 180-181.

44 R. DRENKHAHN, Artisans and Artists in Pharaonic Egypt, in: J.M. SASSON (ed.), *Civilizations of the Ancient Near East* I, New York 1995, 333.

Fig. 1: Stela Brussels E.4860 (drawing by P. Whelan)

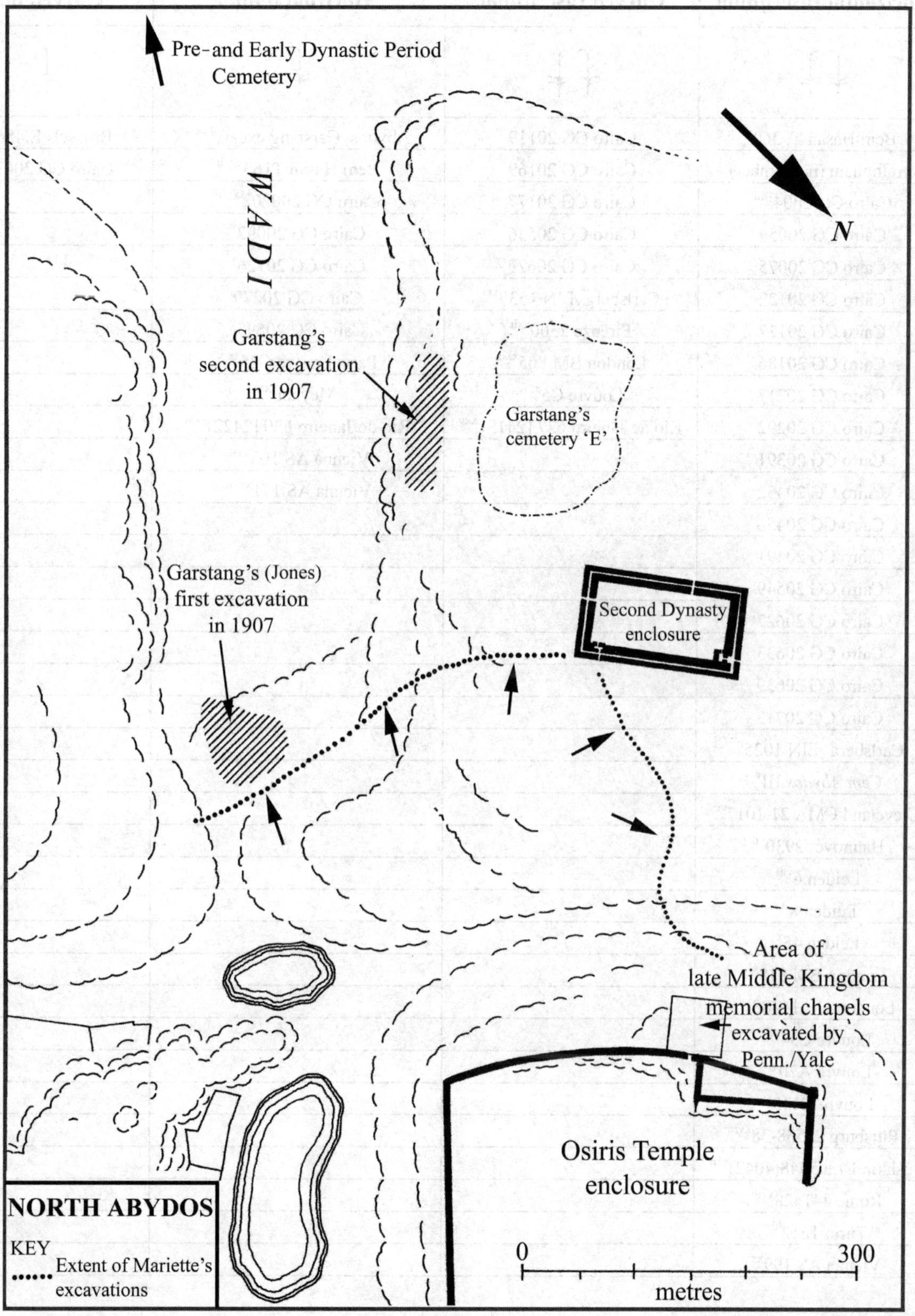

Fig. 2: Map of North Abydos (adapted from KEMP/MERRILEES, *Minoan Pottery*, 106 fig. 36)

Horizontal Inscription	Curved Inscription	Horizontal line	Curved line

Beni Hasan T. 360[i]	Cairo CG 20119	Abydos, Garstang excav.†[xxvi]	Brussels E.4860†
Birmingham (no number) [ii]	Cairo CG 20169	Beni Hasan T163[xxvii]	Cairo CG 20038†
Cairo CG 20048[iii]	Cairo CG 20177	Cairo CG 20020†[xxviii]	
Cairo CG 20059	Cairo CG 20536	Cairo CG 20092†	
Cairo CG 20075	Cairo CG 20629	Cairo CG 20126†	
Cairo CG 20122	Carlsberg ÆIN 1539[xxi]	Cairo CG 20279	
Cairo CG 20127	Firenze 2500[xxii]	Cairo CG 20595†	
Cairo CG 20186	London BM 805[xxiii]	Paris Louvre C25[xxix]	
Cairo CG 20217	Louvre C5[xxiv]	Meylan[xxx]	
Cairo CG 20292	Rio de Janeiro 627 [2419] [xxv]	Rio de Janeiro 630 [2422][xxxi]	
Cairo CG 20391		Vienna ÄS 103[xxxii]	
Cairo CG 20452		Vienna ÄS 171[xxxiii]	
Cairo CG 20456			
Cairo CG 20491			
Cairo CG 20549			
Cairo CG 20627			
Cairo CG 20633			
Cairo CG 20639			
Cairo CG 20713			
Carlsberg ÆIN 1025[iv]			
Cem.Abydos III[v]			
Cleveland CMA 21.1017[vi]			
Hannover 2930[vii]			
Leiden 6[viii]			
Leiden 8[ix]			
Leiden 45[x]			
London BM 318[xi]			
London UC 14488[xii]			
Louvre C34[xiii]			
Louvre A70[xiv]			
Louvre C145[xv]			
Pittsburg 21538-38[xvi]			
Pushkin I.1.a.5348(4042)[xvii]			
Rome 441428[xviii]			
Turin 1612[xix]			
Vienna ÄS 199[xx]			

Fig. 3: Stelae with symmetrically reversed *ḥtp-dj-nsw* formulae composed with a single or two sedge plants

References to Fig. 3:
i) J. GARSTANG, *The Burial Customs of Ancient Egypt*, London 1907, 187, fig. 195; **ii)** D. LINES, A Curious Middle Kingdom Stela in Birmingham, *Journal of Egyptian Archaeology* 87 (2001), 43-54; **iii)** The source for all Cairo Museum stelae: LANGE/SCHÄFER, *Grab- und Denksteine des Mittleren Reiches* I-IV; **iv)** O. KOEFOED-PETERSEN, *Les stèles égyptiennes*, Copenhagen 1948, 18-19, pl. 18; **v)** T.E. PEET/W.L.S. LOAT, *The Cemeteries of Abydos* Part III. – 1912-1913, London 1913, pl. XIII.2; **vi)** BERMAN, *Stele of Shemai*, 93-99; **vii)** M. CRAMER, Ägyptische Denkmäler im Kestner-Museum zu Hannover, *Zeitschrift für Ägyptische Sprache und Altertumskunde* 72 (1936), 86-87, pl. IV.4 (I am grateful to Wolfram Grajetzki for this reference); **viii)** BOESER, *Beschreibung der Aegyptischen Sammlung*, 3-4, pl. V; **ix)** IBID., 4, pl. VII; **x)** IBID., 12, pl. XXXIV; **xi)** *Hieroglyphic Texts from Egyptian Stelae, &c., in the British Museum* IV, London 1913, pl. 46; **xii)** H.M. STEWART, *Egyptian Stelae, Reliefs and Paintings from the Petrie Collection* II, London 1979, 35, pl. 36.5; **xiii)** SIMPSON, *Terrace of the Great God*, 19, pl. 43; **xiv)** P. PIERRET, *Recueil d'inscriptions inédites* II, Paris 1878, 8 (formula not shown); **xv)** IBID., 49; **xvi)** D. CRAIG-PATCH, *Reflections of Greatness. Ancient Egypt at The Carnegie Museum of Natural History*, Pennsylvania 1990, 28-29, no.18; **xvii)** S. HODJASH/O. BERLEV, *The Egyptian Reliefs and Stelae in the Pushkin Museum of Fine Arts, Moscow*, Leningrad 1982, 74 no. 31; **xviii)** F. MANERA/C. Mazza, *Le Collezioni Egizie del Museo Nazionale Romano*, Milan 2001, 93 no. 61; **xix)** A.M. DONADONI ROVERI, *Egyptian Civilization. Religious Beliefs*, Milan 1988, 107, fig. 141; **xx)** I. HEIN/H.SATZINGER, *Stelen des Mittleren Reiches* II (*Corpus Antiquitatum Aegyptiacarum Wien* 7), Mainz 1993, 7, 133-135; **xxi)** KOEFOED-PETERSEN, *Les stèles égyptiennes*, 10-11, pl. 11a-b; **xxii)** S. BOSTICCO, *Le stele egiziane dall'antico al nuovo regno. Museo archeologico de Firenze*, Rome 1959, 33-35 no. 30, pl. 30a-c; **xxiii)** *Hieroglyphic Texts from Egyptian Stelae, &c., in the British Museum* III, London 1912, 10, pl. 40; **xxiv)** SIMPSON, *Terrace of the Great God*, 17, pl. 3; **xxv)** KITCHEN/BELTRAO, *Catalogue Rio de Janeiro* I, 14-23 and II, pl. 1-2; **xxvi)** An unpublished photograph from Garstang's 1907 excavations (Liverpool A.640 - album A07I, 63) shows a group of stelae amongst which is a rectangular stela with cavetto cornice and symmetrically reversed formulae; **xxvii)** GARSTANG, *Burial Customs of Ancient Egypt*, 185, fig. 192; **xxviii)** The source for all Cairo Museum stelae: LANGE/SCHÄFER, *Grab- und Denksteine des Mittleren Reiches* I-IV; **xxix)** P. PIERRET, *Recueil d'inscriptions inédites* II, 4-5 (formula not shown); **xxx)** P. TRESSON, Une petite stèle inédite du Moyen Empire provenant de la Collection du Bois-Aymé, *Kêmi* 1 (1928), 69-82, pl. VIII (= ANOC 68.1, SIMPSON, *Terrace of the Great God*, 22, pl. 33); **xxxi)** KITCHEN/BELTRAO, *Catalogue Rio de Janeiro* I, 35-36, II, pl.11-12; **xxxii)** I. HEIN/H. SATZINGER, *Stelen des Mittleren Reiches* I (*Corpus Antiquitatum Aegyptiacarum Wien* 4), Mainz 1987, 4,9-12; **xxxiii)** IBID., 4,124-128; **xxxiv)** I. HEIN/H. SATZINGER, *Stelen des Mittleren Reiches* II (*Corpus Antiquitatum Aegyptiacarum Wien* 7), Mainz 1993, 7,145-148.

Catalogue

This catalogue lists all objects in this category known to me. Due to limitations of space only a brief description of the physical appearance of each object is given accompanied by a thumbnail drawing showing the categorising feature(s) as well as the position of any incised border lines. All other decorative elements and/or inscriptions are omitted from each drawing, but are described in the accompanying text. All objects are decorated on one side only, except for block monuments N and O. Photographs of each object, except G, are published; hieroglyphic transcriptions and/or translations of texts have yet to be published for objects A, B, C, D, and G.

A New York, Metropolitan Museum of Art 65.120.1

Limestone
H. 30.5 cm W. 42 cm
Owner: *shtp-jb-rʿ*
Title: *mr-mšʿ*
13th Dynasty
Provenance: unknown, Ex collection W. H. Irvine

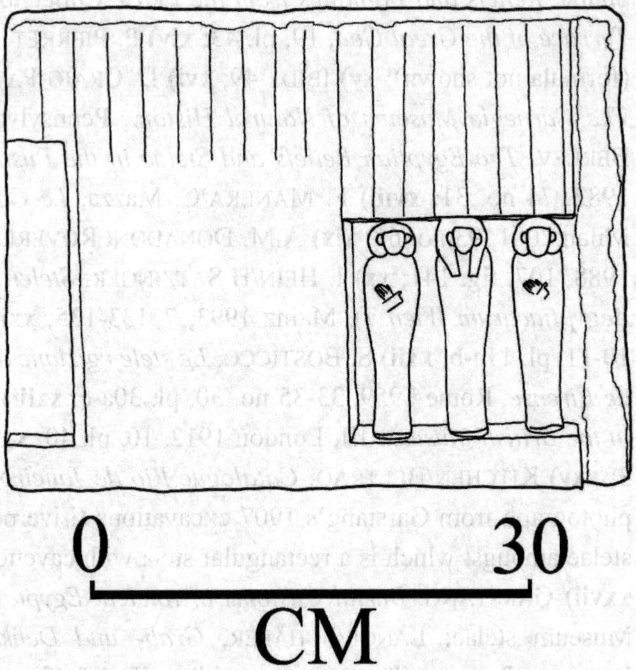

Published:
The Metropolitan Museum of Art: Notable Acquisitions 1965-1975, New York 1975, 66.

Description:
A rectangular slab, the upper half of which is inscribed with sixteen vertical lines of hieroglyphs below which, on the right, is a rectangular niche containing three mummiform figures each bearing a single vertical line of inscription. The central female figure sports a lappet wig and is flanked by male figures each with hands modelled in relief and wearing a "khat" wig. To the left of the niche is a scene carved in sunk relief showing the deceased seated before an offering table piled high with food. A narrow rebate of uncertain function runs down the right edge. On the far left is an enigmatic recess, which may be part of another niche, the bottom of which is aligned with the base of the right niche, while its top is below the short final column of inscription. This slab is associated with object B and both may be fragments from a larger decorated stela or elements from a larger composite memorial.

B New York, Metropolitan Museum of Art 65.120.2

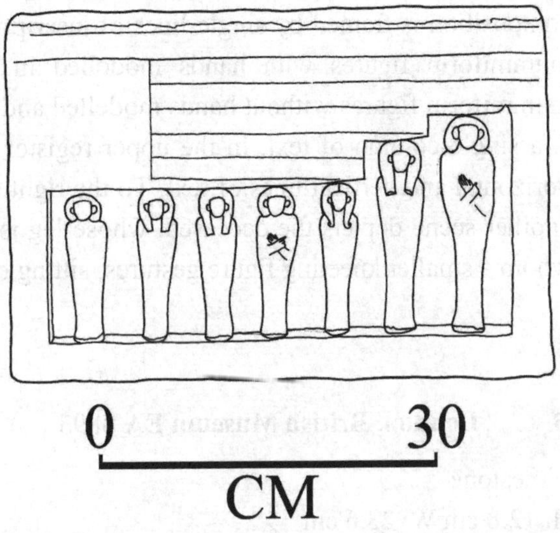

Limestone
H. 30.5 cm W. 48 cm
Owner: *sḥtp-jb-rˁ*
Title: *mr-mšˁ*
13th Dynasty
Provenance: unknown, Ex collection W.H. Irvine

Published:
The Metropolitan Museum of Art: Notable Acquisitions, 1965-1975, New York 1975, 66.

Description:
This is either part of a larger stela or an element from a monument that almost certainly belongs with object A. A horizontal line of inscription across the top of the rectangular slab is followed below by five shorter horizontal lines. On the left a small offering scene shows the deceased facing to the right and sitting before an offering table piled with food. The lower register is entirely filled with a rectangular niche containing seven mummiform figures representing three males and four females, each bearing a single column of text. The top edge of the niche steps upwards twice on the right to accommodate two larger mummiform figures of the deceased and his spouse. All three male figures wear "khat" wigs, but only two have hands modelled in relief. Three of the female figures are depicted with lappet wigs; the fourth sports a Hathor wig.

C Turin, Museo Egizio 1630

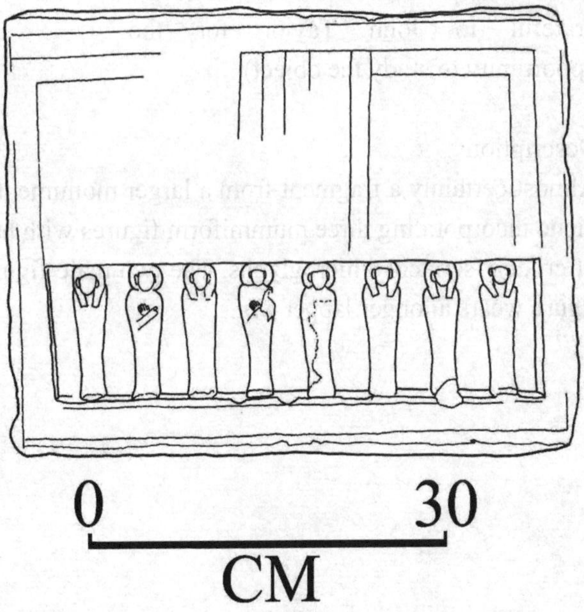

Limestone
H. 45.5 cm W. 35 cm
Owner: *rˁ-pw-ptḥ* (?)
Title: Uncertain
13th Dynasty
Provenance: probably Abydos, Ex collection Drovetti

Published:
A. FABRETTI/F. ROSSI/R.V. LANZONE, *Regio Museo do Torino: Antichità egizie,* Turin 1882, 177; DONADONI ROVERI, *Egyptian Civilization. Religious Beliefs*, 111, pl. 148.

Description:
The rough edges of the slab suggest that it has been cut from a larger stela/monument. The whole composition is framed by single lines of inscription. A niche in the lower portion contains three male mummiform figures with hands modelled in relief and wearing "khat" wigs, and five female mummiform figures without hands modelled and wearing lappet wigs. To the side of each figure there is a single column of text. In the upper register two scenes are carved in sunk relief and framed by horizontal and vertical lines of text. To the right a seated couple face toward the left; while on the left another scene depicts the deceased, whose leg is touched by a smaller standing figure, his spouse, to whom a smaller kneeling figure gestures, sitting on either side of a table piled high with offerings.

D London, British Museum EA 8893

Limestone
H. 12.8 cm W. 23.6 cm
Owner: The owner may be one of the five individuals named *jp.nw*(*w*) (♂); *ttj* (♀); *ḫns* (♂); *ḥw* (♂); *msȝn* (♀)
Title: none indicated
13th Dynasty
Provenance: unknown, Ex collection J. Sams

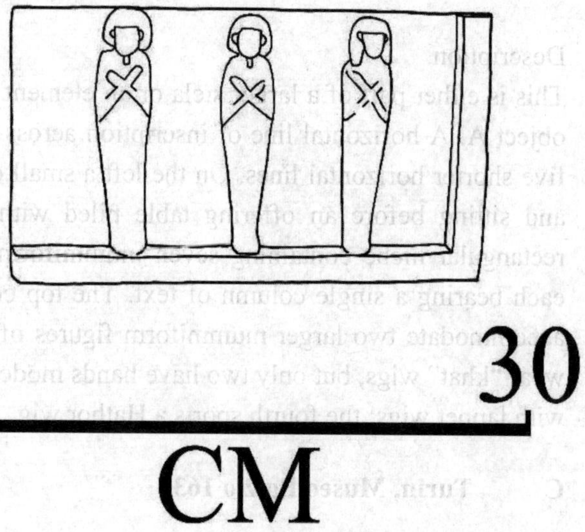

Published:
J.H. TAYLOR, *Death and Afterlife in Ancient Egypt*, London 2001, 114 (I am grateful to John Taylor for the opportunity to study the object)

Description:
Almost certainly a fragment from a larger monument, which preserves the right and bottom edges of a niche incorporating three mummiform figures with hands shown in relief each bearing a single column of crudely scratched hieroglyphs. The two male figures have "khat" wigs and short beards; the female figure wears a longer lappet wig.

E London, Petrie Museum of Egyptian Archaeology, University College London UC 14347

Limestone
H. 30 cm W. 31 cm
Owner: *sbk-nḫt-ḥtp*
Title: none indicated
13th Dynasty
Provenance: Purchased by Petrie at Abydos

Published:
STEWART, *Egyptian Stelae Petrie Collection* II, 34 no. 144, pl. 40; J. CAPART, *Recueil de Monuments Égyptiens* II, Brussels 1905, pl. LVIII; A.E.P. WEIGALL, Some Inscriptions in Prof. Petrie's Collection of Egyptian Antiquities, *Recueil de Travaux Relatifs à la philologie et à l'archéologie Égyptiennes et Assyriennes* 19 (1897), 217; PORTER/MOSS, *Topographical Bibliography* V, 102.

Description:
The rectangular slab appears to have been trimmed from a larger stela/monument and is decorated with two rectangular niches of similar size; the upper one of which contains four much abraded mummiform figures representing three female and one male. Each mummiform figure is embraced by a male figure carved in low relief. The lower niche contains three male and one female mummiform figures, three of which are embraced by male figures carved in low relief. Each of the human-form figures bears a single column of inscription.

F Cairo, Egyptian Museum CG 20497

Limestone
H. 54 cm W. 34 cm
Owner: *jmn-m-ḥꜣt*
Title: *mr ꜥḫnwty*
12th – 13th Dynasty
Provenance: unknown

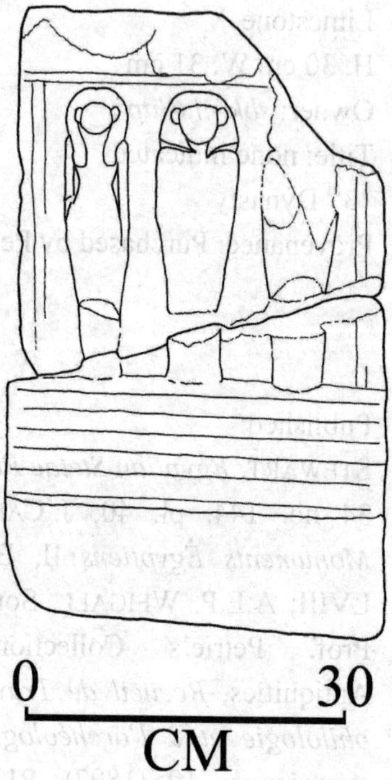

Published:
LANGE/SCHÄFER, *Grab- und Denksteine des Mittleren Reiches* I, 88-89, IV, pl. XXXIII; H.D. SCHNEIDER, *Shabtis. An Introduction to the History of Ancient Egyptian Funerary Statuettes with a Catalogue of the Collection of Shabtis in the National Museum of Antiquities at Leiden* I, Leiden 1977, 63; SIMPSON, *Terrace of the Great God*, 12; FRANKE, *Personendaten*, 81, Doss. 77.

Description:
The top of the slab bears the remains of a cavetto cornice below which a recess (originally a niche?) contains two male mummiform figures and one female figure in human form, all bearing a single column of inscription. Both male figures wear shoulder length wigs with pointed lappets; the female sports a long Hathor-style wig and has both arms tight against her sides. Five horizontal lines of text are inscribed beneath the recess, below which a rebate runs across the width of the slab.

G Paris, Musée du Louvre C44

Limestone
H. 44 cm W. 43.5cm
Owner: *ḥr-bḫn*
Title: none indicated
13th Dynasty
Provenance: Not known

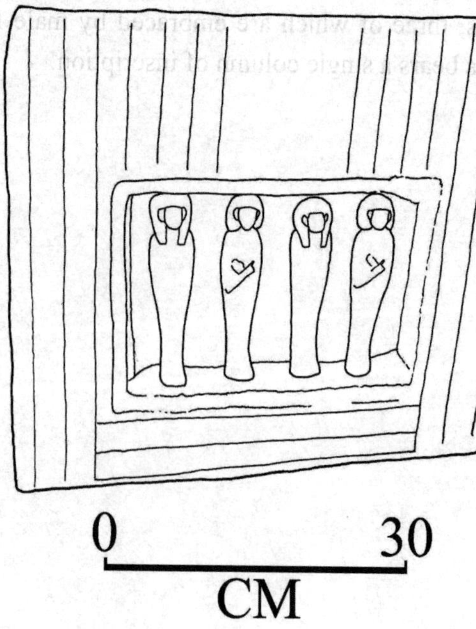

Published:
C. BOREUX, Département des Antiquités Égyptiennes. Guide catalogue sommaire I Salles du Rez-de-chaussé escalier et Palier du Premier Étage Salle du Mastaba et Salle de Baouît, Musées Nationaux Palais du Louvre, Paris 1932, 149-150; FRANKE, *Personendaten*, 133, Doss. 168 and 273, Doss. 435.

Description:
The slab appears to be a fragment of a larger stela or an element from a composite monument. A central rectangular niche contains two male and two female mummiform figures. Both male figures wear "khat" wigs and have hands modelled in relief; the female figures sport lappet wigs. Three of the four mummiform figures are shown embraced by a human figure carved in sunk relief above each of which is a single column of inscription. A central scene carved in sunk relief above the niche depicts offerings on, and below, a low table. Twelve columns of inscription are arranged both sides of the niche and the offering scene; two horizontal lines of inscription run immediately below the base of the niche.

H Cairo, Egyptian Museum CG 20097

Sandstone
H. 46 cm W. 33 cm
Owner: uninscribed
Title: uninscribed
12th Dynasty
Provenance: Unknown

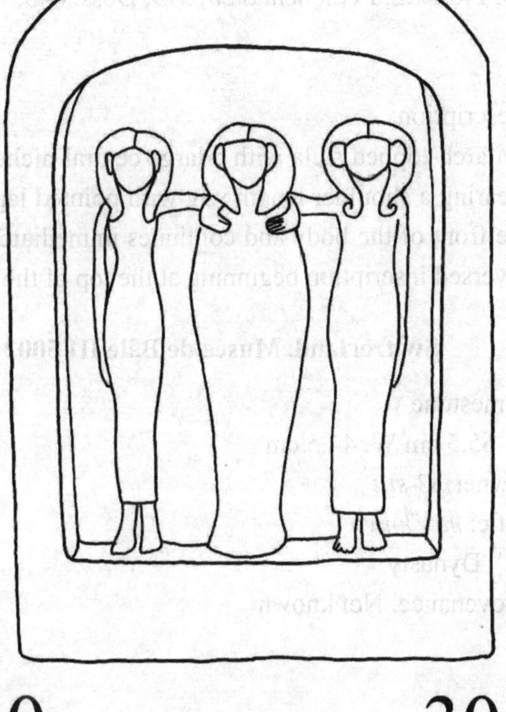

Published:
LANGE/SCHÄFER, *Grab- und Denksteine des Mittleren Reiches* I, 117, IV, pl. IX; VANDIER, *Manuel d'archéologie* II, 487, fig. 296 (lower left); SCHNEIDER, *Shabtis* I, 63.

Description:
An arch-topped stela with a niche containing a central male mummiform figure sporting a shoulder length wig with pointed lappets flanked and embraced by two human-form female figures wearing tight fitting long dresses, both wearing Hathor-style wigs. The object is otherwise undecorated.

I Cairo, Egyptian Museum CG 20569

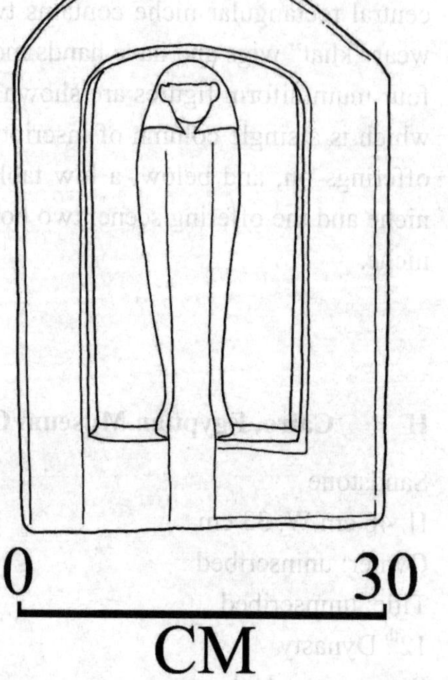

Limestone
H. 43 cm W. 30 cm
Owner: *snb-f*
Title: *mr-pr n(j) wḏ3 n(j) ḫrp k3wt*
12th – 13th Dynasty
Provenance: Abydos; Mariette excavations in the "nécropole du nord"

Published:
LANGE/SCHÄFER, *Grab- und Denksteine des Mittleren Reiches* I, 206-207, IV, pl. XLV; SCHNEIDER, *Shabtis* I, 63; FRANKE, *Personendaten*, 379, Doss. 643.

Description:
An arch-topped stela with a large central niche of similar shape containing a male mummiform figure wearing a shoulder length wig with pointed lappets. A single vertical column of inscription runs down the front of the body and continues immediately beneath the niche and to the left. Two single lines of reversed inscription beginning at the top of the arch run around the niche.

J Switzerland, Musée de Bâle III 5002

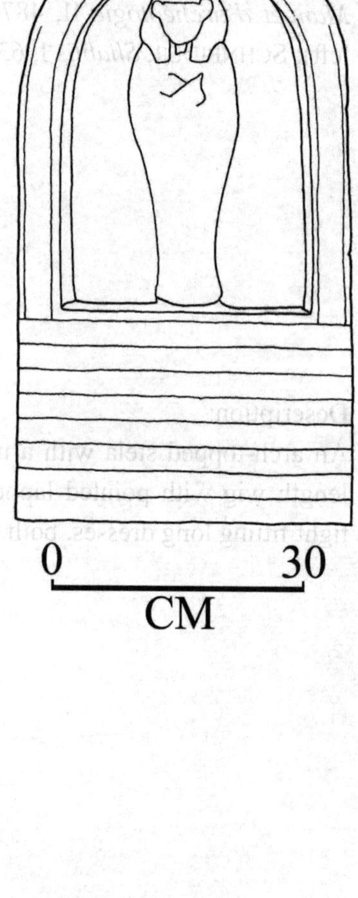

Limestone
H. 65.5 cm W. 44.5 cm
Owner: *s3-stjt*
Title: *mr-ʿḫnwtj*
12th Dynasty
Provenance: Not known

Published:
E. NAVILLE, Une stèle funéraire au Musée de Bâle, *Archives suisses d'anthropologie générale* 3 (1919), 200-205; *Führer durch das Museum für Völkerkunde Basel*, Basel 1930, 16-17, fig. 9; PORTER/MOSS, *Topographical Bibliography* V, 100; SCHNEIDER, *Shabtis* I, 63; SIMPSON, *Terrace of the Great God*, ANOC 1.8, pl. 3; E. HORNUNG, *Geschenk des Nils. Ägyptische Kunstwerke aus Schweizer Besitz*, Basel 1978, 47-48, pl. 153.

Description:
An arch-topped stela with a similarly shaped niche containing a male mummiform figure sporting a lappet wig and with hands modelled in relief. To the right of the mummiform figure, two human-form female figures one above the other are carved in sunk relief at the back of the niche accompanied by inscriptions. Two male human-form figures with accompanying inscriptions are carved in sunk relief to the left of the mummiform figure. Two lines of reversed text begin at the top of the arch and run either side of the niche terminating in line with its base. The bottom portion of the stela immediately below the niche is filled with seven horizontal lines of inscription.

K Cairo, Egyptian Museum CG 20038

Limestone
H. 35 cm W. 29 cm
Owner: *jj-ẖr-nfrt*
Title: *mr ẖtmt* (*mr-prwj ḥḏ mr prwj nbw*)
12th Dynasty
Provenance: Abydos; Mariette's excavations in the "nécropole du nord"

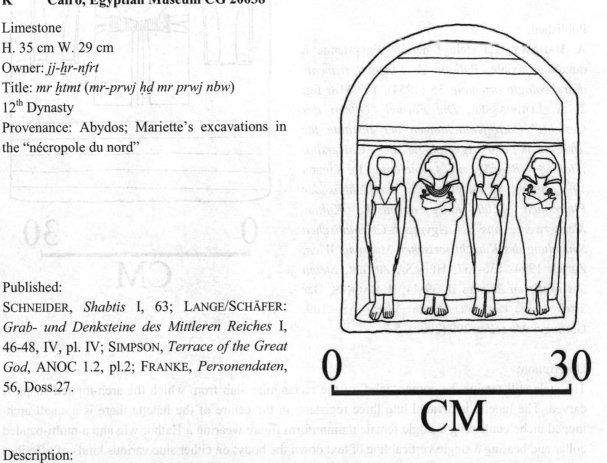

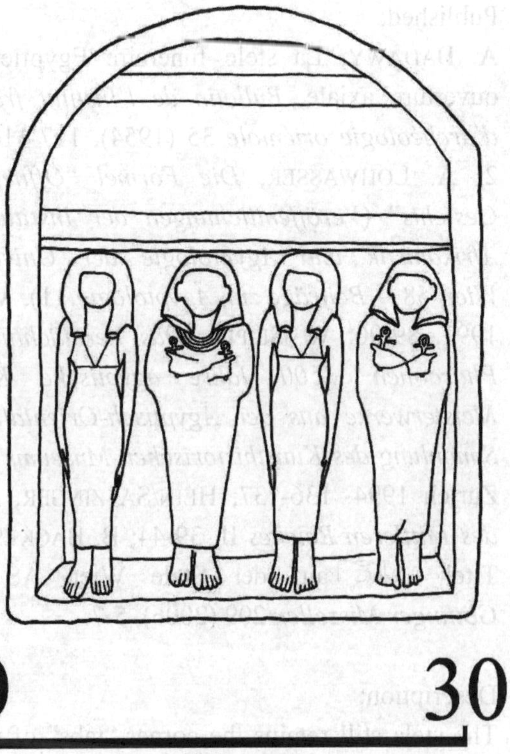

Published:
SCHNEIDER, *Shabtis* I, 63; LANGE/SCHÄFER: *Grab- und Denksteine des Mittleren Reiches* I, 46-48, IV, pl. IV; SIMPSON, *Terrace of the Great God*, ANOC 1.2, pl.2; FRANKE, *Personendaten*, 56, Doss.27.

Description:
An arch-topped stela around the front of which is a raised band bearing two lines of reversed inscriptions which begin at the top of the arch and run down either side of the stela. A slightly recessed panel in the lunette is decorated with two horizontal lines of inscription beneath which an offering scene on the left depicts the deceased seated before a small offering table and with his back to other offerings. On the right, one seated and two standing figures face the deceased. Below this scene is a large rectangular niche containing two male mummiform and two human-form female figures, each bearing a single vertical line of inscription. Both male figures wear a shoulder length wig with pointed lappets and hold ankh symbols in their hands, which are revealed through a tightly wrapped shroud that terminates above the ankles leaving the feet exposed. One male figure wears also a multi-banded collar. Both female figures are shown with a lappet wig and with arms extended at their sides, wearing a tight-fitting strap dress which terminates above the ankles.

L Vienna, Kunsthistorisches Museum ÄS 109

Limestone
H. 45.5 cm W. 35 cm
Owner: *snbf*
Title: *mr-st* (*wdpw*)
13th Dynasty
Provenance: Purchased by Burghart 1821, possibly from Abydos

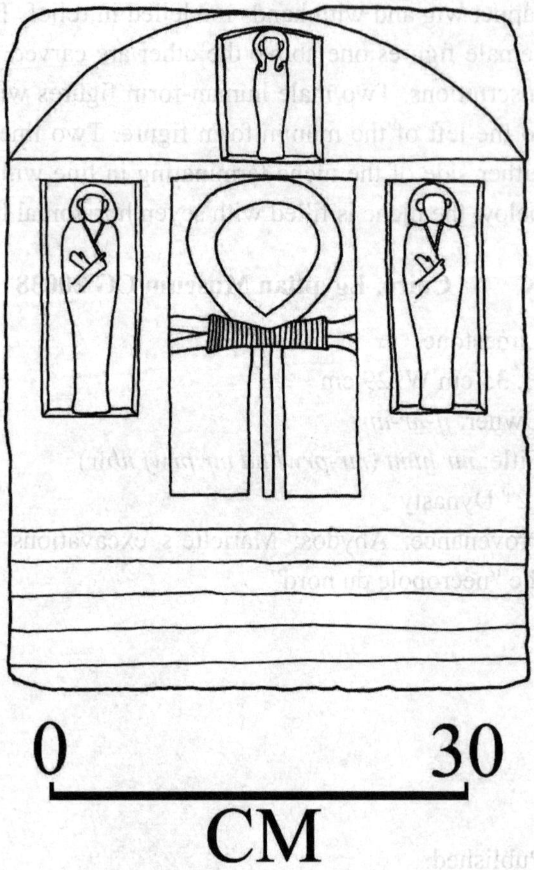

Published:
A. BADAWY, La stèle funéraire Égyptienne à ouverture axiale, *Bulletin de l'Institut français d'archéologie orientale* 35 (1954), 117-118, fig. 2; A. LOHWASSER, *Die Formel "Öffnen des Gesichts"* (*Veröffentlichungen der Institute für Afrikanistik und Ägyptologie der Universität Wien* 58 = *Beiträge zur Ägyptologie* 11), Vienna 1991, 89-90; W. SEIPEL, *Das Vermächtnis der Pharaonen. 3500 Jahre ägyptische Kultur. Meisterwerke aus der Ägyptisch-Orientalischen Sammlung des Kunsthistorischen Museums Wien*, Zürich 1994, 136-137; HEIN/SATZINGER, *Stelen des Mittleren Reiches* II, 39-44; B. BACKES, Der Titel  auf der Stele Wien ÄS 109, *Göttinger Miszellen* 209 (2006), 5-7.

Description:
The stela still retains the corner "tabs" of the rectangular slab from which the arch-topped shape is carved. The lunette is divided into three registers; in the centre of the lunette there is a small arch-topped niche containing a single female mummiform figure wearing a Hathor wig and a multi-banded collar and bearing a single vertical line of text down the body; on either side various kinds of offerings are carved in sunken relief. Directly below this niche is a rectangular aperture incorporating an open-work ankh. On either side of this aperture, separated by a single column of inscription, is a rectangular niche containing a single male mummiform figure wearing a "khat" wig and with hands modelled in relief. The stitched hem of their tight fitting shrouds forms a vee-neck and a single vertical column of text runs down the front of the body. A single vertical column of text runs down the outer vertical edge of each niche. Below each niche is a seated figure facing towards the centre carved in sunk relief accompanied by labelling inscriptions. The lower register is composed of four horizontal lines of inscription.

M Rio de Janeiro, National Museum 635+636 [2427]

Limestone
H. 44 cm W. 43.5cm
Owner: *ḫntj-ḫty-ḥtp*
Title: *mr-pr*
12th or 13th Dynasty
Provenance: Collection Fiengo; gift of Dom Pedro I; probably from Abydos

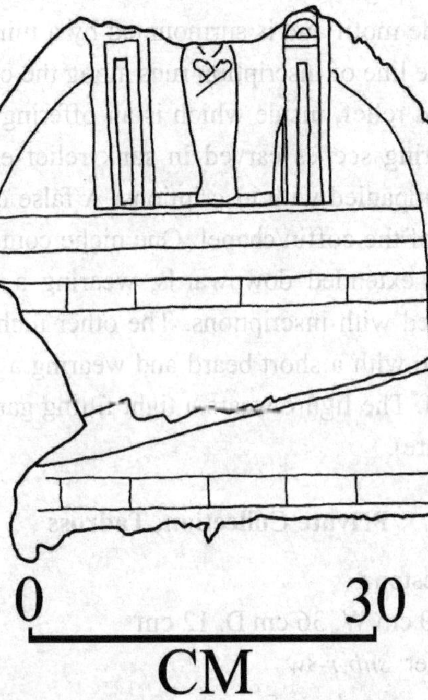

Published:

A. CHILDE, Museu Nacional, Rio de Janeiro (IVa Secção): Guia. Collecções de Archeologia Clássica, Rio de Janeiro 1919, 42 [2427], IX; KITCHEN/ BELTRAO, *Catalogue Rio de Janeiro* I, 47-49, II, 25-26 no. 11.

Description:

An arch-topped stela in a fragmentary condition with a single niche in the lunette which contains male mummiform figure of which the head is missing; the hands are modelled in relief. Two stylised chapels or shrines flank the figure. Directly below the niche are three horizontal lines of inscription followed by a fragmentary scene, carved in sunken relief, of five male figures in human form standing before an offering table. A single horizontal line of inscription runs across the bottom of the stela.

N Bonn, Ägyptisches Museum der Universität L 1675

Limestone
H. 73 cm W. 65.3 cm D. 25.6 cm
Owner: *kms*
Title: *mr-ḫnww*
13th Dynasty
Provenance: unknown, possibly Abydos

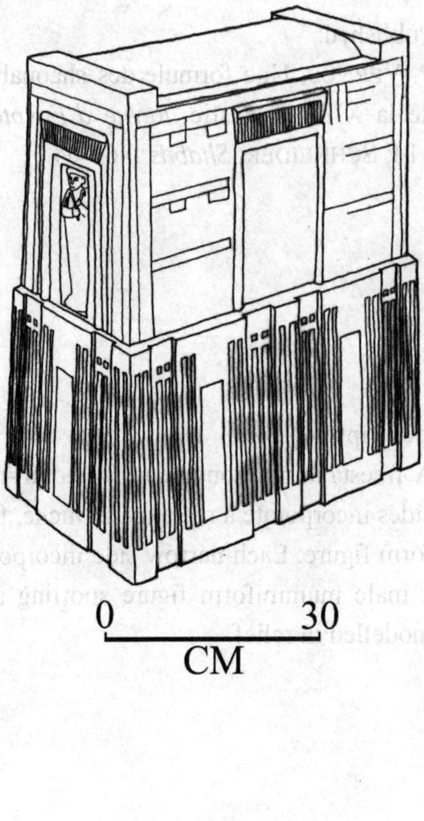

Published:

G. LAPP, Die Stelenkapelle des Kmz aus der 13. Dynastie, *Mitteilungen des Deutschen Archäologischen Instituts Kairo* 50 (1994), 231-252, pl. 37-41.

Description:
A rectangular limestone block carved all-round. The lower part is decorated with a niched palace façade motif and is surmounted by a miniature coffin or chapel with a vaulted lid and upright ends; a single line of inscription runs along the centre. In the middle of each long side a false door is carved in raised relief, inside which is an offering scene with accompanying inscriptions carved in sunk relief. Offering scenes carved in sunk relief either side of the false door depict family members and are accompanied with inscriptions. A false door incorporating a rectangular niche is also carved at either end of the coffin/chapel. One niche contains a male human-form figure standing in a pious pose with arms extended downwards, wearing a short wig and knee-length pleated kilt; the composition is framed with inscriptions. The other niche, also framed by inscriptions, contains a mummiform male figure with a short beard and wearing a "khat" wig, with hands holding the crook and flail carved in relief. The figure wears a tight fitting garment which leaves the lower legs and feet exposed (cf. cover picture).

O Private Collection, Tadross

Limestone
H. 60 cm W. 36 cm D. 12 cm
Owner: *snb-r-ꜣw*
Title: *wr mdw šmꜥ*
13th Dynasty
Provenance: Not known, possibly Gebelein or Abydos

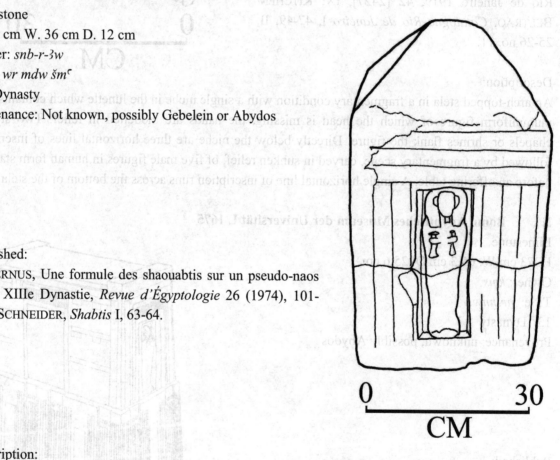

Published:
P. VERNUS, Une formule des shaouabtis sur un pseudo-naos de la XIIIe Dynastie, *Revue d'Égyptologie* 26 (1974), 101-114; SCHNEIDER, *Shabtis* I, 63-64.

Description:
A freestanding monument carved all-round with an undecorated pyramidion-shaped top. Both longer sides incorporate a rectangular niche, framed by inscription, which contains a male and female human-form figure. Each narrow side incorporates a rectangular niche, framed by inscription, which contains a male mummiform figure sporting a lappet wig and a beard, with hands holding two Hes vases modelled in relief.